Sport in the Global Society

General Editor: J.A. Mangan

DISREPUTABLE PLEASURES

SPORT IN THE GLOBAL SOCIETY

General Editor: J.A. Mangan

The interest in sports studies around the world is growing and will continue to do so. This unique series combines aspects of the expanding study of *sport in the global society*, providing comprehensiveness and comparison under one editorial umbrella. It is particularly timely, with studies in the political, cultural, anthropological, ethnographic, social, economic, geographical and aesthetic elements of sport proliferating in institutions of higher education.

Eric Hobsbawm once called sport one of the most significant practices of the late nineteenth century. Its significance was even more marked in the late twentieth century and will continue to grow in importance into the new millennium as the world develops into a 'global village' sharing the English language, technology and sport.

Other Titles in the Series

DISREPUTABLE PLEASURES

Less virtuous victorians at play

Editors

MIKE HUGGINS
St Martin's College, Lancaster

J.A. MANGAN
De Montfort University (Bedford)

FRANK CASS
LONDON AND NEW YORK

First published in 2004 in Great Britain by
FRANK CASS
2 Park Square, Milton Park,
Abingdon, Oxon, OX14 4RN

and in the United States of America by
FRANK CASS
270 Madison Ave,
New York, NY 10016

cax
British Library Cataloguing in Publication Data
A catalogue record for this book is available from the British Libray

ISBN 0-714-65363-2 (cloth)
ISBN 0-415-34598-7 (paper)

Library of Congress Cataloging-in-Publication Data
A catalog record for this book has been requested

Typeset in 10.75 on 13pt Times New Roman by FiSH Books, London
Printed in Great Britain by TJ International Ltd, Padstow, Cornwall

Contents

List of illustrations

List of tables

Prologue: All mere complexities

MIKE HUGGINS AND J.A. MANGAN

Certainly some Victorians took pains to paint themselves as virtuous, solid and respectable citizens. The walls of Leeds Town Hall, that monument to mid-nineteenth-century civic pride and conspicuous urban wealth, list meritorious maxims reflecting the values for which the industrial and commercial plutocracy of Victorian Leeds wanted to be remembered: 'Honesty is the best policy', 'Weave truth with trust', 'Industry conquers all'. Such clichés were a celebration of the world of work and religion, duty and ethics, virtuous commercialism and confident capitalism.

In the past historians have too easily accepted such pious pomposities and sanctimonious rhetoric as illustrating a uniform commitment to respectability, authority, duty and religion. In the early twentieth century historians tended to view Victorianism as an uncomplicated phenomenon; subsequently the nature of Victorianism has been the subject of vigorous debate. Changed cultural and economic values, the world wars, burgeoning hedonism, new historical fashions, political imperatives and even the heritage industry have all influenced the way in which the Victorians have been presented.[1] In the 1960s and 1970s, for example, historians needed a supposedly repressive and repressed Victorian middle class as the hypocritical foil to contemporary 'modernist' sexual liberalism, and to point up the virtues of the working class, and the need for a more inclusive and populist history. Then in the 1980s Mrs Thatcher's mythological world of 'Victorian values' shaped public perceptions of the Victorians as serious, earnest and sober, committed, *inter alia*, to those mantras of Victorian leisure – rational recreation, respectable pastimes and muscular Christianity. The Victorians have thus been the victims of academic *naïveté*, sectional manipulation and political simplification – all in the interest of the peddling of a purified past. This collection is rather more concerned with reality.

Raymond Williams defined culture as 'a whole body of practices and expectations, the whole of living...perceptions of ourselves and our world...a lived system of meanings and values – constitutive and constituting – which as they are expressed as practices appear as reciprocally conforming'.[2] Williams's work provided the stimulus for work on working-class leisure by E.P. Thompson and others.[3] In their work the middle class figures only indirectly. Peter Bailey, Hugh Cunningham and John Walton subsequently viewed popular Victorian mass entertainments such as the music hall, the seaside or the pub mainly from this working-class perspective.[4]

Williams, however, struggled to come to terms with these popular leisure forms. More attracted by 'high culture' – the world of the arts and the intellect – he largely dismissed them as trivial. Likewise, Asa Briggs's work deals with Victorian culture more in terms of provincial and metropolitan 'cultures', in the sense of 'a veneer or polish', and 'refinement of taste and manners'. His discussion of the 'cultural life of a Victorian city' is replete with references to libraries, clubs, reading rooms, theatres and periodicals.[5] This view of an apparently largely middle-class Victorian 'high' cultural and 'respectable' leisure life has been further explored by a number of other social historians.[6] Bob Morris, for example, in his studies of the Victorian British middle class, presents the various voluntary associations, such as choral societies, literary groups and charity organisations, as creating a respectable recreational world in which a range of mainly middle-class interests could be accommodated, a view that also embraces the emergence of sports clubs in the late nineteenth century.[7]

Pierre Bourdieu's work on culture and its relationship to the social order suggests that cultural hierarchies reproduce and reinforce social divisions, and that good taste and reputability help to delineate and maintain social boundaries.[8] His work has had a major impact. By the 1980s 'reputable' and 'disreputable' were being used as valued concepts for an understanding of the cultural life of the Victorian period. Geoffrey Best was one of the first to portray the cultural gulf between 'respectables' and 'roughs' as a sharp, virtually absolute dividing line, which consolidated cohesion between middle-class and working-class 'respectables'. F.M.L. Thompson constructed a polished interpretation of the social history of Victorian Britain as 'the rise of respectable society', with respectability as *the* central Victorian value. In this analysis 'respectability' is represented as a highly specific value system of considerable normative power, espoused by *both* the middle class and the working class.[9] It gave rise in turn to Cunningham's picture of a single, monolithic middle-class leisure culture.[10]

This 'respectability' thesis has not gone unchallenged. Indeed, Bailey first mounted an effective attack on the more simplistic aspects of the supposed differences between the 'respectable' and 'rough' working class some 20 years ago.[11] Yet it is only recently that more direct attacks on the viability of the thesis with regard to the middle class have begun to be launched.[12]

Disreputable Pleasures sets out to further challenge the 'respectability' thesis by examining the extent of disreputability, mainly, but not wholly, in terms of *actual* middle-class leisure experience. In Victorian Britain the debates about respectability formed part of a cultural contest over 'correct' social values and 'appropriate' ways of life. Many members of the middle class attempted to define themselves, and others, in accordance with inflexible conventional values. Their certainties, however, clashed with the ideas and actions of others, and thus were divisive.

The rituals and symbols of respectability served major purposes for many in the middle class. They were integral to the struggle for middle-class dominance in society, integral to attempts to establish social leadership, and integral to the need to demonstrate that their precepts and practices were superior to most of those of the working class. Reputability and disreputability were powerful *leitmotifs* in Victorian life and death, fact and fiction, ideas and language. They set parameters and allowed segregation. They permitted self-serving dichotomous identities – 'refined' and 'rough' – and defined a polarised world of absolutes: virtue and vice, morality and immorality, sanctity and sin, purity and impurity, puritanism and pleasure. The pleasurably disapproving contemplation of the disreputability of other people, places and practices became a moral obsession, providing reassurance, security and predictability for those who aspired to membership of the 'respectables'. The volume of Victorian public rhetoric of moral condemnation, the energy of the reformist drive for rational recreation, the projection of sensationalist negative images in the press and the harsh punishments frequently handed out to transgressors all hammered home the message that decency was crucial. The 'spin' of the decent was unrelenting; the success of the 'spin' was uncertain.

The middle class unquestionably played a central role in the new Victorian sports culture. Consequently these sports were imbued with what Neil Tranter has described as a 'battery of serious purposes', which were intended to transform sport into 'a device thought essential for the continued success of Anglo-Saxon civilisation'.[13] These 'serious purposes' included the improvement of health and physique; personal, civic and national prestige; and personal profit. Participation thus supposedly benefited society by improving personal health, promoting 'right' values and inculcating sound virtues. Sport was also seen as a cultural bond that promoted social stability, although in reality many in the middle class resisted the spread of sport 'down the social ladder' for fear of working-class domination, with its consequent immoral possibilities. The code of the mainly middle-class amateur was designed to keep the working class in proper moral subjection.

Various sports historians have given different degrees of emphasis to the concepts of 'respectability' and 'morality' in their discussions of the late Victorian sports 'revolution'. John Lowerson, in his well-crafted and rigorously researched work on the sports of the Victorian and Edwardian English middle class, suggests that their sports ethic initially was grafted onto 'the great mid-century virtues of Work, Punctuality, Thrift and Respectability'. He recognises, however, that this wavered as play became 'a socially acceptable alternative to Sunday churchgoing for growing numbers of the middle class' by the turn of the century.[14] Richard Holt, in a more general overview, sees the efforts of the middle classes to keep themselves '*morally* [our italics] distinct from the lower orders' as one of their defining characteristics.[15] Dennis Brailsford argues, a little sweepingly, that the various Victorian sports had to accommodate themselves to the growing ascendancy of the middle class and 'that complex of high if sometimes hypocritical moral values known as "Victorianism"'.[16] Neil Wigglesworth, in his account of the evolution of British sport, asserts, equally sweepingly, that 'the new righteous middle class preferred a more recreational involvement in sport...resulting in a strictly codified amateur ethic and the rise of the sporting club'.[17]

Such views are too narrow – a depiction of a more or less monolithic middle-class sports culture, at one and the same time both sanctimoniously and sincerely occupying the moral high ground. These views do scant justice to reality, to the sectional complexities, divisions of interest and diverse attitudes as well as the range of motives associated with sport within Victorian Britain's middle class. These could be different at different ages, in different places and in different social settings. Cultural variations, subcultural divisions and shifting subcultural conflicts and alliances, not to mention individual self-assertion, meant that there was a wide variety of 'lived' cultural experiences within the middle class. Definitions of the morality associated with respectability could be fluid and the use of the term in relation to class identities should be cautiously exploratory rather than assertively confident.

Happily, historians are beginning to concede that the Victorians were far from one-dimensional in their values and actions. Victorian leisure in general, and sport in particular, possessed shades and nuances, general and specific elements. There is, in consequence, a real need for a subtle analysis of Victorian culture in all its variety. This is the primary concern of this collection. The Victorians were multifaceted, leading lives that might entail multiple identities and multiple selves, at different times, at different places and with different companions. They could, and did, live not in one but in several worlds. This collection challenges the overly simplistic binary class division of reputable and disreputable leisure and sporting identities, and, it is to be hoped, provides a more subtle and nuanced view of the ways in which the apparently more disreputable aspects of sport co-existed with the reputable. The collection has its roots, in part, in Bailey's earlier work on the situationally contingent nature of Victorian pleasure, and the extent to which working-class behaviour was more or less respectable depending on context, income and opportunity.[18] It also draws on Huggins's more recent work, which drew attention to the multiple settings in which the middle classes could participate in less respectable pleasures.[19] Yet it is only a beginning.

The collection takes subject matter from a cross-section of mainland Britain, including Wales, Glasgow and Edinburgh, Yorkshire and Lancashire, London and the Home Counties. It covers activities as varied as horse-racing, rugby and recreational reading, and deals with great British rituals such as the Grand National, great British institutions such as the universities of Oxford and Cambridge, and watershed British moments such as rugby's 'great split'.

The essays concentrate on the middle class, whose involvement, investment, participation and spectatorship underpinned the sports 'revolution' of the late nineteenth century, and, through complex processes of cultural hegemony, cultural proselytism and cultural imperialism, made *the* major contribution to national and global sport as a cultural and social entity.

In the 'contested cultural space' of leisure, sports that were reputable when sensibly indulged in by the more affluent could become disreputable when 'wastefully' taken up by the less affluent. In this respect, many sports were respectable for some and not for others. However, what constituted 'respectable' behaviour was always a fluid and dynamic category, highly responsive to changing circumstances. Victorian attitudes, of course, changed over time, and the frontiers of respectability were constantly in flux, so the temporal aspects of behavioural contexts are significant. Croll and Johnes, for example, show how in Wales the *cnappan* form of folk football became once more respectable and regarded nostalgically as part of a romanticised pre-industrial age, once its unruly and violent behaviour was safely in the past. Nevertheless, respectability, puritanism and sobriety in Victorian life, while powerful social forces, were not the only forces. As the chapters in this collection illustrate, middle-class Victorian sport was linked to such disreputable activities as gratuitous violence, obsessive gambling, sexual licence and excessive drinking. The latter, in John Burnett's neat phrase, 'liquid pleasure' was, of course, a major 'recreation' of the period,[20] while hedonism, controlled and uncontrolled, was an integral part of manly sports. 'Sensual recreation' entertained and educated individuals, maintained and sustained relationships, and aided and abetted communal well-being in different ways, but no less successfully than 'rational recre-ation' did.[21] Hence its attraction and survival.

Thus, Victorian society was characterised by the co-existence of reputable and disreputable patterns of behaviour, usually linked to highly specific contexts. There were some middle-class Victorians who stuck inflexibly to a 'strong' puritan respectability and accepted it as a life-organising principle in all situations. There were other Victorians who had a more flexible and pragmatic respectability, in which actions were judged as appropriate or inappropriate as the situation demanded. Few, except some very rich or some very poor, had consistently disreputable lifestyles. The middle class is not to be equated invariably with inflexible segregation. Reality was more complicated. There were separation and integration, heterogeneity and homogeneity. Participation in disreputable as well as reputable pleasures cut across classes, as well as existing within them. Furthermore, there was a necessary and often thick patina of 'overt' decency and 'covert' indecency. It is useful to remember that at least one of the members of the royal family privately enjoyed an excess of drinking, gambling and sex. Prince Albert Edward (later Edward VII) trod the public stage with the outward appearance of dignified respectability. His private life was rather different.

When considering the cultural contexts of less reputable behaviour, social class is not necessarily always the best analytical tool to employ. It can be an analytical labyrinth. As David Cannadine has recently reminded us, contemporaries employed several different models and languages of class.[22] Nevertheless, as several chapters in *Disreputable Pleasures* make clear, differences over respectability associated with aesthetic taste and sporting behaviour were consistently used as powerful symbolic weapons between classes (and generations), and respectability used in this way was often closely linked to a defensive and offensive class rhetoric. However, the chapters also make clear that the various class 'leisure cultures' of Victorian Britain overlapped, making for a complex reality.[23] Some sports, such as horse-racing, brought all the classes together in shared enjoyment, making sense of Patrick Joyce's notion of 'the people'. Joyce argues that working 'people' possessed a spectrum of identities that in many cases involved the sharing of values, attitudes and loyalties with those from other social groups.[24] In beginning the difficult process of mapping out and providing a more detailed survey of the multiple leisure settings in Victorian Britain, *Disreputable Pleasures* likewise challenges simplistic representations of homogenous class attitudes and actions.

Cultural historians, of course, are now coming to realise that, while class remained a powerful determinant of leisure choice, late Victorian 'leisure culture' was pluralistic. As already noted, definitions of respectable behaviour were highly dependent on time and place. What this collection makes clear is just how important life-cycle stage and location were as determinants of sporting identity and behaviour.[25] Less respectable behaviour was much more common at certain times in the middle-class life cycle. Adolescents, younger unmarried males and older married men whose families had grown up were most prone to such behaviour. Sites of social solidarity, visibility and significance – the home, the pub, the church or chapel, or the workplace – strongly influenced lifestyle priorities. However, locations hidden from the potential control and pressure of family, the workplace and the church or chapel self-evidently reduced the need for respectability, and, of course, were far more likely to offer opportunities for disreputable lifestyles.

The first section of *Disreputable Pleasures* considers some of the places of 'privileged play' in which members of the more wealthy middle and upper classes could indulge themselves, and the extent to which these were associated with activities that would be looked upon disapprovingly in other social settings. Schools and universities are both dealt with in some detail. The seaside and spas, music halls and racecourses also provided escape from irksome social constraints, where respectability could be relatively easily abandoned.

The Victorian public schools, in all their variety, were crucially important educational institutions. They developed the cult of athleticism. They lay at the heart of Britain's imperial mission. They were the matrix of later global sport, and in their late Victorian manifestations they helped to foster the codes of militaristic manliness, fair play and team spirit. J.A. Mangan's chapter in *Disreputable Pleasures*, however, brings together material on the concomitant violence, brutality and sadism that some middle-class pupils experienced. For too many boys 'the public school experience was nasty, brutish and not short enough'.[26] The violence of the Victorian public school has been, understandably, a much less trumpeted aspect of its enduring publicity. It provided both licit and illicit pleasures, for both boys and masters.

Among the more titillating images and major anxieties in Victorian literature were the sinful pleasures of the young, unmarried middle-class male. He enjoyed more free time than his elders and sometimes applied himself more to play than to work.[27] The behaviour of some university students, then as now, reveals an irresponsible, frivolous and immoral lifestyle. Mangan's chapter on Victorian university life sheds illuminating light on this fascinating feature of the Victorian establishment. 'Oxbridge' presented itself as the training ground for developing 'character', necessary for the confident administration of the empire and for entry to an assured ruling elite. Yet for many students Oxbridge was not a source of self-discipline, but a place of privileged play on the river and games field, and, as various disciplinary books reveal, of disorderly, rowdy and undisciplined behaviour within college and beyond college walls. Nineteenth-century athleticism came to predominate over the aesthete and the academic in student life. It sustained indiscipline, anti-intellectualism and philistinism, and it was encouraged by some university dons for various and contradictory reasons – both pragmatic and altruistic – to maintain control of bored students, to develop their 'character', to maintain college recruitment levels and to adhere to classically rooted ideals.

The liminal nature of certain locations such as the racecourse, the seaside and the music hall, or the anonymity of large urban areas such as London, Liverpool, Manchester or Newcastle upon Tyne, rendered them particularly attractive places of disreputable play. Simultaneously they confronted and sustained decency, allowing individuals to slip into or out of disreputability as the choice took them. John Pinfold discusses the involvement of the Liverpool middle class in local races, especially the Aintree meetings, and provides vivid evidence of the extent to which the races provided opportunities for middle-class drunkenness, gambling and association with prostitutes, all activities looked on tolerantly by the authorities. Pubs, hotels and betting clubs in Liverpool, he states, continued to offer facilities for betting, including illegal cash betting, throughout the nineteenth century, although betting clubs were in decline by the later 1890s. Many of the Liverpool magistrates, he asserts, were lenient in their attitudes to both on-course and off-course betting, and, where members of their own class were involved, unwilling to interfere too actively. The largest bookmakers of the city were regarded as wholly respectable by the local press. Pinfold explores the more dubious aspects of the lifestyle of James Maybrick, a Liverpool cotton merchant, and his US-born wife Florence, both representative of at least a segment of Liverpool middle-class society. Their lives shed a bright light on one member of the city's merchant community and highlight the need for more extensive local studies of less respectable as well as respectable Victorian middle-class behaviour.

The Victorian belief that disreputability could be located, described and categorised was created partially through the period's media. The local press provided colourful insights into the practices of bourgeois culture.[28] Certainly the media provided vicarious opportunities for the enjoyment of disreputable pleasures, and helped to shape attitudes to both respectability and 'non-respectability'. In the second section of the book the three chapters by John Springhall, David Scott Kamper and Mike Huggins consider the ways in which the Sunday press, 'penny dreadfuls' and comic cartoons variously dealt with less acceptable pleasures. The chapters by Collins, Pinfold, and Croll and Johnes provide a further rich fund of local newspaper coverage. The fast-growing towns and cities of the Victorian age gave local journalists opportunities to write about a wide range of doubtful pleasures. Their approach was often pathological, episodic and sensational, with allegedly 'typical' rather than first-hand description, dialogue and action. Their mix of prurience and censoriousness, which positioned them on the moral high ground, coupled with graphic description, was hugely popular. The later *News of the World* had its Victorian antecedents.

The popular press became increasingly sensationalist in its content and coverage as the nineteenth century went on. By the 1890s the Sunday newspapers were particularly popular and commercially successful, with about two million copies being sold each week, largely to the lower middle and working classes. Kamper describes how these newspapers helped to define the terms of class-based cultural debate, in which claims to respectability could be articulated, accepted or denied. Some middle-class moralists refused to read these supposedly lower-class, 'grubby' newspapers, as evidence of their own respectability. Newsagents claimed to dislike Sunday trading but were unwilling to lose newspaper sales. The newspapers themselves were careful to frame detailed crime reportage and coverage of sport, especially horse-racing and betting, within a condemnatory rhetoric of respectability. However, although betting was an inflammatory issue, almost all the Sunday papers provided racing tips, and defended the betting of their working-class readers as legitimate, honest and decent, while condemning excessive and dishonest gambling by the rich. In short, the public and the press attempted to have it all ways.

Thanks to elementary state education, adolescents, literate and semi-literate, were more and more a part of the reading public in late Victorian society. Springhall shows how 'penny dreadfuls' and 'bloods' created a new commercial market among middle-class as well as working-class adolescents.[29] These penny part serials and cheap weekly periodicals, with their details of low-life London, prurient and risqué tales of women in peril and school stories with sport thrown in, were aimed mainly at working-class boys, but targeted also the sons of the middle and lower middle classes. Certainly Springhall suggests that much of the middle-class 'moral panic' associated with these comics derived from a fear that their own sons and daughters were as much at risk from contamination by them as the children of the urban poor were. With alternative images to biblical morality these entertaining and indecorous periodicals had a clear appeal.

To lapse briefly into esoteric jargon, there has been a recent emphasis on the 'linguistic turn' in sports history writing.[30] However, relatively little attention has been devoted to what might be termed a 'visual turn' in the study of Victorian leisure, which may seem somewhat surprising, given the emphasis placed on media images of sport in the twentieth century.[31] Mike Huggins attempts a thorough and thoughtful analysis of the varied nature of visual sporting humour in two contrasting periodicals, *Punch* and *Ally Sloper's Half Holiday*, and of the patterns, themes and narratives that characterised their satirical sports coverage. Victorian sporting cartoon artists were faced with the challenging task of interpreting the significance of the sporting revolution that their society was experiencing. The resulting cartoons cover the concerns, expectations and prejudices of audiences and artists, and reveal associated beliefs about the 'respectability', or otherwise, of sporting behaviour. Huggins paints a complex, shifting picture of attitudes to the role of sport in masculine identity, in the inter-relationships between classes and sexes, in male social relationships and attitudes, and in male concerns over the essential nature of femininity. *Inter alia* he discusses the evolving metropolitan and provincial attitudes to dominant ideologies such as athleticism.

The last three chapters explore middle-class (and working-class) violence, vice and virility, in a variety of regional and sporting settings. Tony Collins shows how attitudes to hacking, brutality and aggression within middle-class rugby changed over time, an important theme first developed in *Rugby's Great Split*, his prize-winning book on the origins of rugby league football.[32] In the 1860s and 1870s such behaviour was generally seen as legitimate, and was viewed approvingly as 'manly' and 'British'. Rough and robust approaches still characterised some 'gentlemen' and former public school teams in the 1880s, and their gamesmanship and emphasis on winning were a long way from any 'Corinthian' ideal. The game's traditions of violence were initially part of its appeal, even if they became increasingly antithetical to some sections of middle-class public opinion. Collins demonstrates that it was only in the 1880s, when such tactics were successfully used against these teams by the working-class players then entering the game in large numbers in Yorkshire and Lancashire, that these traditions were 'un-invented'. They were replaced by a utilitarian ethical system of 'fair play', used in part to justify continued control of the game by the public-school-educated.[33]

Croll and Johnes offer an original interpretation of the ways in which the dominant leisure images of 'virtuous Wales' and Welsh Nonconformity during the late nineteenth century need to be reconsidered. They provide a revealing picture of the ways in which the 'aesthetics of vice' developed in South Wales. It is hardly surprising that, with the increased urbanisation, industrialisation and commercialism of South Wales, the frontiers of respectability were constantly shifting in response to changing attitudes, making healthy, formerly eyebrow-raising pursuits such as female cycling acceptable and rendering previously taken-for-granted brutal street ball games unacceptable. Increasingly as the nineteenth century progressed, Welsh aspirants to respectability came face to face, not always unwillingly, with louche behaviour through the extensive reporting of a 'disreputable' Wales in the pages of the local press. Thus, reading about sordid and sinful ways of life became a widespread pastime, making readers vicariously 'veritable connoisseurs of the disreputable', while at the same time confirming their decency through 'inescapable' vicarious involvement.

Not surprisingly, given the 'double standards' of the time, less respectable sporting recreations were much more likely to be found in all-male settings, rather than in mixed or all-women settings. There were, for example, many men-only clubs, with their betting, billiard-playing and bookmaking, scattered across the face of urban Britain, from the Victoria, the Turf Club, and the Junior Tattersalls Clubs in London to the Waterloo, Camden and Grosvenor Clubs in Liverpool. Detailed investigation of the records and minute books of the more respectable Victorian sports clubs, all almost incidentally the result of a concern with amateurism and professionalism, reveal that for many members their main role was social.[34] Sport was not always 'improving', and ribaldry, drinking and betting could often be found in even the most 'respectable' of clubs. Members of cycling clubs, for example, faced accusations in the 1890s that 'they fill themselves with liquor to the accompaniment of vulgar and often obscene songs'.[35]

Hamish Telfer explores the socially exclusive male world of the late Victorian Scottish harriers clubs. These clubs first emerged in Glasgow and Edinburgh in the mid-1880s, and by the 1890s they were popular in cities across Scotland. Dundee alone supported some 17 harriers clubs between 1887 and 1890. The larger and more prestigious clubs could have an active membership of up to 100 or more. These clubs placed a strong emphasis on gentlemanly sociability and some acquired town club rooms, with lounges, overnight accommodation and other facilities providing a persuasive veneer of respectability. They organised regular winter Saturday cross-country runs in a variety of venues, booking good-quality hotels and socialising energetically afterwards. Although there were individualistic competitions, many events had a strong emphasis on teamwork and collective performance, with 'packs' running together following 'hounds'. If 'conviviality lies at the heart of sport', in the case of the harriers clubs Telfer makes it clear that single-sex conviviality was certainly as great an attraction for many members as the sport itself.[36] All-male socials and 'smokers', with their drinking, smoking and revelry, were far more of an attraction than the inhibiting sobriety and propriety of the mixed Grand Annual Dance.

The less respectable aspects of sport, then, were largely, although not entirely, a male phenomenon. Both the emergence of the entrepreneurial and professional middle class, and the rise of the evangelical movement, gave fresh impetus to a view of women 'as carriers of social and religious virtue' in the private, domestic sphere.[37] However, as indicated in the chapters by Pinfold and Huggins, middle-class women were sometimes able to publicly break through the male 'glass wall' inhibiting their personal conduct. However, as in the case of Mrs Maybrick, more often than not they experienced moral opprobrium if they transgressed the limits of decorum. Historians could usefully explore more fully middle-class women's participation in leisure of the time, which was often linked to the sinful. Successful female athletes, such as pedestrians, for example, were often portrayed as women with questionable reputations.[38] The opponents of cycling, for their part, saw it as indecent practice, while any closeness between near-naked bodies during mixed bathing smacked of depravity.[39]

Victorian middle-class women developed ways of exploiting sexual double standards. Women frequently got men to place bets 'for them', often receiving the winnings in the form of a pair of gloves, but invariably avoiding paying out on a losing bet. In mixed sports women could get away with behaviour that etiquette forbade to men. Numerous accusations of female cheating seem to suggest that while, in public, women were placed on pedestals as paragons of virtue, in sport they were allowed the licence of immature children. On the Victorian croquet ground a peculiar sort of role reversal could take place, which enabled women to jettison their expected passivity and dominate – indeed, humiliate – men, mixing flirting with tantrums, wrangling and argument.[40] In 1893 Lewis Carroll went so far as to claim that 'croquet is demoralising society. Ladies are beginning to cheat at it terribly, and if they are found out, they only laugh and call it fun.'[41]

Respectability clearly was adapted to circumstances, occasions and events. The same actions could mean different things to different people in different places and at different times. The overriding conclusion to be drawn from *Disreputable Pleasures* is that 'respectability' was a quicksilver phenomenon, reshaping itself to environment, gender, age and time.

There was a period complexity associated with respectability that, as yet, has not been fully appreciated, recorded or understood. What is equally clear is that the full extent of the obverse has suffered the same fate. If the former has been over-emphasised, the latter has been under-emphasised, certainly in relation to the Victorian middle class. Future investigators will surely rub their hands at the prospects of plunging them further into the layers of disreputable pleasures that this collection has barely, but, we hope, stimulatingly, exposed.

Part 1:

The privileged pursuit of dubious pleasures

1

Bullies, beatings, battles and bruises: 'great days and jolly days' at one mid-Victorian public school

J.A. MANGAN

Plus ça change ... ? Well, perhaps:

> The Michaelmas term begins, the football season gets under way, there is a nip in the evening air and the heart sinks as one reads those announcements posted by fee-paying schools in yesterday's paper. Yes, the dreaded YK Swotski is Head Boy, the Fourth of November will be held on Nov. 6, together with a performance of *If* in College Chapel. JSB Outstanding-Greaser is Keeper of the Mixed Grill. What memories seem to rise within me as I look at those cryptic blocks of text.
>
> Think of the smell of carbolic; the awful afflatus of the organ on that first Sunday evening, as hundreds of pupils, their mothers' Mitsouko still on their cheeks, whimper their way through 'Abide With Me'. Think of that little British microcosm, with nothing ahead but violent games and teasing and the howling of the school dog, and no girls save the Chaplain's daughter. Think of the privations, think of the cabbage, think of what it felt like to have your head kicked as you lay face down in the mud of some far-flung playing field at four o-clock as darkness fell and the sleet intensified.
>
> And what did it feel like, my friends? It felt absolutely marvellous, of course. Totally top-hole. It made me what I am. It was a first-rate preparation for life.[1]

Another irreverent modern commentator has sent an equally satirical dart winging its way to a bull's eye:

You can't expect a boy to be vicious till he's been to a good
school. So wrote Saki, and, although he was joking, the joke was
funny because it was also true. Schools have long been recognised, in our literature and by the man in the street, as dens of
vice, distinguishable from prisons in their capacity to encourage
bad behaviour.[2]

In the second half of the nineteenth century 'a good school' meant 'a
good public school', which meant invariably bullies, beatings, battles and
bruises. Marlborough College by the 1870s was 'a good school'. The
Schools Inquiry Commission of 1868 (the Taunton Commission) put
Marlborough College and Rugby, with Marlborough College in first place,
far ahead of all the other schools in terms of the number of Open
Scholarship holders at Oxbridge. It also commented:

> The kind of education given at Eton, at Rugby, at Marlborough,
> whatever may be its drawbacks, has at any rate received whatever
> stamp of public approval can be considered to be given by over-
> flowing numbers. And it is not too much to say, that what chiefly
> wins this approval is not so much what these schools teach, as the
> training which is given by their school life.[3]

In the same decade, the Oxford University cricket eleven included five
Marlburians, and the 12th man was also a Marlburian.[4]

All was not quite perfect. Of the Marlborough of the time, Sir Lionel
Earle wrote, with a laconic display of the proverbial 'stiff upper lip': 'The
education was wooden and in my opinion unenlightened...The food was
bad and there were considerable outbreaks of boils.'[5] Edward Lockwood, in
his *The Early Days of Marlborough College*,[6] wrote of Lent in the earlier
pre-Clarendon Marlborough: 'On Wednesdays and Fridays my only food
was stale bread washed down by water from the pump, and we used to
search for pignuts to satisfy our craving.'[7] On food, or the absence of it, the
Kemble Notes ('Marlburiana') state that:

> after a leg of mutton had been cut down to the bone, the bone
> itself was held up on the fork, dexterously severed by a sharp
> blow, and the two bones placed on two plates as a helping for two
> boys. Any boy's plate coming up after this had to beg from
> another table or the poor boy had nothing.[8]

Starvation was not the only ordeal. It was not only the daily diet that was bad, Earle remarked, so was pupil behaviour: 'There was much bullying, and young Burne-Jones, the son of Sir Edward Burne-Jones, the painter, was so heckled for writing home daily to his mother that he ran away and was found after three days in a starved condition in Savernake Forest.'[9] Earle added, surely unnecessarily, that his parents 'very wisely took him away'.

Unendurable 'ribbing' was only one torment. The *History* of 1923 records that all the boys in the mid-1840s were taught in one room. In the winter most were frozen. They might have seen the flames of the log fire at the end of the room in school hours, but the only time they felt its warmth 'was when they got a great deal more than they liked, and were submitted to the ordeal of "roasting", a familiar form of torture in those days'.[10] Shades of Flashman! Earle too had something to say on school torture: 'Among all the tortures invented by... the Marlborough bully, the suspending of small boys in sheets over the bannisters of the upper corridor of a House is, perhaps, the most blood-curdling.'[11]

To his reminiscences Earle attached as a conventional rider the smoothly diplomatic comment that he believed that Marlborough in the 1930s was one of the best of the public schools – as indeed it was, but only a few years earlier it had seen some celebrated bullying of the so-called 'hereticks', a group of aesthetes that included Anthony Blunt, John Betjeman and Louis MacNeice. Betjeman's description of 'Big School' in his verse autobiography *Summoned by Bells* provides merely a flavour of their defiant suffering:

> Alas for them, that wrapped in swaddling clothes
> Are A House's special care,
> Who dread the 'bloods' that turn their collars up,
> Wear coloured socks and paste their hair.
>
> Alas for them, I say, when plunged from thence
> To pan barbaric Upper School,
> Whose aspect grim within is not denied
> Where hardy, stubborn athletes rule.[12]

Nevertheless, Betjeman had it easy. The early days were by far the worst: 'in the general hurly-burly no mercy was extended to the weak. They led a life of oppression, though they had at least the consolation of seeing and knowing that their companions in misfortune were numerous.'[13]

Whether or not this was a consolation is now impossible to know. Some sort of consolation was certainly necessary. In response to 'most attempts to awaken the chords of memory' associated with those early moments of Marlburian history, it has been remarked, it was the 'bitter cry of the weak and the oppressed' that was 'the prevailing note'.[14]

James Franck Bright has left an account of Marlborough about the time that G.E.L. Cotton was appointed headmaster in 1852. The school, he remembered, 'was in a very bad state'.[15] Apart from savage bullying,

> There was a fixed hostility to the masters. The organisation of games was scarcely perceptible. The arrangement of the school buildings lent itself to disorder – immense dormitories and schoolrooms in which certain privileged boys were allowed to sit out of school hours, where they cooked illicit meals, but where it was nearly impossible to read or study; and an enormously big school, the scene of all sorts of pranks and bullying, into which all the unprivileged were crowded.[16]

There is much more in the same vein set down by pupils and masters of the time. However, Marlborough was not exceptional: it was typical. It had its idiosyncrasies, but it also had its commonalities. As an anonymous contributor to *All The Year Round* in 1879 remembered of the school in the 1840s: 'In literal truth we were not worse than any other set of boys, and our outbreaks did not arise from any inherent wickedness, but were the venial ebullitions of youthful spirit inadequately watched and restrained.'[17] Sir Lionel Earle's recollections are, therefore, quite typical of his generation (and in some aspects, of later generations), and indeed repeated over and over in the autobiographies, memoirs and reminiscences of Victorians.

Bullying was a commonplace pleasure of the bigger mid-Victorian public schoolboy. J.S. Thomas, in his 'Reminiscences' of Marlborough of the 1840s, noted that the real brute in the school was the school bully and added that he himself had witnessed

> acts of which the only explanation could be that the author delighted in inflicting torture. I remember a big fellow who was in the habit of calling small boys to him and running pins through lobes of their ears, and on one occasion I saw him vary this practice by using a penknife instead of a pin.[18]

Such memories, he added, somewhat gratuitously, made thoughts of Marlborough hateful. Another cruel amusement he described involved thoughtless fellows who by way of amusement tied sheets together and with these dropped small boys over the balustrade from the top of A House to the basement – clearly an early form of involuntary indoor bungee jumping.[19] The bullies of B House employed a variation of this amusement, letting boys down the well of the staircase in a carpet-bag: 'a very dangerous proceeding; for, to say nothing of the fright, it is evident that a knot which slipped would probably cause death, as B House is several storeys high.'[20]

Virtually every part of the school available to the boys was used by the ingenious bully: 'One "sport" was 'to make small boys run across an arch in the court . . . the boys ran from the shelter of one pillar to another; and the big boys "shied" at them with heavy sticks as they ran.'[21] Another amusement of the time involved getting the victim to lift the skin of the back of his hand and cutting it off with scissors.[22] Surely this was bad enough. However, according to Bright, at pre-Cotton Marlborough 'there was a great deal of bullying of a severe character; one boy, for instance, was periodically half-hanged; another tall ruffian used to take a small boy into Savernake Forest and, giving him 12 yards' start, proceeded to pot at him with a pistol.'[23]

Such were merely some of the 'disreputable pleasures' of mid-Victorian Marlborough. They certainly do not exhaust the list.[24]

Marlborough College was the brain-child of a West Country cleric keen to create a (boarding) 'School for the sons of Clergy'.[25] Its wet August opening day in 1843 is described in the *Centenary Commemoration* of 1943 in a series of sharply remembered impressions of a then very young entrant. First he described the approach to the school: 'The barren downs without hedgerow or habitation, rolling in grey monotony to the horizon, the interminable white road, the sombre copses looming indistinctly through the driving mist – all seemed inexpressibly bleak and dismal.'[26] They were portents of things to come.

If the location seemed uncongenial, the arrival of scores of rowdy West Country scions of the regional priesthood, among others, was disastrous for one well-adjusted species of the amphibious population: 'One group of lads were engaged in hunting frogs, which abounded there, and great heaps of the slain were prominently in view. Every hole and corner was carefully explored.'[27] The sacerdotal fathers of these rumbustious offspring promptly left them to it: 'The parsons soon grew weary of the scene and retired to spend a quiet evening at the Ailesbury Arms', while the young entrant wisely sought to 'ingratiate himself with a tough-looking sturdy lad' under whose wing he hoped to shelter in safety. It was not to be. The advances were resented, and this local 'Tom Jones' irritably 'aimed a furious blow with a thick frog-slaying blugeon at my head'.[28] Fortunately it missed. So the scene was set for at least a decade of Marlburian rural recreations.

The site of this slaughter was the Mound. There is a description of it by the earlier fortunate survivor of the attempted bludgeoning:

> A long terrace, bordered by prim rectangular flower-beds, and terminating in an artificial ruin, looked down on a straight and formal canal, on the other side of which a grove of lofty limes and poplars rose out of the thickets of a wilderness, and a huge Druidic mound reared its eccentric cone crowded with waving foliage, and ascended by a spiral walk which wound imperceptibly to the summit. The mound and wilderness were surrounded by a moat, half of which crept sluggishly through a jungle of reeds and rushes, whilst the other half meandered amongst strawberry-beds and cabbages, and was overhung by apple-trees.[29]

The slaughterers were a motley bunch:

> We were a unique assemblage. Most of us saw each other for the first time, and we came from widely distant quarters. Every English county had its representative and the sister island mustered strongly. There was a boy from Lydd, and a boy from Castlebar; Britons from the Land's End, and Cumbrians from the mists of Skiddaw; the Londoner confronted the Welsh mountaineer, and the East Anglian listened with astonishment to the brogue of Ulster.[30]

Their appearance was, to say the least, 'picturesque',

> ...as we were not restricted to any particular dress, and many of us came from remote places where the fashions of the day were unknown, or regarded with pious abhorrence. Wide collars falling to the shoulders and terminating in a large frill; caps made of horsehair, bulging out like air cushions, or sticking up in whalebone pinnacles; pantaloons of glaring colours lent variety to this crowd. One poor boy entered the arena in a white beaver hat![31]

'Tom Jones', mentioned above, was fortunately a little clumsy with his bludgeon. However, despite the fact that many were the sons of men of the cloth, apparently early Marlburians became adept at wielding a somewhat slimmer stick, the 'squaler',[32] as a weapon for killing wildlife. The 'squaler' in the early years of Marlborough was 'as much a part of the ordinary equipment of a Marlborough boy'[33] as the cricket bat would be in later years. It was a canehandle with a lead top about the size of a pear. Marlburians used it to deadly effect to kill rabbits and hares, and sometimes deer. Many boys could throw it a considerable distance with force and accuracy.

A good number of the boys 'were allied by blood or other affinity to the landowning class, and came from a stock to whom field sports and the instincts that develop into them were a second nature'.[34] Not surprisingly, therefore, most of the school 'looked to field and forest for their recreation'.[35] There was an abundance of both on their doorstep. The view has been expressed that a 'barbaric instinct of slaughter and adventure inherent in English men was [thus] fostered by the surroundings of the place, as well as to a great extent by the origins of the boys', with the result that these young men 'developed naturally into poachers, rat-catchers and even raiders of poultry-yards, at the bottom of all of which was the crude sporting instinct brought from West Country homes, and forced very often into illicit channels'.[36] There were ample opportunities. There was 'a numerous wild population of fallow deer, hares, rabbits, and squirrels; hawks, crows, magpies, jays, starlings, and wood-peckers; and in the remote depths shyer creatures, such as the badger and the ring-ouzel, find a home; or the intruder is liable to be frightened by a red stag suddenly and fiercely lifting his antlered head from the fern'.[37]

Thomas summed up the pre-1851 Marlborough generation as follows: 'We were a birds'-nesting, poaching, trespassing rabble, the scourge and the horror of the neighbourhood.'[38] He does not appear to have any reason to have indulged in exaggeration: quite the reverse.[39] Elsewhere Thomas insisted that poaching, in his time, had been 'very rife in the school'.[40] One Marlburian, he remembered, reduced poaching to 'a regular system' and was 'professional' in his approach:

> Now poaching had, as I have stated, been very rife in the school. Indeed, one boy, if he was correctly reported, had reduced it to a regular system. He had a big overcoat with large inside pockets, in which he was able to carry the divided stock and barrel of a gun. Half a dozen small boys were compelled to accompany him, with whom he resorted to some small coppice in the neighbourhood. They were stationed at intervals around the outside of the coppice, with instructions that in case of danger they should run in from the threatened quarter and give the alarm, whereupon the whole party hastened out and away from the opposite side. So

long, however, as no alarm was raised, the sportsman, accompanied by a dog which was kept for him by some cottager, systematically hunted and shot the coppice.[41]

The masters were certainly faced with rough, tough specimens of British rural boyhood:

An Irish boy opened a sort of Cave of Adullam, and gathered about him all the discontented spirits. Another boy, a native of Devonshire, was so loquacious and argumentative, and had so little notion of subordination, that no one could act with him. He also drew aside and revolved in his private orbit, forming a club for himself of such boys as were willing to render him implicit and unquestioning obedience. For some years there were several rival clubs in the school, until at last the fittest survived.[42]

These Marlburians, not surprisingly, more than held their own with the local 'moonrakers',[43] the uncouth and largely unintelligible local rustics. There were frequent 'serious and unseemly conflicts':

On one occasion some drovers, on their way to Pewsey market, met a party of boys. Words passed between them, and from words they came to blows. The drovers fought with great fury, using their sticks and whips, and any weapon they could seize; but they were beaten off, and so severely mauled that they determined to prosecute their assailants, and obtained permission from the head-master to come to the college and identify them. Accordingly, one day whilst we were at dinner, two ghastly figures entered the hall, [and] were led round the tables with grave solemnity by our fat butler. Their faces were woefully discoloured, and their noses and foreheads plaistered with horizontal stripes.[44]

The boys had their illicit pleasures. They were not alone. The masters, it seems, had theirs:

The masters faced with these period middle-class delinquents frequently resorted to beatings to maintain control. Nevertheless, these beatings certainly were far from being simply an instrument

of discipline. Rather they appeared, on occasion, to be opportunities for sadistic enjoyment, despite the early assertion that
'...promiscuous caning...at that time by no means peculiar to
Marlborough,...from the very first...seems to have been a
tremendous engine of discipline there.'[45]

Beatings could be both a licensed and licentious Victorian public school
'sport':

The penchant for using the birch on every possible pretext, which
was so often displayed by schoolmasters not only of the famous
public schools, but also in other scholastic establishments
throughout the country, suggests that these pedagogues were
sometimes imbued with motives other than those to which they
gave public utterance. This much is implied in the following
satirical couplet from *The Rodiad*:

'Delightful sport! whose never failing charm
Makes young blood tingle and keeps old blood warm.'[46]

Consequently, there could well be some truth in the assertion: 'It is impossible that among the [Victorian] schoolmasters of Britain there were not many
who derived conscious sexual pleasure from the practice.'[47] The latitude
allowed to these tormentors was extraordinary to modern minds sensitised by
guidance counsellors and gentled by European Union legislation.

Marlborough masters handled the cane enthusiastically. Even the well-
disposed among the early pupils at the school – there were some –
considered that the term 'brutal' was the only one that adequately fitted the
systematic floggings the boys endured: 'in the depths of every magisterial
desk at that time lay a cane...a weapon of hideous length and terrible
circumference'.[48] It did not remain in the desk for long: 'At frequent intervals and upon slight provocation these formidable flails leapt...from their
lurking-places and descended upon the backs of the trembling culprits.'[49] All
this before a large, excited audience of pupils in one huge classroom holding more than 200 boys. F.A.Y. Brown, one early pupil, recalled that the
boys took pride in taking the beating without flinching and that his brother
'did his back up tight, as a sort of defiance to the master, and kept it so;
though his jacket was cut to pieces, and his back...was scored across from
shoulder to shoulder, with 7 or 8 blue and yellow weals that took up to three
weeks to heal'.[50] Another boy stood up to 30 strokes from another master.[51]

Figure 1.1. A public flogging in Eton. Source: George Macdonald Fraser, *The World of the Public School* (London: Weidenfeld & Nicolson, 1977). (Originally from *Recollections of Eton* [1870].)

Brown retained in adulthood 'the sound of the master's drawing his heavy armchair back, so as to clear the deck for action; and the hush which ran through the schoolroom as the boys looked up from their work to see who the culprit was, and who was the executioner.'[52] Thomas too, retained a lasting memory of the moment when boys who, among other things, failed in their work were punished, stating chillingly:

> Probably no one of us who lived in the upper school-room, at the time of which I am speaking, could hear that peculiar sound which is made by a heavy oak chair when pushed back over a hollow wooden stand, without involuntarily looking round. It always betokened the rising of a master to inflict corporal punishment. The familiar sound produced an instantaneous silence, and a concentration of all eyes on the spot indicated. There stood the victim and the executioner. If the latter was notorious for the strength of his right arm, it was a matter of no small interest to us to see whether his victim's pluck would suffice to bring him victorious through the limited number of strokes which custom and decency enjoined. If he never flinched or uttered cry, we regarded him as a hero who had scored one against the redoubtable wielder of the rod of justice.[53]

Lockwood too, and, he suggests, others, took the unhappy memory of the pushed-back chair with him into adulthood, and in his case, into empire:

> The grating noise, made by the master's chair as he rose to make his rounds, or knout us in the school, is one of those familiar sounds, which I imagine has often been recalled by many an old Marlburian. I have fancied that I heard it in the lonely Indian jungles, and whilst lying on the banks of the sacred Ganges; and although night-mares seldom trouble me, that sound [takes] the place of other terrors which troubled sleepers see.[54]

Lockwood has left an horrific description of the impact of the 'flail' on his own back: 'The knoutings which I received from my master's reverend arm, turned my back all the colours of the rainbow.' He recorded also the insensitive cruelty of the highest authority: 'when I screamed from the fearful torture they produced, the headmaster would send a prefect down to say that if I made such a "horrid noise" he also would have a go-in at me, when my master had done his worst'.[55] When Lockwood returned home and 'was undressed and put to bed by my tender-hearted nurse, she viewed my back with the utmost horror and indignation. But she was told that as the punishment had been administered by reverend men called to the ministry, I must have deserved every blow I got.'[56] In reality, God appeared to be on the side of the devils, not the angels.

Lockwood's description of beatings in tandem certainly arouses the suspicion that perversion as much as punishment was the motive: 'occasionally two masters would be caning at the same time in time with the rhythms of blacksmiths hammering on an anvil'. Another pupil of the time recalled an occasion 'when a master lost control over himself in his efforts to bring some note of pain from a particularly heroic victim. The former gave up exhausted, but the latter had to be consigned to the sick-room, where strips of his shirt were extracted from his lacerated back'[57] by the newly appointed school doctor. As neatly summed up in *The Whippingham Papers*:

> This is the way with schoolmasters; their fashion
> Is to flog boys for silence as for speech;
> If a boy blubbers while they lay the lash on
> They dry his tears with a fresh cut for each;
> If he won't cry, it puts them in a passion,
> And they lay twice as much upon his breech;
> So, if you cry, you're flogged; and if you don't,
> You're flogged for impudence because you won't.[58]

As mentioned earlier, Marlborough was in no way exceptional. The English public schools, famous and less famous, were:

> notorious for the whippings inflicted there...[They] had an unsavoury reputation throughout Continental Europe as the home and headquarters of flogging, both domestic and educational. When one considers the widespread references in English literature to public school and university floggings, and the zeal for the infliction of corporal punishment displayed by so many of England's most famous educationalists, there seems little wonder that such an idea became ecumenic, and that, with continual repetition, it acquired an exaggerated force.[59]

It was certainly the case that:

> 'Mid folks of high degree, the rod's astir –
> At Eton, Harrow, Rugby, Westminster,
> Six days in seven making due sensation
> Among the best posteriors of the nation.[60]

Marlborough posteriors, of course, also felt the rod.

The appearance as well as the actions of masters could produce terror. Lockwood mentioned one zealously sadistic Marlborough teacher of esoteric and, no doubt for some, frightening appearance:

> One of the masters, when he came upon us unawares perpetrating any peccadilly [*sic*] would exclaim, as he seized us by the hair or neck, 'Slippery fellow, I've got you at last!' He also affected a highly polished satin stock with an iron buckle which fastened it behind, the end sticking out several inches and presenting in the distance a formidable horn or pigtail, and as this from long usage had become much frayed, the boy who sat next to me in school exercised his wit in writing a poem; describing the master's supposed search through the various shops in the town for a new stock of the same antiquated shape and pattern, describing it as 'one of the old sort, buckle behind'. This description being incomprehensive to the shopmen, various forms of banter, in which the words 'slippery fellow' were freely used, filled up the poem which at last concluded, by a cupboard, fastened by a rusty lock unused for a century or more, being opened and disclosing the long sought for article. On which the joyous purchaser skipped out of the shop, very fast, crying,
>
> > 'Slippery fellow, I've got you at last!
> > The old sort, buckle behind!'[61]

Here is Lockwood on the brutality of yet another master:

> There was a boy who was only seven when he arrived at school; he sat near me, and one day he whispered that he thought he could eat a house [*sic*], meaning that he was very hungry. It was resur-rection-day, on which a réchauffé was served up... hunger had

made my neighbour reckless, and he demanded a second slice; and then the dreaded Inspector stood before him...The master eyed his victim for some moments, which, though they may have been pleasant enough to him, were agony to the wretched boy; and at length, pulling out the well-known pocket book, he said, 'Come to my desk when the school bell rings, and I will cane you.'[62]

Understandably, Lockwood added: 'How gladly the entire school would have hailed the sudden appearance of the Editor of *Truth* or the Secretary of the Society for the Prevention of Cruelty to Children on the scene, to stay the reverend arm.'[63]

Lockwood, as well as the boy who sat next to him, recruited irony in the form of black humour to sustain him in his recording of his Marlborough experiences: 'There was a tradition in the Lower School that, if any master raised his aim above his head whilst in the act of caning, he was liable to be fined a bottle of the best champagne', and then added that if this penalty was ever enforced in his case, he certainly never received his share. He suggests that possibly it was enforced in the staff's 'Common-room' and the masters drank his health while hoping, at the same time, that 'the dose would be repeated soon'.[64]

If classroom beatings were spontaneous, the ceremony of the headmaster's beating was a calculatedly solemn and sombre ritual:

A birching by the Head Master has...been the most awesome of scholastic functions in every age, and Marlborough in these days fully maintained the fearsomeness of the occasion. The Head Master, bearing always, as part, no doubt, of the insignia of office, a bunch of keys, was wont to move in solitary state to his desk in the upper schoolroom, followed by the trembling culprit. The former then took his stand upon the raised dais, the sinner immediately in front of him, and a prefect upon either hand. The Head Master then made a brief speech to the assembled school, dwelt on the nature of the offence, and pointed to the crushed figure in front of him as a warning to all evil-doers. Then, amid an awful silence, and in mournful procession, the master, the criminal, and the two prefects wended their way to the sixth-form class-room, from whence in due course proceeded sounds calculated to make the undetected sinner outside reflect seriously upon the error of his ways.[65]

Thomas has provided an equally frightening description of the ritual associated with the headmaster's public floggings of pupils:

> there was another sound which was associated with the infliction
> of a flogging. This was the jingling of a bunch of keys. Why these
> were carried by the Master on this particular occasion I do not
> know, but almost invariably as he advanced to his seat of state in
> the upper school-room he held his bunch of keys in his hand.
> Attracted by the sound we looked up. The Master was advancing
> followed by the culprit. He took his stand on his raised dais, the
> culprit before him. Two prefects, who were to act as assessors,
> placed themselves on his right and left. Then the Master, in a
> short speech, explained the character of the offence for which
> retribution was about to be exacted, and a few words of warning
> were added to point the moral. He descended, and the melancholy
> procession of Master, culprit, and prefects proceeded to the Sixth
> class-room. The door closed, and the sound of the birch rod, not
> seldom accompanied by cries of distress, brought home to our
> minds the severity of this – the utmost penalty of the law.[66]

If moral reflection was an eventual consequence of this flogging ritual, a
more immediate consequence was general anticipatory excitement.

Of course, as has already been made abundantly clear, flogging was
commonplace in all the public schools of the time, not just Marlborough,
with the result that: 'flogging was given prestige by the public schools and
imitated elsewhere; the assumption being that what was good enough for
public schoolboys was good enough for everyone else'.[67]

Arguably Eton has the fullest records of flogging left by pupils and they
provide flesh to the skeleton[68] offered by more reticent Marlburians. John
Lewis Deleware remarked in an article 'Eton Thirty Years Since', published
in *Macmillan's Magazine* in 1875, that:

> I cannot close this paper without adverting to two extremely singu-
> lar institutions, much cherished by the authorities of my day as
> accessories to their system, and which indeed seem to me admirably
> to illustrate that system. One was the theory of 'bounds', and the
> other the practice of public flogging. In neither case, if I were
> endeavouring to explain the matter to an educated Frenchman,
> should I feel quite sure that he believed me to be speaking the truth.[69]

Figure 1.2. A public school birching. Source: R.G. Van Yelyr, *The Whip and the Rod* (London: Gerald G. Swan, 1941).

He remembered that 'some half-dozen to a dozen boys were flogged every day'.[70] At Marlborough, too, 'public floggings were a regular feature of daily life'.[71] 'Marburiana', referred to earlier, included the statement: 'I have seen as many as twenty boys just waiting to be birched.'[72] Indeed, Matthew Wilkinson, the first headmaster, who opposed corporal punishment, at least in theory, at one moment in his headmastership, stated in a letter in the late 1840s: 'Flogging has been much more common at Marlborough than Eton.'[73]

At Eton 'anyone who chose might drop in' for a beating by the head-master. If the offence was heinous (smoking or drinking, for example) or the individual famous (a member of the eleven) there would be a crowd of up to 100 who 'would throng the staircase leading up to the headmaster's room, flattening their noses against the balustrades and the oaken doors, struggling and elbowing for places, vociferating, chaffing, fighting, in the intervals of peeling oranges and cracking nuts, just for all the world as it is said that many used to go on outside Newgate'.[74]

As Oxford and Cambridge are often bracketed together, so Eton is invariably bracketed with Harrow. It is interesting, therefore, to find that beatings by the Harrow headmaster Charles Vaughan in the 1840s more than held their own with those of the great Eton headmaster and beater Keate in their degree of incalculable brutality:

> As Arnold's disciple, Vaughan had strong views about beating: he approved of it. Alone in the Fourth Form Room, with only Custos as a witness, the head used a birch – 'swishing' – on the exposed backsides of culprits. Whereas Wordsworth's birches were reput-edly feeble, being old, big, and bushy, Vaughan insisted on a new birch for each 'swishing' (leaving his used ones to the furious Under Master Oxenham), ordering each one to be reduced in bulk so as to sting more. These he kept locked in a cupboard (also to his deputy's rage). When, on one occasion, its lock was blocked up as a prank, Vaughan threw a tantrum, threatening to punish the whole school (by then, February 1847, over 250) unless the perpetrators confessed. Following Arnold, Vaughan did not beat often or recklessly, but when he did he meant it to hurt. He would deliver six, eight, or ten cuts and draw blood, leaving birch buds imbedded in the wounds that could last for a fortnight.[75]

Was the drawing of blood another of Vaughan's disreputable pleasures? Eventually he resigned because of a homosexual affair with a pupil. At Marlborough birching by the headmaster was in the privacy of his room, but the audience left outside relishing the groans or screams inside no doubt would have reacted in much the same way as did Etonian voyeurs.

As is well-known, in the late nineteenth century the public schools became widely known for their subscription to playing team games. However, Esmé Wingfield-Stratford touched on a perennial reality of these schools in the late nineteenth century and the early twentieth century when he wrote of Eton at the turn of the century that flogging was as much a form of athletics as compulsory games, and added that there was little shame involved, and less justice and responsibility. The fact of the matter was that the big boys enjoyed beating the little boys. Indeed, they were proud of any talent to inflict the maximum pain: 'Any, or no excuse, was considered good enough for the command "bend over"! Housemasters, in his experience, could be just prone to this pleasure, and appetite naturally grew by what it fed on.'[76] More generally, R.G. Van Yelyr concludes that:

> Even where no sadism was existent at the time of commencement the career of schoolmaster, the regular practice of whipping was almost certain to develop it. Even in the case of the onlooker, there is a risk of developing a liking for cruelty. Much more, therefore, may one expect such a development in the actual flogger. The reality of this danger is indicated in the revelations of schoolmasters themselves, who have confessed to the experiencing of pleasure in the infliction of punishment, often to their own consternation.[77]

Without question at least some of those who were beaten also got a perverted pleasure from being beaten, as Donald Pearsall has pointed out:

> One outcome of the public school predilection for flogging, was that in later life, while many public schoolboys found being flogged a painful and humiliating experience, and looked back on it with horror and disgust, there were others, though they cannot have been many (so wide and diverse were the excuses for a swishing), who escaped. And there were others who forsook the pleasures of the block when they discovered the delights of heterosexuality. But even after these three categories have been cleared, there were considerable numbers of young men anxious and often desperate to recapture the lost sensations, and for them the flagellation brothels thrived.[78]

It appears that in 1838 flogging 'supported 20 splendid establishments'[79] in London and was known as 'the English vice'; this was before many public schools had been created. It was not without reason, then, that in the second half of the nineteenth century, 'flagellomania, while almost totally absent in France, Spain and Italy, was widespread in Britain'.[80] One famous former public schoolboy was the poet Algernon Charles Swinburne, who wrote in 1879 in *The Pearl*, a pornographic magazine, of learnt early pleasures:

> Any boy that enjoys
> A fine flogging to see,
> I give leave to stay here
> With Frank Fane and me.
> They will see his white bottom,
> When they see it again,
> I don't think they'd fancy
> It belongs to Frank Fane.[81]

There was a vast literature of flagellation produced during the Victorian period. However, if it was vast:

> The audience to which this literature was directed was ... limited. It was restricted in the first place, of course, to those men to whom this perversion appealed; but it was further and even more rigidly restricted in point of social class. The literature of flagellation in Victorian England assumes that its audience had both interest in and connection with the higher gentry and the nobility... It further assumes that its audience had the common experience of education at a public school. Many works are set at school – 'Birchminster', for example – and the anonymous authors style themselves 'Etonensis' or 'An Old Boy'.[82]

To return to Marlborough, Lockwood provides a succinct summary of his, and others', schooldays there in which beatings loomed large, providing an alternative to William Cory's view of schooldays as 'days of sunshine and youth':

> At length the time arrived when I was to spend my last half-year at school; and when I arrived at Marlborough, in August, 1851, I knew no more of the subjects which formed the curriculum of the

school, than I did when I first arrived eight years before; and what otherwise might have been the joyous spring-time of my life had been, with a few bright intervals, little better than a dreary winter of chronic hunger and fear of impending evil in and out of school. No one had ever made the feeblest effort to teach me anything, and the cane had completely failed to drive the Latin grammar into my head. Nor was I alone in this misfortune, for most of the other boys who arrived at the school without having been previously 'grounded' rowed in exactly the same boat with me.[83]

In a succinct understatement worthy of the original Sparta itself (it too, of course, had its flogging rituals) the centenary publication *Marlborough College 1843–1943*, commented of this period: 'It was certainly a rough and rigorous life.'[84] This publication also contains the following bland comment: 'It is clear from the records and reminiscences of later years that for many boys, if not for all, the life was often, to put it mildly, far from happy. Hunger, fighting, bullying, floggings and fines are the recurrent themes of too many early accounts . . .'[85]

It comes as no surprise, therefore, to read this reasonable observation of Marlborough in its early years: 'For the weak, the sensitive or the studious it must have been a terrible place.'[86] In such unpleasant conditions, it has been calmly noted, 'Even before the end of 1847 there seems to have been a great many miserable individuals in the school who had come to the conclusion that life there was not worth living', with the result that, in the autumn of the same year, 'the number that ran away is quite unexampled in the history of the place'.[87] Things got so bad that one of the college's founders[88] admitted to considerable nervousness when 'traversing' the streets of London, 'lest he should perchance come face to face with the infuriated parent of some escaped Marlburian demanding his lost son!'[89] Disappearances became so frequent and the response of the authorities so ruthlessly desperate that one form that had been 'gated' *en masse* after one of their number had absconded took to mounting guard over suspected fugitives and disciplining returning escapees.

Thomas set down the details of one runaway's 'sympathetic' beating from his self-policing peers:

It was a Saturday night when licet had been called at tea, [and] there was an immediate exodus from the hall. I had no idea of the cause, but of course I rushed out to find out what was up, regardless of the increased cravings of the stomach which would follow from my abridged meal. I found that all were flocking to the Upper School. There a vast circle had been formed, and about the centre of it was a solitary individual, unknown to me, sitting or standing at his desk. I was informed that he was about to be thrashed publicly. The ministers of justice had not arrived, and, to beguile the time, now and again a dictionary, or other book, would be thrown at him from the circumference; but without much effect. At last two big fellows of his form stepped forward and gave him a thrashing – not a very severe one, as far as I remember.[90]

Acute misery was the stimulus to flight.[91] More than 50 years later, George Orwell's ruthlessly honest essay 'Such, Such were the Joys' set out with poignant clarity his recollections of his early twentieth-century school-days, providing an enduring image of many generations of small public schoolboys that, arguably, fits the young mid-Victorian Marlburian like a glove:

It is curious, the degree – I will not say of actual hardship – but of squalor and neglect that was taken for granted in upper-class schools of that period. Almost as in the days of Thackeray, it seemed natural that a little boy of eight or ten should be a miser-able, snotty-nosed creature, his face almost permanently dirty, his hands chapped, his nails bitten, his handkerchief a sodden horror, his bottom frequently blue with bruises.[92]

For Orwell, and most assuredly for many small Victorian Marlburians, at least in the second half of the nineteenth century, 'In winter, your nose ran continually, your fingers were too numb to button your shirt...and there was the daily nightmare of football – the cold, the mud, the hideous greasy ball that came whizzing at one's face, the gouging knees and the trampling boots of the bigger boys.'[93]

For the powerful and the pugnacious, however, there were certain well-established enjoyments. Fist-fighting was a frequent pleasure (for winners and audience) in mid-Victorian schools, as in the wider society. It had time-honoured legitimacy. Thomas Assheton-Smith, who boasted that he had learned nothing at Eton (1783–94) but had enjoyed his cricket, rowing and boxing, 'earned lasting fame for his bloody hour-long fist-fight with a fellow pupil, Jack Musters, who, Nimrod once remarked "could have leaped, hopped, fought, danced, played cricket, fished, swam, shot, played tennis and skated with any man in Europe".'[94] It was clearly little wonder that Assheton-Smith won acclaim for the defeat of such a physical paragon. Thomas Hughes, of course, provided the moral licence for public schoolboys to beat each other senseless: 'Fighting with fists is the natural and English way for English boys to settle their quarrels.'[95] He urged his youthful readers to 'learn to box, then, as you learn to play cricket and football. Not one of you will be the worse, but very much better for learning to box well.'[96]

According to John Chandos: 'up to the 1840s boys battled in bloody combat on any pretext, "hardly a day passing", according to Gladstone, "without one, two, three or even four more or less mortal combats".'[97] Sometimes the consequences of fist-fighting were far less admirable than Hughes claimed, and indeed could even be tragic. Tim Card, a recent historian of Eton College, slides smoothly and swiftly over such activities at pre-Clarendon Eton with the urbane comment: 'Prize-fighting was admired nationally, and the boys settled their quarrels with their fists – on the most notorious occasion a son of Lord Shaftesbury was actually killed.'[98] Down the decades this death mattered little in maintaining Eton numbers. Ofsted inspectors today may have considered a barefisted fight of some hours that ended in a death somewhat over the top, but sensible parents then, and before and after, had the clearest priorities: 'the School's main draw was the desire of parents to have their sons in a school that enjoyed royal favour, and where they would met the right company'.[99]

At mid-century Marlborough, it seems, there occurred the rather odd paradox that the early bully 'was scarcely ever pilloried, but the combatants in a square stand-up fight seem, when caught red-handed, or rather red-nosed, to have been for some reason or other the special objects of official wrath'.[100] Nevertheless, it was stated later, of the mid-century years:

> Fights at this period, and for a long while afterwards, were frequent and fierce. Neither were they confined as in more recent times to the middle and junior parts of the School. Among the many notable contests that distinguished the first five years, one, fought at 6 a.m. in the fifth-form room between two of the biggest fellows in the School, seems to stand out prominently. It lasted an hour, and resulted in a drawn battle, both combatants, however, being relegated to the sick-room to recover from their injuries and meditate at their leisure upon the punishment which was surely meted out, in those days, to the detected pugilist.[101]

Figure 1.3. A fight in the 1840s at Fleuss's arch. Source: A.C. Bradley, A.C. Champneys and J.W. Baines, *A History of Marlborough College* (London: John Murray), 1923.

Fleuss's Arch was the venue of formal fights.[102] Fighting, however, as noted above, was not restricted to the Arch. In fact, it took place virtually everywhere: 'in the court, the field, the school room, the dormitory'.[103] However, 'for the more formally arranged encounters Fleuss'[s] Arch was recognised as the appropriate spot, unless the principals were leading fellows in the school. In that case the Upper Fifth was sometimes [as has been made clear above] selected.'[104] In these instances all arrangements would have been carefully made beforehand, and 'a plentiful supply of water and towels would have been brought in, after breakfast the combatants and their personal friends would adjourn to the classroom, and, with the doors barricaded, there was no danger of disruption until the school-bell necessitated dispersion'.[105] The *History* of 1923 recorded of the legendary contest described earlier:

> Almost lovingly have Marlburians of this period dwelt on the famous fights... A celebrated one at this particular time took place in the fifth-form class-room, where the desks ranged in semicircular form constituted a kind of amphitheatre, and lasted from breakfast till ten o'clock school. The last really notable

contest, we fancy, that took place was in 1863. The arena on this occasion was the Upper School. The fight was a lengthy and stubborn one, and both combatants, fellows in the lower fifth, were knocked out of time and their faces out of recognition. The one was a young patrician with more spirit than physique; the other was a sturdy Irishman. Nearly the whole School, except, of course, the sixth, were present at the fight; and even a group of small boys from A House had the temerity to cross the forbidden threshold and mingle in the crowd.[106]

Thomas earlier provided further detail about the famous fifth-form fight: 'two fellows, strong of limb and of indomitable pluck fought', he recounts; 'one was [later] a humble-minded, earnest Christian man and the other was [later] a soldier who died in India'.[107] In stressing later careers Thomas was making a point. There was for all concerned, he stressed, nothing brutalising in these encounters: 'Swollen eyes and bleeding noses did not absorb interest' so much as 'the pluck, the endurance, the indomitable resolution... in full play.'[108] His laudatory comments could have been written by Thomas Hughes.

However, the motives of spectators were not always so laudable. Brown described how, when he was a young Marlburian, 'a bully backed another boy' to beat him and they were made to fight, '...he willing, I not. He had some science, and I had none, and he beat me hopelessly; his fists seemed always in my face. I felt the defeat, but chiefly the injustice of being made to fight, for the amusement of the bigger boys.'[109]

In mid-century Marlborough the fighter's, not the games player's, courage and skill were celebrated. This is perhaps insufficiently appreciated. In 1852 one newcomer to Marlborough recalled that when he joined the school, rather than the captains of cricket and football or other athletic heroes, his fellow pupils pointed out to him with bated breath, as he sat in Hall for his first meal, the hero of the last fight, who had battered 'a bigger antagonist into temporary blindness', and had himself lost so much blood that he was 'too weak to cut his own meat at dinner'.[110]

Of course, pleasures were not invariably denied the powerless, nor were they inevitably disreputable. Whatever the sufferings of many young Marlburians of the time, and later, the young are extraordinarily resilient and Thomas could state matter-of-factly of Marlborough of the late 1840s: 'Yet, after all, we were not all unhappy. We formed stronger friendships from the fact that they sprang up and grew amid many hardships.' The escape routes to happiness were the local forest and downs: 'If we were not safe within the

College gates, we were safe and happy as we explored the recesses of the forest, or wandered over those grand old downs...The cuffs and kicks did not hurt much when you came to regard them as only natural and proper.'[111] Later Orwell also made the same point:

> No-one can look back on his schooldays and say in truth they were altogether unhappy. I have good memories...among a horde of bad ones. Sometimes on summer afternoons there were wonderful expeditions across the Downs or to Beachy Head... And there were still more wonderful midsummer evenings when, as a special treat, we were...allowed to wander about the grounds in the long twilight, ending with a plunge in the swimming bath at about nine o'clock.[112]

Despite such escape valves, at Marlborough various early pressures steadily mounted, and relations between boys and masters, in particular, steadily deteriorated to a state of permanent 'natural enmity'.[113] An early revolt was nipped in the bud in 1847, when a master, 'noted above all his colleagues for nerve, promptness, and decision',[114] confronted a belligerent school in 'the big schoolroom' during preparation, thrashed several of the biggest and drew the sting of an uprising. It was in 1851 that the boys experienced arguably the ultimate 'disreputable pleasure' any schoolboy can enjoy, and anticipated the film *If...* by many schoolboy generations, on the occasion of the 'Rebellion'.

After 1847 the number of pupils at Marlborough grew considerably. It has been asserted that 'the old-fashioned methods of intimidation by cane and confinement...proved hopelessly inadequate',[115] with the result that 'the bully grew more ferocious, the poacher more audacious and the breaker of bounds more regardless of the law'.[116] In direct consequence, in 1851, it has been claimed: 'Between October and December...there was more or less constant and violent war between the boys and the school authorities... during which one side smashed windows and furniture, set fire to rooms and assaulted officials, while the other side flogged and expelled with desperate diligence.'[117] This was the period of the Rebellion.

Wilkinson himself called the outbreak of violent confrontation a 'Rebellion'. It finished him. Soon after it, he 'resigned early...and retired to a country living'.[118] This controversial uprising has never been forgotten, for good reason: 'The great rebellion of 1851 is the event that stands out above all others in the early days of Marlborough.'[119] Perhaps it should have come as no surprise. It was 'the climax of the insubordination that for a long period had been growing and ripening. The School had, in fact, got thoroughly out of hand, demoralised in its own life, and a scourge to its neighbours.'[120]

Among other things, the boys grew increasingly more sullen in the face of mass punishments. There was a cycle of repression, resentment and retaliation. A main focus of resentment was the Gate Sergeant, C.T. Peviar,[121] 'a little bumptious man, with a prying nose, small sharp black eyes, and eyebrows habitually elevated', who was expected to keep a record of bad language and bad behaviour. This he did with 'more zeal than tact'. 'He appeared', stated Thomas, 'to regard the entire body [of the school] as 500 individuals all delinquents *in esse* or *in posse*, and himself as the acute myrmidon of the law who had to catch us tripping.'[122] Consequently he was loathed. The one-storey brick box at the gates in which he lived frequently came under attack by stone-throwers.

On one October evening in 1851 a serious attack in force was launched, with the result that the 'whole School was confined to their classrooms after dusk *sine die*'.[123] The event was described some years later by a witness of the time as follows. Startled by a heavy crash against the door, Peviar

> looked out, but was driven back by a shower of stones and brickbats, and, thinking there was some design upon his life, retreated with his wife and baby into the wash-house at the rear of the premises. Meanwhile, the hurricane of missiles continued, and did not cease until the door, windows and many of the tiles were smashed, and his chimney-pot shivered to atoms.[124]

Eventually he summoned up courage to look out on a deserted Court.

The 'hit and run' tactics in the dark were to be expected. The school of the 1840s lent itself to night-time 'warfare': 'the rabbit warren of ill-lit buildings offered endless possibilities not only to the adventurous but also to the ill-disposed for whom smoking and stone-throwing (a habit that persisted well into the 1870s) seem to have been the main occupations'.[125]

There was now a surge of extreme indiscipline. Work was disrupted, windows were smashed, an imposed curfew was ignored and masters who attempted to keep order, it has been stated, were pelted and hissed. On 1 November Wilkinson rescinded the system of wholesale punishment and confinement, but also expelled one rebellious ringleader. On 5 November the school expected to celebrate Guy Fawkes Night: 'It has been the custom from all time, or more strictly speaking, since the school was founded in 1843, to have fireworks and to remember the fifth of November.'[126] They were not allowed to do so. However, 'the school determined they would have fireworks; and they did!'[127] Five o'clock was fixed 'for the opening of the fray'.[128] One eyewitness later reported that at five o'clock sharp a rocket shot up from the centre of the court and 'the revolution had begun'.[129] The court was ablaze with fireworks for the whole of the evening, and the boys let them off in classrooms under the desks and in the classroom fires. Masters were powerless to do anything and all that night 'the row continued and the echoing of B House rang with continual detonations. The whole College for the next two days reeked of gunpowder.'[130] It appears that throughout the night of 5 November the masters, 'for the most part quiet studious men . . . were completely out of their element in a scene of violence, in darkness among unseen enemies, and distracted by flying brickbats, sudden explosions and the crash of falling glass'.[131]

Authority, initially stunned and paralysed, acted on 7 November and expelled five boys. This merely made matters worse. One of them was extremely popular: 'As this hero of the hour drove off, the entire school broke out of gates in a mass, and followed his fly the whole way up the High Street, shouting and cheering with wild enthusiasm.'[132] The townsfolk joined them. Then on the boys' return, the local miller, 'the sworn enemy of the School',[133] was jeered at and jostled, and later protested strongly to the headmaster. The boys now returned to the school and rushed 'with vengeance in their hearts to the room in which the Headmaster was sitting, groaned, hooted, hissed and, by way of a more forcible demonstration, smashed every pane.'[134]

With the ringing of the school bell, the boys returned to their classrooms, and when the masters arrived 'the uproar broke out again, and all authority was defied with groans, slamming of desks, and stamping of feet. Windows were smashed, desks were broken, and anarchy reigned everywhere throughout the week.'[135] Various aspects of this anarchy, apparently, involved the thrashing of Peviar by one of the school's champion fighters; setting fire to the wooden wings of the old rackets court; and the tossing of fireworks into fires against which masters were standing.[136]

Wilkinson appears to have suffered most:

> Down went the Doctor's crimson throne, forms, chairs and desks were overturned and smashed, and the floor was soon strewn with grammars and dictionaries, and Latin and Greek classics.
>
> Emboldened by impunity, the marauders flew to a higher game. Adjoining the schoolroom was the headmaster's classroom, a sacred chamber, replete with painful associations. In it the doctor kept his pages, including the manuscript of Sophocles which he was

preparing for the press; it was the scene of the daily tribunal for the trial of all grave offences; it likewise contained the stock of birches, and the record of crimes and punishments, and was the common place of execution. The shadow of a fear hung over it, and many a boy had abandoned hope here as he entered the gloomy portal.

All this was not forgotten. The door was broken open, the detested twigs were scattered to the winds, the furniture was smashed, the records torn up, the large inkstand flung through the window, and Sophocles dragged forth and burnt.[137]

Brown was a witness to this act – at a distance. He stated simply, 'the manuscript was in his desk. The boys took it out and burnt it.'[138] Thomas too was a witness to the destruction of Wilkinson's manuscript. He was more outspoken:

One act reflects disgrace on all concerned. In the Master's desk was found an interleaved and annotated edition of Sophocles. I remember seeing this in the hands of a big brute, who, with an opprobrious remark on its author, threw it into the flames. We learnt subsequently that it was an edition of Sophocles which the Master was preparing for publication, and now all his labour was thus ruthlessly destroyed. It is only fair to the offender to say that his act was one of culpable thoughtlessness rather than of deliberate malice. I remember the circumstance precisely, and I am certain that I am interpreting his action aright.[139]

Wilkinson capitulated at the close of the week. The school was assembled and a statement of their grievances was requested. They demanded the return of all privileges taken from them in the previous four years. This was agreed, subject to a contribution to the cost of repairing the damage done and a proper apology. These terms were complied with and the 'worst of the storm' passed.

On one later Sunday, however, a fresh disturbance occurred. It 'consisted in the burning of the masters' desks, including registers and punishment books; chairs, forms and other articles being piled on the flames'.[140] However, it was a limited not a general uprising and several perpetrators were successfully expelled. Floggings continued 'in a spirited and wholesale fashion' – one batch of 28 pupils were 'condemned and executed *en bloc*'. Such forceful actions seemed to bring major disruption to a close.

There is controversy over the extent of the Rebellion. In fact, throughout all the spread-out disturbances, Wilkinson reported, 'despite the disorders, work has continued as usual and latterly it has shown a general improvement'.[141] It was wise, of course, in his own interests to play down the 'Rebellion'. Perhaps, understandably, on occasions he did just this. On others, however, as will be seen shortly, it served him to be brutally honest. The diary of a boy at school at the time also contrasts the normal with the abnormal, as in his entry for 6 November: '...Fireworks let off from 5½ – 6½. Lots of windows were broken after chapel...played football.'[142] So perhaps normality oddly existed with abnormality.

Memory, as L. Warwick James, at one time the school's archivist, has remarked, does play strange tricks. It can shrink *and* enlarge remembered moments. This must be borne in mind. Nevertheless, there was an uprising, there was violence, there was destruction of property and papers, and it did go on for some time – spasmodically if not consistently. There is, in my judgement, no reason to believe that the harsh descriptions, by loyal supporters of the school such as Thomas and Bright, of the period that included the Rebellion are overdrawn. There is always the possibility of a tendency on the part of those who have served or belonged to institutions, understandably, to present them in the best light. For example, in his *Recollections of Schooldays at Marlborough College, 1848–1851*, printed privately in 1918, Canon W. Gildea made light of the Rebellion and, indeed, the excesses of pre-Cotton years. To be quite frank, he seems to have existed at Marlborough with 'his head in the clouds'. He certainly protested an institutional innocence too much. Perhaps his recollections help to put the early years in a somewhat 'more balanced' perspective, but in reality the times were against him.

What went on at Marlborough went on at other public schools of the period, but the rough and ready behaviour of Marlburians was a period commonplace. Indeed, Warwick James stated as much himself: 'There is, in fact, little in the spare-time occupations of Marlburians during the 1840s and '50s to differentiate him from boys in other schools.'[143] Gildea simply tried too hard to 'set the record straight'.[144] Without doubt, he failed.

Perhaps most damning of all for Gildea's fragile memory are passages in the letters written at the time by Wilkinson himself, especially with regard to the Rebellion. In a letter to the school's Council, dated 11 November 1851, Wilkinson wrote '...on 5 November a combined assault was made, more or less in all the houses, by throwing out of the rooms into the court and still more into the open space in the interior of houses A and B large quantities of squibs, crackers and other such things'.[145] To a parent of an expelled boy he wrote: 'I am sorry to say I have been obliged to send your son away... for heading a confederacy of insurgents and have made violence with fireworks etc. etc. etc. and done much damage to property and endangered life.'[146] With regard also to the extensive letting off of fireworks, he wrote, on another occasion at this time, of 'riotous attacks with stones after dark on persons and property, [and] a very wholesale discharge of fireworks in improper places, etc., etc.'.[147] In yet another letter he wrote of 'an attack made *in* and *from* every House with crackers, squibs, etc...'[148] Finally, he wrote to a colleague '...of the great disorder and outrages that were had amongst us on the fifth and the following day. The rioting grew to a head. Fireworks were thrown *in* and *from* all the houses through the night and in abundance – windows continued to be broken...'[149]

In other letters of the time Wilkinson refers to other aspects of the pupil uprising. To one parent of an expelled pupil he wrote: 'It is with much pain and concern that I have been obliged to send your son home for taking a very active and prominent part in an outrageous rebellion.'[150] To another parent he wrote that the parent's son had taken 'a mutinous part... violently throwing large flints... in an attack on one of the officers of the College'.[151] With regard to the initial attack on Peviar, Wilkinson wrote: '...a mischievous spirit has shewn itself in the College and broken windows in abundance are part of the result, but besides great injury and alarm is occasioned to persons employed whilst in the regular discharge of their duty'.[152] Again, 'We have had a series of outrageous attacks (on windows and persons employed in the court, etc.) that at last grew in spite of caution to a sort of mutiny.'[153] Finally, Wilkinson also wrote of the Rebellion that 'much damage to property' was done and 'life endangered with fire'.[154]

Thomas remarked of Wilkinson, with some charitable insight, that he was an inexperienced boarding school headmaster saddled with equally inexperienced masters, limited resources and a rapidly increasing pupil population: 'His task was desperate and it was only through failure that defects could be discovered and remedies applied.'[155] Wilkinson's successor, G.E.L. Cotton, the unwitting creator of the eventually castigated public school Games Cult,[156] benefited from Wilkinson's inadequacies. He correctly understood them and set matters right.

A final comment: Gildea, it seems, was incensed by the description of the Rebellion and the 1840s in the College *History* of 1896. It is interesting, therefore, to find that G.T.L. Carwithen, who was at Marlborough from 1850 to 1856, wrote in a letter dated 8 September 1913: 'I have been much interested in the History of Marlborough College... I read the Chapter on the Rebellion Half very carefully through and I do not hesitate to say that every word of it is true.'[157]

By the time peace had been restored, Wilkinson, quite understandably,

Figure 1.4. The 'blood' in full regalia. Source: *The Captain*, vol. XLII, no. 247, October 1919.

had had enough. In the first half of 1852 he resigned and retired 'to the tranquil Wiltshire parsonage of Market Lavington, and to the more congenial life and work of a country clergyman'. For the boys the beatings, bullying and bruising continued, somewhat reduced, but the battles for possession of the school ended entirely. Marlborough's Rebellion was the last great public school uprising, but 'the disreputable pleasures' of public schoolboys went on for a great deal longer.

Public schools have been and remain controversial. In the early twenty-first century successful adaptation, intelligent readjustment, and subscription (and attention) to the pursuit of excellence, among other things, excite resentment in some quarters. It might be appropriate, therefore, to end with these comments from a recent letter by one Richard Reynolds to the *Daily Telegraph*, headed 'Tom Brown Would Not Recognise School Now',[158] written in response to an earlier critical view by someone called Bella Bathurst of her post-war independent school:

> As a fellow boarder in a single-sex institution, I can spot many of the aspects of boarding school life in a fog of academic and emotional underdevelopment. Narrow and petty teachers, often violent and impressively numb-skulled fellow pupils, sexual confusion and unfulfilment... it all comes back like the chill of an early morning (cold) shower or the stinging burn of a cane stripe on my undeserving bum.[159]

Reynolds adds, however, that 'I am not sure where Bella has been since school, but years have elapsed and boarding schools have changed a lot... almost any private boarding school has a level of teaching, pastoral care and facilities that were indeed limited to the best few when Bella and I were at school. And the children seem happy.'[160] *Plus ça change...? Sometimes it is simply not true.*

Bloods, blues and barbarians: some aspects of late Victorian Oxbridge

J.A. MANGAN

> You exhibit no sympathy with us, no interest in our somewhat limited universe . . . you contemplate us as a set of lamentable barbarians; we regard you as a species of pitiful sheep (Open letter to a Don in *Granta*, January 1898).

In October 2001 the Dean of St Catharine's College, Cambridge, Dr Peter Tyler, imposed strict rules to control drinking in the wake of cases of alcoholic poisoning, a drunken female student vomiting in and around the Senior Common Room, another female undergraduate being virtually carried out of hall due to extreme drunkenness and an 'excess' of drunken, naked girls running across college lawns[1] – and all this while St Catharine's was sinking to the bottom of the academic league tables. The women-only Alley Catz dining club was investigated for its initiation ceremonies, which demanded that initiates drink large quantities of alcohol 'to prove their worthiness to join'. An anonymous third-year student was reported as remarking, 'At the end of the day you have to make a choice whether to drink or get a good degree.'[2] In the light of a fall from 11th to 18th in the Thompkin's (Performance) Table of the 24 colleges in 2000, there seems to have been some truth in this assertion. An associated editorial in the *Daily Telegraph* stated: 'Without condoning any of these incidents, they are just the sort of thing that has been going on for centuries at our ancient universities. Indeed, they might be thought of as a defining Oxbridge feature . . . the only innovation is that women are now at it.'[3]

Such activities were unquestionably unremarkable 100 years earlier at many 'Oxbridge' colleges, except for two things: they certainly did not include women,[4] who were not yet admitted to exclusively men's colleges; and they included the 'hearties' who populated many of the colleges. It was the time of bloods, blues and barbarians.

In October 1893 Ewart Grogan, later an African adventurer, settler and entrepreneur and, among other things, the first European to traverse Africa from the South to the North (most of the way he was accompanied by black

Africans, who are unsung), arrived at Jesus College, Cambridge, indisputably a 'hearties' college, famed for its philathleticism, its philathletic dons H.A. 'Black' Morgan and E.H. 'Red' Morgan, and the success of the college boat on the River Cam. At the time of Grogan's appearance 'Black' Morgan was the Master, and 'Red' Morgan (not a relative) was the Dean and Senior Tutor.

Grogan had spent the previous year ranging 'all over the Alps in search of new challenges: from Zermatt to the north side of the Rhone valley to the Dents du Midi, east of Champéry'.[5] He was exactly the type of undergraduate to win favour with 'Red' Morgan, who ensured Grogan's entry to the college. Morgan presided 'over Grogan's interview and sitting of the entry exam to read law, thoughtfully shutting his prospective student in a room filled with all the reference books necessary to secure a pass'.[6] Grogan passed. Grogan subsequently never visited his law tutor and never attended lectures. His intellectual interests were more eclectic. He read widely, showing an interest in medicine and a clear aptitude at mathematics. Ignorance of law posed no problem: his knowledge was hardly put to the test.[7] Exams were not compulsory and he took full advantage of this.

Grogan was more conscientious at his play: he rowed for a time, played rugby, at which he won his college cap, and proved to be a far from inadequate hammer-thrower. He was no intellectual philistine, however. A popular member of the Cranmer Debating Society, he was already a superb debater. Above all, however, he earned a Cambridge reputation as a renowned practical joker. In 1896 came his *pièce de resistance*:

> One afternoon, he spotted a small flock of sheep that had meandered their way from Jesus Common to feed on the geraniums in the college gardens and, having had a particular 'Smug' tutor in his sights for weeks, saw an opportunity not to be missed. Believing that the man would be dining late, and 'having nothing better to do', Grogan and a 'New Zealand pastoral friend' proceeded to herd the sheep into the hapless tutor's rooms. Unfortunately for both Grogan and the don, the latter was not out for dinner but had gone to London for the night. When he returned the sheep had eaten most of his carpet, his tablecloth and his prized aspidistra. Worse still, his rooms 'stank like a shearing shed' and were uninhabitable for weeks.[8]

Grogan's Cambridge career thus came to an abrupt end. He returned to the Alps, 'reached the summit of the Matterhorn and made a number of other testing ascents'.[9]

Grogan clearly possessed an imaginative talent for the outrageous, but he was simply one in a long line of rowdy, undisciplined, recalcitrant Cambridge students. By way of illustration, the Disciplinary Books kept by the Senior and Junior Deans of St John's College during the mid-Victorian period cast an interesting first-hand light on the student behaviour of the time. These two Deans for decades had the unenviable task of being responsible for student discipline: 'The statutes of 1580 prescribed two deans, one of whom must be a bachelor of theology and a senior, the other a Master of Arts. This was presumably to provide effective disciplinary supervision for all students within the College.'[10] It is clear that in 1867 the Junior Dean was responsible for first- and second-year men, the Senior Dean for the rest.[11] Both deans were clerics. Arrangements continued in much this way until the middle of the twentieth century.

The Deans' Disciplinary Book for 1853 provides a flavour of student life in college at the time, and makes for lively and, at a distance, amusing reading. One bane of the life of the Junior Dean in the mid-nineteenth century was a student by the name of Acourt, who was admonished on one occasion for a disorderly fencing match in his room after midnight, 'which made a visit by the Dean necessary'. He was admonished, but to little effect. It is recorded that the very next night he and some of his friends visited another student's room, and 'caused great disorder and mischief'; in the early hours, still with his friends, he returned to his own room, allowing them to continue 'to be disorderly'.[12] This time he was 'gated' for a fortnight and reported to his tutor. On another occasion, with a student friend by the name of Snow, Acourt was caught pistol-shooting in Snow's room. Later he was requested not to keep several guns in his room. Other anti-social acts included disorderly parties, noisy games and noisy singing. To top all this off, he was 'very neglectful of chapel'.[13]

The Dean had a lively time of it that year and no doubt in other years. On one occasion another friend of Acourt's, called Cotton, was reported to his tutor for letting fireworks off in college and being at a disorderly drinking party in a friend's room, 'which awoke the Dean, Tutor and others'. The Dean, upon investigation, found him 'half-intoxicated and riotous'. Another student by the name of Simpson held a disorderly party one evening, which again awoke the Dean, the Tutor and others. In the Disciplinary Books there are, in fact, continual references to 'disorderly parties', 'noisy parties', 'disorderly and noisy behaviour', and 'intoxicated and riotous behaviour'.[14]

Students appear to have come and gone at will, despite the nightly curfew. There are continual references in the Deans' Books to students being absent from their rooms all night. One student clearly decided that he had had enough of the puritanical restrictions of St John's and, to the chagrin of the Dean, married 'a girl from Hawkston of doubtful character', the daughter of a publican there. They were married at the register office in Cambridge on 5 January 1858 'without the knowledge of relatives'. It is recorded that he 'then lived at Hawkston a riotous life'.[15]

There is much in the same vein in the Deans' Disciplinary Books. They paint a picture of a general self-indulgent hedonism rather than of sober industry. In the main, the dons apparently were reputable; the students, it appears, were not. Increasingly as the second half of the nineteenth century progressed, the student 'barbarians', such as Grogan, took to the newly created and continually expanding playing-fields: the public school 'bloods' (successful athletes) strove to become university 'blues' (even more successful athletes). It demonstrated their manliness; it improved, where necessary, their career prospects; it was preferable to Latin, Greek and mathematics. For the most part, the students remained 'barbarians', but fencing with swords and shooting with pistols were largely replaced by playing with rugby, soccer and cricket balls – and many took their acquired skills with them into the wider imperial society when they left the universities.[16] Games-playing, in the words of the Victorian journalist Hedley Peek, became a 'mania'.

This 'mania' inspired the following comment by Peek in the *Fortnightly Review*, at the time of Queen Victoria's Diamond Jubilee in 1897: 'the last 15 years had witnessed one of the most remarkable revolutions in popular taste to spread throughout Great Britain and Ireland, not to mention many other countries. Sport of various kinds had become "not only the ruling passion of the people, but well nigh the chief topic of conversation"'.[17] Perhaps he was too close to events. With greater perception, he would have appreciated that Britain had witnessed not merely a recreational but an educational revolution. Educational fashion had produced social change – change that was neither casual nor spontaneous. The 'mania' that Peek remarked upon had been introduced deliberately into the upper-class educational system. There it became known as 'athleticism'.[18] Initially it was seen as an antidote to hooliganism. Later it was seen as training in imperial leadership. Eventually it became considered as an unfortunate obsession. By 1897, however, it was part and parcel of life in both the public schools *and* their 'finishing schools', the universities of Oxford and Cambridge, for much the same reasons.[19] These reasons hardly require rehearsal again here. They have been discussed extensively elsewhere.[20]

Hugh Kearney has described in *Scholars and Gentlemen: University and Society in Pre-Industrial Britain, 1500–1700*[21] how he came slowly but surely to appreciate that a university curriculum exists, not in a vacuum, but in a social universe. Universities are as much social as intellectual institutions. Kearney frankly admitted that this was a self-evident truth, but went on to make the interesting observation that it was often hidden from view: 'Too often official histories were portraits without warts, resembling old-style business histories commissioned as subtle pieces of advertising.'[22] Kearney wrote of Oxford and Cambridge up to 1800; the interest here is in late Victorian and Edwardian Oxford and Cambridge. Is Kearney's stricture true of them then? As I have asked on another occasion: 'Have they too often suffered from what may be termed "Kearney's PR syndrome"?' What, in reality, was the late nineteenth-century 'Oxbridge' of many students and not a few dons? Was there a dominant ethos that influenced the lives and determined the lifestyles of many, if not most, undergraduates and some dons?[23] How accurate is T.B. Howarth's assertion in support of J.B. Priestley's comment on the lost generation of the 'Great War', namely, 'that nothing would shift him from the belief, which he would take to the grave, that the generation to whom he belonged, destroyed between 1914 and 1918, was a great generation, marvellous in its promise'?[24] Howarth offered some illustrative Cambridge exemplars:

> Geoffrey Hopley of Trinity went down in 1914, by which time he had secured a double first in the History Tripos, passed all his bar examinations in one year, [and] won a cricket blue and a heavy-weight boxing blue. He died of septicaemia after being shot by a sniper. In the very last months of the war Geoffrey Tatham, Fellow and Junior Bursar of Trinity, and already a historian of distinction, was killed as a mere captain, aged 34. James Woolston of Pembroke, a Professor of Mathematics in South Africa, died of wounds as a lance corporal. D.H. Baynes of Clare, with a first in Mathematics and another in Natural Science, was killed, aged 32 ... Philip Bainbridge, killed in September 1918 as a Second Lieutenant, had won a first in both parts of the Classical Tripos.[25]

To what extent were these tragic heroes archetypal representatives of a generation? In short, how accurate is Priestley's nostalgic sentimentality?

If it is accurate, then what of the caustic assertion by Noel Annan that for much of the late nineteenth and early twentieth centuries the 'ancient' universities of Oxford and Cambridge were 'little more than finishing schools for public schoolboys'?[26] Rowland Prothero (later Lord Ernle) once wrote, 'Life in the universities has been exclusively described in the autobiographies of men whose subsequent careers were only the fruit of their brilliant triumphs of school and college. As in boyhood and youth, they belonged to that distinguished minority who made the fullest use of their educational opportunities'.[27] Now this is a quotation to linger over and chew on:

> It hints at a widely unrecognised reality. 'Oxbridge' between 1875 and 1914 was more a place of privileged physical play than it was a centre of meritocratic cerebral effort. To fashion a simile, it was like a bottle of milk, which, far from being heavy with rich cream, was in fact of very moderate quality, with only a thin creamy layer at the rim and a considerable quantity of watery residue.[28]

There should be no beating about the bush. 'Life in late nineteenth century Oxford and Cambridge revolved around a public school modus of prejudices and predilections,'[29] and this public school 'modus' was obsessively athletic. There was a very good reason for this. The athletic relationship between school and university was cyclical. Worshipped 'bloods' at school became admired 'blues' at university and were enthusiastically head-hunted by the schools as games masters, who in turn sent their 'bloods' on to the universities. In this way Peek's 'mania' was sustained and reinforced.

Figure 2.1. 'Mentor and Telemachus'. Source: *Punch*, 15 June 1872.

In the universities, as initially in the schools, it had a mixed reception. There were watchful enthusiasts:

> A contributor to *Blackwood's Magazine* in 1866 wrote with hesitant approval of the passion excited by athletic contests, which 'has become, to the vast majority of the undergraduates, the great interest of the academical [*sic*] year'. Things had got to such a pitch, he argued, that it was now a matter of some doubt as to whether matters of the mind could hold out 'before the popular glories of the palaestra'.[30]

However, there were less cautious enthusiasts. A contributor to the *Contemporary Review*, only a little later, laid stress on university sports as 'being a main element in teaching a youth to fulfil his baptismal vow by keeping his body in temperance, soberness and chastity'. Other commentators were less sure. T.H. Huxley remarked sardonically, at about the same time:

> When I think of the host of pleasant, monied, well-bred young gentlemen, who do a little learning and much boating by Cam and Isis, the vision is a pleasant one; and, as a patriot, I rejoice that the youth of the upper and richer classes of the nation receive a wholesome and manly training, however small may be the modicum of knowledge they gather, in the intervals of this, their serious business.[31]

The truth of the matter is that athleticism (the cult of games) took over Oxbridge to a considerable extent in the late nineteenth century. These universities became for many, if not for all, places of privileged play on the rivers and games fields. This should occasion little surprise: 'the average undergraduate was merely...the average public schoolboy transferred to conditions affording him rather greater scope for his essentially schoolboy impulses'. Consequently: 'In a manner never before or since duplicated, late-Victorian and Edwardian university life was an extension of the English public school. It was a sporting life, centred not so much around horses and hounds as around the river, the cricket pitch and the football field.'[32] It is clear that:

Between approximately 1875 and 1914 there was a new and heady fashion abroad in the universities. River and games field had moved close to the centre of collegiate life. These elements are not to be dismissed as insignificant to the history of these famous institutions... they stood as symbols of period values, of an upper-middle-class educational system and culture. They were more than casual recreational venues. They represented contradictory and powerful social forces: moral idealism, class conspicuous consumption, social insulation, circumscribed hedonism, unconscious and defiant quixotry.[33]

In plain truth, it cannot be claimed that at this time the two ancient universities were centres of general cerebral excellence: quite the reverse. For the majority the significance of river and pitch was considerable. In the late nineteenth century a belief in the moral value of sport became increasingly apparent. Subscription to this belief was

disseminated enthusiastically by alumni throughout the public, state and colonial school systems of Motherland and Empire. And the ramifications of ethical inspiration were even more widely dispersed. It is far from notional to suggest that the activities characteristic of the rivers and playing fields of late nineteenth-century Oxford and Cambridge were load-bearing supports underpinning the moral structure of British and imperial society. Attitudes, relationships and administrations owed much to the ethical imperatives of the playing fields.[34]

This is not to say, of course, that the studious were not to be found, that intellectual matters were set aside, that scholarship was not fostered. What was true of Cambridge was equally true of Oxford. There existed three cultures:

predominantly of the mind, predominantly of the body, and of both mind and body. In short, there were reading men, rowing men and men who attempted both. All three types persisted throughout the Victorian and Edwardian eras. W.E. Heitland recalled [of Cambridge] that, in the 1860s, the 'quiet reading men... often went for long walks in the country... [these] meant close companionship and exchange of views, and were in truth, a valuable part of the varied processes that made up university training'. The longevity of this life style is well illustrated by the experiences of Arthur Eddington who, as a hard-working and reserved under-graduate at Trinity College in 1902, could not afford time for football or cricket, but enjoyed strenuous walks with a fellow undergraduate of like persuasion. In contrast to such inoffensive exercises, non-reading men, who, according to Heitland, were many in his day, did not have enough harmless amusements as analgesics against the pain of occasional contemplation. They despised walking: 'the exercise was too humdrum to suit youths with no ideas to exchange and prone to intellectual rest'.[35]

Rowing was established early at Oxford and Cambridge, but after 1860 playing games had become the fashion in the expanding public school system[36] and a little later it also became the fashion at the two universities. Rowing never lost its pre-eminence, but games grew in popularity. After 1870 the changed topography of the two cities of Oxford and Cambridge makes this plain. They were physically transformed. Oxford and Cambridge became dotted with new playing fields belonging to the colleges. Their fields eventually spread into the adjoining countryside. Without these facilities the fortunes of some colleges could wane, with them the fortunes of some waxed.

As noted earlier, a moral advantage was claimed for the new cult of games:

A university witness declared to the Public Schools Commission of 1864, that a notable improvement in the moral character of the average undergraduate had recently occurred because of the introduction, chiefly due to the public schools, of new athletic movements. He observed that cricket had greatly increased; fives and racquets courts had been established; 'athletic sports' had been introduced and an excellent gymnasium won substantial support.[37]

It was claimed by the same observer that, as a consequence, hunting, idle driving and riding had fallen off; happily, expensive habits and temptations to immorality had been reduced. His optimism should be taken with a large pinch of salt. In effect, one form of student 'barbarism' was now to replace another. This was clearly recognised at the time. One Oxford don, Mark Pattison, yearned for the presence of learned and scientific men, and savaged the new 'barbarized athlete',[38] while the French essayist Hippolyte Taine, as did Noel Annan later, rightly considered the universities merely extensions of the public schools. In Taine's view, life at Oxbridge 'proved the soundness of the Platonic reflection that the lives of thinker and athlete were incompatible; much-used muscle and large appetites precluded subtle philology, and elevated philosophical speculation.'[39] Enthusiastic as he was for river pursuits, Leslie Stephen has provided for posterity an amusingly candid description of a mid-nineteenth-century oarsman in *Sketches by a Don*:

> He resided at the University for, say, 800 days, excluding Sundays and vacations. Of those he passed 790 on the river; and during nine of the remainder he was laid up by a sprain caused by his exertions. The remaining day, which he wasted in lionising his mother and sisters, he will regret as long as he lives. Years afterwards he will date events by the University races of that time. The Crimean War, he will say, broke out in the year of 'the 18-inch race' – i.e. the race when Oxford beat Cambridge at Henley by that distance...Every morning, he was up at seven o'clock, and took his tub after half an hour's trot. His breakfast, according to a superstition not yet extinct, was raw beef-steak; his supper was oatmeal porridge. He measured his wine (except on occasional jollifications) with the careful eye of a gaoler distributing an allowance. He did not smoke, for fear of injuring his wind. The only ornaments in his room were cups or 'pewters' won on the river. His dress always included the colours of his boat-club. His library consisted chiefly of the Boating Almanac and the back numbers of *Bell's Life*. His conversation varied only by referring at one season to the sculls, and at another to the 'fours'.[40]

Public school mores and 'varsity' manners were now sometimes indistinguishable. For one thing, loyalty to the house became loyalty to the college. Peer pressure (and, as will be seen, don pressure) resulted in an informal but effective compulsion to play. Prothero wrote of his late nineteenth-century student days at Balliol: '"It was the duty of all who had the necessary physique...to do service", while E.E.C. Firth found himself on the Isis in his first week "learning the science of rowing at the 'request' of a senior member of Pembroke."'[41] The cult even made its impact on the selection of college appointments, as this comment by a far from unsympathetic observer of the manifestation, Lewis Farnell, reveals:

The ceaseless exigence of the athletic claim expressed itself in various ways – by inroads in the proper time of study claimed by home and foreign matches; by the withdrawal of scholars and exhibitioners from intellectual work...by attempts of headmasters to influence our scholarship elections by athletic testimonials; by the attempt to influence even elections to tutorial fellowships by athletic considerations.[42]

Dons could and did exert pressure on students in pursuit of college athletic success, which brought institutional celebrity. Zealous adherents to the cult of athleticism, which absorbed quite a few dons in late Victorian and Edwardian Oxbridge, included Leslie Stephen, E.H. Morgan and H.A. Morgan at Cambridge, and Charles Clovely Price, William Ince and Lewis Farnell at Oxford, with the result that on one occasion *Punch* published the following sarcastic verse:

Who cares a hang for a first in Greats
And Academic glory?
Dull bookworm, come and see the sights
And shut *De Oratore*!
Learn what a thing a man might be
And think to win a pewter
More splendid than a first,
Like me, your Tutor.[43]

Whether enthusiasts or critics, no one disputed this state of affairs. It would not be too frivolous to accept almost at face value the words of the lugubrious Rector of Lincoln College, Oxford, Mark Pattison, mentioned earlier, and state that for many at Oxford and Cambridge the colleges were boarding schools in which the elements of rowing and games were taught to youths:

An enthusiasm for sport became so acute, and activities on river and playing field eventually became so pressing, that the hour of dinner in college was moved back 'from 3 o'clock to 4 o'clock and then to 5 or even later', and eventually 'the timing of cricket matches to begin at 12 noon effectively cut down the lectures which could be attended to one per morning'.[44]

In all truth, for many among the *jeunesse dorée* 'memories of Oxford and Cambridge throughout the second half of Victoria's reign were frequently those of idle years of cricket, fives, racquets and billiards, when work weighed lightly on the conscience and the river and the games field engrossed many students. One disillusioned Uppingham scholar found Cambridge minds of the time not, in reality, much occupied with lofty themes, and the eyes of the time 'if open at all, more likely to be fixed on some vision of Cam or Thames than on the deep flowing river of Thought'.[45]

This situation outlived the Victorian age. 'It cannot be denied', remarked Frank Rutter in his *Varsity Types: Scenes and Characters from Undergraduate Life*, published by Heffer's of Cambridge in 1911, 'that the visitor to Oxford and Cambridge is often impressed with the idea that recreation and amusement form the real work here, and that study is merely useful insofar as it goes to fill up some corner of the day's routine, which cannot be otherwise allocated.'[46]

Such a state of affairs attracted its critics. Foremost among them was *Punch*. It continually lamented an odd academic state of affairs. In the last quarter of the nineteenth century the magazine 'systematically monitored the evolution of muscularity at the universities, and consistently shot small, sharp, verbal barbs in the direction of philathletic staff and students'.[47] One early and accurate volley fired off in 1873 included the sardonic suggestion that 'Corpus' might well acquire a new interpretation in the light of recent Cambridge happenings. *Punch* kept up a steady fire over the years. On occasion verse replaced prose as the satirical arrowhead:

> Carfax College was plunged in gloom,
> And a cloud hung over the Common room,
> For alas, the College no longer held
> The place that she did in the days of old.
> There had been a time when she used to shiver
> Unless she remained at the head of the river.
> And Carfax men were wont to yield
> To none in the cricket or football field.
> But now the glory was all departed,
> What wonder the College was broken-hearted?
> 'Twas years since she'd boasted a bat of note
> Or a single man in the Varsity boat.
> Why, worse – well might the dons turn pale!
> Last year – I shudder to tell the tale –
> There happened that which appeared to portend

The fatal beginning that marked the end.
Last year – they did their best, no doubt,
To hush up the horror, but truth will out –
Last year, by some curious freak of the fates,
A Carfax man took a first in Greats.[48]

This is the opening passage of 'Getting the Blues: A Story Founded on Fact'. The verse recounts how, due to the energetic enterprise of its Master, who made sure that he met the Sydney boat, Carfax obtained the services of a great Australian oarsman, 'Tom Brown', and the college's performance on the Cam was transformed from defeat to success.

Punch did not let up. It was persistent in its persecution of the philathletic ambience. Yet another sarcastic jingle lamented the prevalent state of affairs in which the athlete proved to be a more efficacious college advertisement than the Senior Wrangler.[49] Early in the twentieth century, in plain prose and in a more sober vein, the magazine called for the 'de-athleticising' of the universities, and the removal from them of 'blues' and 'bloods'.[50]

The rapid rise and increasing importance of modern sport at the two universities is clearly demonstrated in Table 2.1.

Table 2.1 First sports meetings between teams or players from Oxford and Cambridge universities across four quarter-centuries, 1825–1925

1825–50		1851–75		1876–1900		1901–25	
Cricket	1827	Racquets		Golf	1878	Swimming	1902
Boat race	1829	doubles	1855	Polo	1878	Gymnastics	1908
		singles	1858	Cross-country	1880	Epée	1913
		Tennis	1859	Lawn tennis	1881	Winter sports	1922
		Steeple-		Hockey	1890	Table-tennis	1923
		chasing	1863	Water polo	1891	Squash	1925
		Athletics	1864	Bandy	1895	Fives	1925
		Rugby	1872	Skating	1895		
		Soccer	1874	Boxing	1897		
		Bicycling	1874	Fencing	1897		
				Ice hockey	1900		
				Lacrosse	1900		

Source: H.M. Abrahams and J.B. Kerr, *Oxford versus Cambridge* (London: Faber & Faber, 1931).

One by-product of university muscular zealotry should again be noted: the circular causality by which esteemed games-playing graduates returned to the schools to fashion new 'Oxbridge' 'blues' and then, in time, new public school housemasters, who strove to turn their 'bloods' into 'blues'. As a direct consequence of their success, Charles Tennyson commented despairingly,

> the mechanism of work at the University is as nothing compared with the vast machinery of play...Cambridge life still shows traces of that fundamental principle of British education, the belief that while limitless exercise is essential to the production of a sound body, a sound mind can only be produced by a studious and deliberate inactivity.[51]

In the tercentenary edition of the magazine of Sidney Sussex College, the *Pheon*, one fellow and tutor of the college was quite savage in his condemnation of the almost all-consuming growth of athleticism. Subscription to the ideal of *mens sana in corpore sano*, in his view, 'had produced not a *mens sana*, but a *corpus vile* in which King Nous did not sit upon the throne'.[52] A more gentle comment, in the form of a rather obvious pastiche in the Downing College magazine, the *Griffin*, described the new fashion in more kindly words:

> The RC chimes the hour of closing day,
> The hockey team winds slowly home to tea,
> The Oarsman homeward plods his weary way,
> And leaves the quad to darkness and to me.[53]

No college better exemplifies the (Matthew) Arnoldian 'barbarianism' of students than Jesus College, Cambridge. This is evident from the pages of the college magazine of the period, the *Chanticlere*: 'In the main it is hearty, philistine, considerably taken up with athletics and preoccupied with the associated issues which so greatly concerned the English public schoolboy of the period – athletic heroes, successes and regalia.'[54] The college magazine, a replica of the typical period school magazine, was replete with letters on sports facilities, obituaries of athletes and editorial complaints about a paucity of literary articles.[55] Indeed, in 1894 the disillusioned editor remarked that he could not remember the last time there had been a literary contribution. It was a sign of the times that the first number devoted 18 pages out of 28 to boating, cricket, rugby, soccer, athletics and lawn tennis. It was also a sign of the times that, while the *Nineteenth Century*, the *Saturday Review* and the *Spectator* remained unread, the *Sporting Times* was 'generally torn in two one hour after it had arrived, so eagerly do men dispute the proud privilege of reading that high-class paper'.[56] It was equally a sign of the times that in 1899 meetings of the recently established debating society were poorly attended, while in contrast, a meeting called to discuss the desirability of a blazer for the Jesus College Athletic Club 'was a large one and many men spoke'.[57]

Inevitably, in such circumstances:

> sporting doggerel of a cheery moralistic nature so familiar to the reader of the *Harrovian, Lorettonian, Uppingham Magazine* and similar products...appeared in *The Chanticlere*:

> > 'O Batsman play the game, or a "duck" will blot your fame;
> > Don't shiver when the umpire sings out "PLAY!"
> > But be wary, wise, and ready; play 'em straight and true and steady.
> > And watch the ball and gently feel your way.'[58]

However, the clearest indication of college priorities was the scrupulous recording of the athletic achievements of freshmen (see Table 2.2).

Table 2.2 Public school backgrounds and athletic achievements of the freshmen of Jesus College, Cambridge, 1893

Beck, A.C.T.	Marriott, H.S., Bradfield
Bower, G.F., private	Sadler, H., Durham (4)
Breakey, H., Eliock (1)	Sedgewich, J.S., Lancaster (1)
Brydone, P., Lancing (2)	Siddons, A.W., King Edward's,
Busby, G.H., Repton (2,3)	Birmingham (1,3)
Chapman, W.T., Loughborough (2,3)	Skrimshire, H.F., Gresham (3)
Coode, A.T., Fauconberge, Beccles (2,3)	Stevens, H., Beaumont (2)
Dickson, A.C., Rossall	Swanson, A.W., Loretto (1)
Exton, G.G., Oundle (1)	Thomson, W., Ripon (1,3)
Ford, E.B., Hastings	Thorburn, K.D.S.M., Wellington (1,3)
Harries, O.W., Bury St Edmunds	Turner, W.G., Chatham House (1)
Harvey, Winchester	Walton, H.G., Newcastle
Lucas, R., Cheltenham	Whitty, R.F.L., Felsted (2,3)
Maclaren, W.V., St C., Merchiston Castle	Wigram, G.E., Bradfield
Maddison, J.R.S., Durham	Woolston, Wellingborough (2,3)

(1) 1st XV Rugby colours
(2) 1st XI Association Football
(3) 1st XI Cricket
(4) First boat

Source: Mangan, 'Oars and the Man'

The archetypal Jesus student of the time appears to have been B.H. Stewart, who graduated in 1896. In his *Reminiscences* he wrote bashfully: 'To anyone who should pick up this little booklet... I feel under an obligation to state that it is concerned mainly with sport – touching lightly on cricket, football, running, swimming, rowing, gymnastics, golf, tennis and boxing, with chess, billiards and cards thrown in.'[59] He ended an apologia for his sporting life with a pretentious and sententious homily in verse on games as a training for life, which no doubt for him set three years of pleasant hedonism in self-justificatory moral perspective:

> And if you're beaten – well, what of that?
> Come up with a smiling face.
> 'Tis no disgrace to be knocked down flat,
> But to lie there, that's disgrace.
> The harder you're knocked, the higher you bounce,
> Be proud of the blackened eye
> It isn't the fact that you're licked that counts,
> But *how* did you fight – and why?[60]

One 'jaundiced' Jesus undergraduate of more serious disposition, and not much given to games, remarked of the college of the period that 'it was a medieval foundation which in the course of modern progress had passed from the housing of religious women to the production of... highly trained oarsmen'.[61] Late Victorian and Edwardian Jesus was indeed famed for its rowing. The remarkable performances by Jesus on the Cam owed a great deal to H.A. Morgan and E.H. Morgan, introduced above. It should come as no surprise that both men had been masters at Lancing College during the emergence of athleticism there, which they enthusiastically encouraged. Over a period of time they literally transformed Jesus. In the 1850s the college had suffered a serious and continuous drop in student numbers, but after the appointment of H.A. Morgan as Tutor, in 1864, there was continuous growth. The reason was provided later by the college's historian, Arthur Gray, who pointed out that in the 'seventies... the college sprang into... athletic prominence' and added that this 'was not unnaturally accompanied by a great rise in the number of undergraduates'.[62]

It would be a mistake to suppose that 'Victorian and Edwardian Jesus was essentially the product of hearty schoolboy enthusiasts, who danced to their own tunes despite the feeble piping of despairing dons'.[63] In reality, another similarity between the Oxbridge colleges and the public schools of the day was the support that athleticism, in theory and practice, received from the authorities. H.A. Morgan, in the influential role of Tutor with responsibility for entries,

> filled it with undergraduates, and then endowed it with a soul – a soul of energy and patriotism. He gave to one and all a just cause of pride in their College, and warmed their courage at the fire of his own enthusiasm. In all sports... he took the keen and intimate interest of one who had practised them... For half a century he encouraged the College boat by his voice and presence; he watched its rise and fall upon the river with the stern enthusiasm of a general watching his army in the field, and his enthusiasm was rewarded by so long a list of victories as has never been claimed by any other College in the world.

In the 1870s the college, previously the sixth largest at Cambridge, became the third largest, after Trinity and St John's. The reputation of Jesus oarsmen was the main reason. The college was 'Head of the River' for 11 years, with the result that the 'inflow of freshmen became phenomenal'.[64] In a manner of speaking, rowing fame made its fortune. It was later stated that 'the position of the College boat on the river was an index of the prospects of the College'.[65] In fact this was true, for better and for worse. In the 1880s boating was considered overdone – even for the times. Numbers declined due to 'an over-emphasis on rowing... coupled with [the] rowdiness and idleness of many of the rowing men'.[66] The Rhadegund Society for the leading athletes, established in 1874 and the most prestigious of the college's clubs, led the way in this hooliganism.[67] Even H.A. Morgan recognised that the goose was overcooked: at one stage he noted with displeasure that the college had become 'nothing but a boat club' and actually hoped for a fall in fortunes on the river.[68] Later, in the 1890s, with E.H. Morgan, a man obsessed with sport, as Tutor, numbers rose again. The main reason was clear. Jesus was once again 'in the front rank of every branch of sport'.[69]

E.H. Morgan was certainly 'a philathlete of extreme persuasion' and 'a large man with a large voice'; he was a forceful disciplinarian.[70] Once described as one of nature's bullies, he was both feared and disliked by Jesus masters and many fellows, as these lines, penned in a moment of dangerous bravado by a fellow don, reveal:

Red Morgan: I am the tutor, bursar, butler, dean:
I rule the College with imperial sway.
The very Master owneth me supreme,
The Fellows tremble and my rule obey.

Chorus: The Czar of Russia and our gracious Queen
Are not so potent as our noble Dean.[71]

As a forceful disciplinarian he was usefully influential at one level – control of the students.

Punch's arrows, tipped with vitriol, did not miss E.H. Morgan. He was once lampooned in *Punch*, in a piece entitled 'Muscular Education', as R.E.D. Morgan (he had a red beard), a confident advocate of an exciting new preparatory school where the boys were trained 'to the real require-ments of modern life (rowing, cricket, football, swimming, racquets, boxing, hockey, billiards, poker, run and spill)', while extras (charged extra for, of course) included reading, writing and arithmetic.[72] Perhaps *Punch* did gild the lily a little. However, the scrapbook of E.H. Morgan in the Jesus College Archives throws a bright light on his interests. It has page after page of sporting memories – Morgan's feats on the cricket pitch, telegrams from various dons on Jesus successes at Henley, details of his administrative responsibilities in the university's boating and athletic clubs, and so on.[73]

In summary, if H.A. Morgan was nothing more than 'a glorified head-master with a taste for rowing', E.H. Morgan was 'a glorified games master with an obsession for games'.[74] Like 'Gramsci's intellectuals, their role was to spread and legitimise new convictions, to colonise fresh conceptual terri-tories, and to win over young minds to bodily pursuits.'[75] In their defence, it should be pointed out that there was a utilitarian purpose to all this, just as there was in the public schools. The acquisition of a 'blue' certainly helped future careers and it must be recognised that, as in the case of the school 'beaks', the motives of such college dons as the Morgans were complex. After the 1850s the collegiate ideal proposed by some dons out of self-interest – to make daily life less boring and students less hostile – was rede-fined to lay emphasis on personal influence in the interests of character formation. Men such as Leslie Stephen led the way. The colleges benefited. To an extent this new emphasis did promote student respect and improve institutional image.

However, there was more to it all than this. Utilitarianism went further – much further. In truth, 'Some casuistic dons, like some "beaks", were little more than perpetual public schoolboys. Others were calculating realists to whom institutional athletic repute meant institutional prosperity. Yet others were common-sense pragmatists who followed the expedient practices of mid-century public school headmasters. They promoted the river and the playing fields as necessary mechanisms of control.'[76] Both public schools and universities, of course, had precisely the same problem: 'sizeable numbers of students in the grip of boredom born of restriction'.[77] The colleges did not always resolve this problem, although, using traditional procedures, they went to considerable lengths in their attempts: 'College lectures, College examinations, compulsory chapel and dinners in hall had a disciplinary purpose, and "a variety of punishments – admonitions, rustication, expulsion, prohibitions and literary impositions – were customarily meted out for violations".'[78] In the second half of the nineteenth century athleticism gave them another means of control. It came just in time. It should be appreciated that, with the greatly increased wealth of mid-Victorian Britain, the related expansion of the public school system, the new ethos of athleticism and the associated university reforms, the colleges witnessed the arrival of a horde of 'hearties'. Those who were most successful in controlling the horde, men such as Henry Latham, H.A. Morgan or E.H. Morgan, were unequalled 'in the power of controlling full-blooded undergraduates, [making] it their business to encourage all forms of bodily exercise, above all rowing'.[79] It should equally be recognised that

> athleticism at the late Victorian ancient universities, without question, 'has been too lightly dismissed, casually overlooked, even purposefully reduced'. The reason is not hard to find. It does not, of course, accord with modern values and pretensions. To maintain this casual or calculated neglect, I would suggest, is to fail entirely to grasp the atmospheric essence of an era and a system. There can be little doubt about its presence, its popularity and its pervasiveness. It was strongly manifested in distinct and pronounced ways: in the striking change of topography, in the content of magazines, in the nature of *Valetes* and obituaries, in comment in subsequent biographies, autobiographies, memoirs and reminiscences, in critical and supportive commentaries, in the qualifications required for careers (especially in teaching and imperial service), and, not least, in the period references, enthusiasms and activities of a number of dons ... [80]

While it is important to appreciate a necessary concern with control, it is important also to appreciate that, in addition to Benthamite utilitarianism,

there was Homeric idealism. Greek *and* cricket, for example, represented
the ideal Cambridge of Walter Headlam: 'if I had not been a Grecian', he is
reported to have said, 'I should have been a cricket pro'.[81] Headlam and
others subscribed to the Athenian concept of 'the whole man'. It was
certainly something of a romantic vision in the universities of the late nineteenth century, but it did exist. There were at least two points of view
regarding this vision: 'The sanguine, like Richard Livingstone, could be
confident that an ancient Athenian would be at ease among "the well-devel-
oped in body and mind" at Oxford and Cambridge; the sceptical, like
Matthew Arnold, were of the view that such an Athenian would have speedily recognised that he was in the presence of Barbarians.'[82]

In the light of the evidence above, it would be short-sighted not to recognise that:

> The fact of the matter was that the compelling ideology of
> athleticism had captured the public school system, and its strongly
> indoctrinated products moved *en masse* into the ancient universi-
> ties and shaped them in their image. The consequences were
> paradoxical: student energy was both dissipated *and* concentrated;
> collegiate order was promoted *and* disrupted; tension between
> dons and students was exacerbated *and* reduced.[83]

It would be foolish not to recognise that there was yet another classical
influence, that of Sparta: sport, it was believed, produced a manly puritanism. In the words of R.C. Lehmann, a university oarsman:

> will have suffered much, he will have rowed many weary miles,
> have learnt the misery of aching limbs and blistered hands, . . . he
> will have laboured under broiling suns, or with snow storms and
> bitter winds beating against him, he will have voluntarily cut
> himself off from many pleasant indulgences. But on the other
> hand his triumphs will have been sweet, he will have trained
> himself to submit to discipline, to accept discomfort cheerfully, to
> keep a brave face in adverse circumstances; he will have learnt
> the necessity of unselfishness and patriotism . . . [84]

It would be unwise also not to recognise that Lehmannism was in part a set
of ethical beliefs translated into action with wide political, social and political resonances, exemplified superbly by three Jesus men in later life: James

Robertson, Headmaster of Haileybury from 1884 to 1890; Charles Hose, imperial administrator in Borneo at about the same time; and Cecil Earle Tyndale-Biscoe, a missionary educationalist in Kashmir a little later – but that is another story, which has been told elsewhere.[85]

It must not be thought that, due to the efforts of men such as the Morgans, most dons and students 'now lived happily ever after'. The student magazines of the late nineteenth century were often tart in their comments on the fossilised don, and complaints of lack of sympathy on the dons' part with the athletic enthusiasms of the students were frequent:

> Who for me doesn't care a pin
> But notwithstanding, thinks no sin
> To rake my golden shekels in?
> My tutor.
> Who studied all his youthful days
> And won the prizes in the Mays
> And cannot understand my ways?
> My tutor.[86]

Another contemptuous undergraduate claimed that to be a don:

> ... is to know at length
> The Pedant's rich reward in blinded eyes,
> And fading strength,
> A palsied heart too dull to sympathise
> With human joys,
> A head that aches at every slightest noise,
> And – worse beyond all question –
> Constant indigestion.[87]

Yet another undergraduate got his own back on Mark Pattison: 'From the general mass of the college he held himself almost completely aloof. He showed no interest in rowing, football or any of the athletics, which formed such an invaluable part of an Oxford education. This was undoubtedly a great misfortune.'[88] This undergraduate extended his criticism to the college dons in general: 'the whole tendency of college life was to draw strong lines of demarcation between don and undergraduate, a bad arrangement for both. The latter are reduced to schoolboys; the former are isolated to an extent unknown in any reputable school.'[89] The efforts of Leslie Stephen and others to transform the image of the dons in the eyes of the students was clearly only partially successful.

In conclusion, late nineteenth-century Oxbridge was characterised by what would be seen today, at least in their excess, as 'disreputable pleasures': many students played rather than studied. 'The Reign of Athletics is at hand', one astonished Oxbridge student reported back to Stonyhurst at the turn of the century.[90] The reasons were complex: 'indulgence, rationalisation, expedience and idealism were the confused, contradictory or complimentary characteristics of the enthusiastic . . . the causes of this enthusiasm were [also] complex. Glorified schoolmasters in the vanguard of fashion, the prevalence of public schoolboys, the College "blood" as hero, concern with control, restructured leisure, ethical imperatives'[91] – and, no doubt, the absence, at least from the colleges themselves, of young women.

Not even *soi-disant* intellectual King's College, Cambridge, was safe. Shane Leslie recalled that King's men were 'very hearty in groups', and that there was a watchful discouragement of the aesthete and an encouragement of the hearty:

> It was during his time that a third-year man was actually discovered using a hot-water bottle: 'This was considered a disgrace to the college and Hope-Jones challenged its owner to run the quarter mile round the front court on a wintry dawn. It was agreed that the challenger should run stark naked, while the challenged wore as much clothing as he wished. The race was won by the less encumbered party and the offending hot-water bottle was duly confiscated and sent to Doctor Barnardo, with the compliments of the Provost, the Fellows and Scholars of the college.'[92]

Thank God, no doubt, for electric blankets, central heating, mixed colleges and modernity.

Dandy rats at play: the Liverpudlian middle classes and horse-racing in the nineteenth century

JOHN PINFOLD

In his pioneering history of horse-racing Wray Vamplew stated that 'There is no hard evidence that the middle class attended race meetings. Certainly the respectable middle class would not go racing'.[1] More recent work by Mike Huggins has challenged this view,[2] and this study seeks to throw further light on the debate by looking at the involvement in racing and betting of the Victorian middle classes in Liverpool. It will also consider whether the ostensibly 'respectable' middle classes may in reality have been indulging in some decidedly unrespectable activities in their leisure time.

'Salford lads, Manchester men, Liverpool gentlemen': this sardonic phrase, more often employed outside Liverpool than within it, nevertheless expressed an important truth, that Liverpool, although containing many industries within its boundaries, was not primarily an industrial city, but rather was a commercial centre, where trade rather than manufacturing was king, and merchants formed the local elite. B.G. Orchard, who compiled an extensive biographical dictionary of Liverpool's merchants, wrote that he regarded a merchant 'as a benefactor to humanity', and added that 'creators of wealth, unrefined though they often are, deserve more honour than do those who, inheriting what others amassed, become their superiors in general knowledge, refinement and grace'.[3]

This lack of refinement, characteristically ascribed to newly rich, self-made men, was what struck many observers of Liverpool's wealthy middle classes. In his novel *Perversion* the Rev. William John Conybeare drew a deliberately crude picture of one merchant family. The women are vulgar snobs, while the men are 'thoroughly well-informed on all that concerned their business, but indifferent to more general topics: evidently absorbed heart and soul in the one great object of making money'.[4] Their single-mindedness, even ruthlessness, in this regard gave them a 'shady reputation' outside the city, and especially in rival ports,[5] but even within Liverpool itself awkward questions concerning the morality of their business dealings could be asked. A local weekly, the *Porcupine*, for example, asked in 1866: 'Are there any speculating men of untainted character in Liverpool? Can any touch cotton and not be defiled?...The depth of commercial duplicity which has been opening up in certain quarters of the Liverpool business world during the past few years will probably never be fully sounded'.[6]

Liverpool merchants were also known as heavy drinkers. Samuel Smith, a cotton merchant and a temperance reformer, memorably commented: 'As Ephesus was said to be a worshipper of the great goddess Diana, it might be said that Liverpool was a worshipper of the great goddess Beer'.[7]

The nature of many of the trades in which the Liverpool merchants were engaged involved a good deal of speculation, and the connection between the cotton trade in particular and gambling was one that was often made at the time. The *Porcupine* regularly ran articles on 'Cotton gambling'. In one of these, a satirical piece entitled 'Mr Porcupine Abolishes Betting', it was reported that on the Exchange floor could be found 'betting, booking and gambling of all descriptions', and that there were busloads of merchant princes 'who had been discovered in the act of arranging bets'.[8] Later in the nineteenth century *The Liver* posed the pertinent question 'why these financial betting men should occupy any better social position than the turf betting men', and gave the answer that 'perhaps the financial bookmaker occasionally makes bigger hauls than his brother on the turf. As we all know, money commands position.'[9]

The merchant princes constituted Liverpool's elite, but the middle classes were much more broadly based. In particular, the commercial nature of Liverpool's businesses meant that the city provided employment for as many as 17,400 clerks.[10] Some of these were well-off and lived in substantial houses in the affluent suburbs of Aigburth or New Brighton; others were barely able to scrape a living. Yet there appears to have been a feeling in Liverpool that 'a clerk is a gentleman and an artisan is not', and it was reported that 'commercial clerkship is to the middle classes what the Church is to the aristocracy, a refuge for sons who are capable of nothing else'.[11] Nevertheless, the merchants tended not to recognise their clerks as gentlemen, even though, such was the self-made nature of Liverpool society, many of them had started out as clerks themselves.[12]

The consequence was that the term 'gentleman', as used in Liverpool, meant something different from what it may have meant elsewhere. The Liverpool crusading journalist Hugh Shimmin answered the question 'What is a gentleman?' thus: 'all one can be sure of is this, that a man who is called

Figure 3.1. The Grand National Steeplechase – crossing the brook. Source: *The Sporting World, c.* 1845, author's collection

so occupies a certain social position, and has done nothing glaringly opposed to the rules that govern society, [but] his moral qualifications are not necessarily known anything of'.[13]

The newly rich merchants of Liverpool were keen to enhance their social standing. One way in which they could do this was through involvement in hunting and other equestrian sports, which might bring them into closer contact with county society. This can be seen in the career of E.J. Thornewill, a corn merchant who was a partner in the firm of Segar & Tunnicliffe from 1861 to 1898, as well as being on the boards of the Liverpool, London & Globe Insurance Company and the Liverpool Union Bank, and whose wife was a niece of W.E. Gladstone. It was said of Thornewill that 'he would come in quite early to the office, well-equipped with overcoats and field glasses',[14] and he gained considerable success as an owner, most notably when Gamecock won the Grand National of 1887 and followed this up with a second triumph in the Champion Chase, also at Aintree, the next day. Perhaps significantly, Thornewill chose to race under the pseudonym 'Mr E. Jay', but it seems likely that his real identity was well-known on Merseyside, as it was said that most of the money placed on

Gamecock, which started at 20–1, came from local people.[15] Thornewill also later became a director of the new Hooton Park racecourse on the Wirral.[16] Another Liverpool businessman who was successful as an owner was R.C. Naylor, who was a member of an old Liverpool family, and a partner in the respected banking firm of Leyland & Bullins. His greatest success came with Macaroni in the Derby of 1863.[17]

Not all Liverpool merchants who went in for racing or hunting knew as much about horses as Thornewill did, and their attempts to use equestrian sports for social climbing are amusingly satirised in a series of verses called *The Lays of Cotton Broking*, which were written by Edward Bradyll, himself a cotton broker, and published in 1865:

> And many a man who first began
> With scarce a coat to his back,
> Thought it the thing, now that Cotton was king,
> To become a sporting crack.
>
> There was many a one in the hunting field
> Who didn't know how to ride,
> And was told by the plough-boy urchins there
> He had better get inside!
>
> To don a scarlet coat, and go
> To the meet, became him well;
> He loved to be seen in the collar green,
> Like a Cheshire County Swell!
>
> And a man who hadn't a seat at all,
> Now thought it a matter of pride
> To ride full tilt at a six-foot wall,
> With a ditch on either side.[18]

This view was echoed later in the century by Orchard, who noted that the Liverpudlian middle classes, unlike their contemporaries in Manchester, had 'a widespread fondness for field sports which has led them . . . to keep horses in the country'. The upward social mobility that this brought them, he thought, made them 'less influential in giving a high tone to local sentiment'. Moreover, even among the Liverpool merchant classes there were 'some very black sheep in the flock', who included 'gamblers, profligates [and] infatuated lovers of sport'. There were, for example, 'many young fellows, men of means, who ... devote themselves to the lower forms of sport – wild riding, rat-killing, hard-drinking, fisticuffs between others for pay, or amongst themselves for amusement, every distraction which may seem not unnatural and is excused among sporting miners, prosperous grooms, and others of the lower class which lives by gambling or the turf'.[19] Nor was this interest in the turf confined to those at the top or bottom of society, for even among the clerks, most of whom aspired to respectability, there were those who 'while at the desk talk of the Star Music Hall or the coming race'.[20]

Although Liverpool races can be traced back to the late sixteenth century, they had fallen into abeyance after 1786, and the nineteenth-century interest in racing in the city can be dated from the late 1820s, when the traditional summer meeting was revived first by John Formby, on a course at Maghull, and then by William Lynn at Aintree.[21] Horse-racing immediately became popular, and within ten years it was reported that it had 'decidedly hit the taste of a vast number of Liverpudlians'.[22] Crowds as big as 40,000 were reported. Lynn staged four meetings a year, including the Summer meeting each July, which rapidly developed into one of the premier fixtures in the racing calendar, and the Liverpool Grand Steeplechase, which, as the Grand National, developed into the most important steeplechase of the year. Both meetings became unofficial local public holidays, attended by 'thousands of the residents of Liverpool and the neighbourhood of all ranks'; at the Grand National in 1879, for example, 'the fashionable attire of ladies and people of good position' was mixed with 'the tattered and dirty clothing of the Liverpool roughs and street urchins', and around the bookmakers could be found 'members of nearly every class of the community'.[23]

Because of the Grand National, Aintree has understandably attracted the most attention from turf historians, but it should also be remembered that in the nineteenth century there were many other meetings within a 20-mile radius of the city centre. These included not just the long-established and prestigious meeting at Chester, but also now long-defunct meetings at such places as Old Roan, Ormskirk, Croston and Southport to the north, and at Rock Ferry, Storeton, Parkgate and Hoylake over the water on the Wirral.[24] As early as the 1820s Liverpool had its own sporting paper, *Bethell's Life in London and Liverpool Sporting Register*, which covered pugilism as well as racing, and later in the century the city supported a twice-daily racing paper, the *City Racing Record*.[25]

As elsewhere, there was opposition to horse-racing from Nonconformists, Evangelicals, social and moral reformers, and a significant portion of the local press, led by the *Liverpool Mercury*, whose owner and editor, Egerton Smith, was a consistent opponent of racing on moral

Figure 3.2. 'Trying to tool a tit'. Source: *The Road*, author's collection

grounds. Nevertheless, this opposition may have been more vocal than effective. Augustine Birrell, born the son of a Baptist minister in Liverpool in 1850 (and eventually Chief Secretary for Ireland in H.H. Asquith's Liberal government), remembered that in his youth there had been a marked distinction between those inhabitants of Liverpool who were not allowed to go to the Grand National and those, 'the large majority', who were; rather wistfully, he recorded that he was, 'as usual', in the minority.[26] In a typical piece of 'Scouse' humour, when the Rev. S. Gamble Walker announced that he would preach at the Price Street Wesleyan Chapel on the Grand National, he received through the post a card advising him to recommend the Prince of Wales's Ambush II in his address to the congregation.[27]

It is clear from the newspaper reports of the time that the middle classes attended the races at Aintree in large numbers. In 1836, for example, at the first running of the Grand Steeplechase, it was noted that 'the assemblage was composed principally of the middle classes'.[28] Three years later, among the great crowd that witnessed Lottery's victory and the christening of Becher's Brook were 'merchants and wealthy manufacturers'.[29] F.C. Turner's picture of this event shows that many of the crowd had travelled out to the races in their own carriages, a long line of which can be seen stretching all the way from the grandstand to the Sefton Arms. This suggests that many of the crowd were wealthy enough to be have their own transport and also, perhaps, that many of them had gone in groups of relatives or friends. Sometimes newcomers, accustomed to the attacks on racing in the newspapers, could be quite surprised at this. R.H. Fry, a prosperous Liverpool draper, remembered that on his first visit to Liverpool races, in 1869, 'The first thing that struck me...was the number of my friends I found there. Persons of undoubted respectability and position were there, not the mere rag, tag and bobtail whom I had expected to see'.[30] There is also some evidence to suggest that the racecourse authorities went out of their way to arrange things to suit the convenience of Liverpool's merchant elite. In 1879 it was alleged that the day of the Grand National had been moved from the traditional Thursday to Friday so that the members of the Dock Board, who previously 'had a severe struggle between duty and inclination', could attend, and this change was said to have been instigated by Samuel Stitt, a well-known iron merchant.[31]

In the mid-1850s Hugh Shimmin gave a graphic description of the crowd at the Liverpool Summer meeting:

> Here are earls, viscounts, noble lords, honourable captains, gallant admirals, members of Parliament, magistrates, aldermen, town councillors, merchants, brokers, publicans, business men of every grade and many men of questionable character...Many of the men have, as magistrates, presided at county sessions lately; others have spoken at public meetings on the duty of making earnest efforts to purify and regenerate society. Several have been found on platforms, supporting, either by their presence, purse or advocacy, missions to the benighted heathen, the Additional Curates', the Pastoral Aid, or Home Church Building Societies; and some of them will no doubt, if they succeed today, stand an extra dozen of champagne in the evening, or make a very handsome donation to some religious or benevolent association.[32]

This comment is interesting for its suggestion that the racecourse was a place where normally respectable people could let off steam and behave quite differently from how they might have at home or at work. Going to the races was a day out, and the racecourse, like the seaside, was a place where different rules applied. Nor was this necessarily a bad thing, for even Shimmin, who was no friend of horse-racing, had to admit that out in the centre of the course one could see 'what a neat style of pic-nic [*sic*] can be done. How speedily bottles can be opened and emptied, and how pleasant and affable even Liverpool merchant princes may become under the influence of good air and healthy appetite.'[33]

If this was true of Aintree, it was even truer of the smaller meetings that took place in the environs of the city. The Croxteth Hunt meeting that took place in April 1870 at Halewood was attended by 'the elite of Liverpool', many of whom had travelled out in family carriages or omnibuses hired for the occasion. At the course 'Pic-nic fashion the carriage people drew forth from safe recesses portly hampers containing all the delicacies of the period.' In between races they were entertained by music provided by a German band, and there were also shooting and archery stands, height and weight machines, and a photographic tent to tempt the racegoers. Yet even at a small meeting such as this one, which seems more akin to a modern point-to-point meeting, there were other less respectable temptations on offer, in the form of thimble-riggers and card-swindlers.[34] The atmosphere at these meetings is succinctly summed up in a report on Hoylake racecourse, which had 'a fashion of freedom from conventionality much and justly prized'.[35]

At Aintree there was all this and more, much of it of a decidedly unrespectable nature, for, as the *Porcupine* remarked, 'it is manifest that the attraction of the day is based upon revelling and what can be made by betting'.[36] First, there was alcohol. This, of course, was true of all race meetings, but there is some evidence to show that there was more drinking at Aintree than elsewhere. One journalist who attended the Grand National in 1870, for example, thought that the crowd differed from that at all other sporting gatherings, and that one of its distinguishing features was the openly expressed desire for 'a big drink afterwards'.[37] That this was something that was common to all classes is clear from Shimmin's account, in which he reports that after racing 'In the booths dancing is general, and men half and wholly drunk stagger about in all directions', and that the police had their work cut out 'in keeping the respectable people within bounds, for drink is now telling on all'.[38]

Drunkenness may have affected all classes of racegoer equally, but they did not receive equal treatment from the authorities when they were apprehended for drunkenness. Returning from the Grand National in 1879, four young men, all of whom bore 'well-known names' and enjoyed 'consider-able social position', were stopped by the police for drunkenness, and for driving their carriage too fast and on the wrong side of the street. One of men then attacked the constable with a whip. After a scuffle several of the party were arrested and taken to the bridewell. At the police court they were subsequently convicted of drunkenness and assaulting the police and were fined 20 shillings (one pound) each, an unusually high sum. Thus far the authorities had behaved perfectly correctly, but what distinguishes the case is that it was deliberately heard very early in the morning before any reporters were in the court. Moreover, once the newspapers did discover what had happened they were asked not to report the case or make public the names of the defendants. All the local papers appear to have complied with this request. Nor was this the end of the affair, for the Watch Committee subsequently reduced both the constable who had made the arrest and the bridewell-keeper by one rank; this involved both a loss of pay and the disgrace of having their names read out on parade as having committed a misdemeanour. This blatant injustice caused a storm of protest and several people who had witnessed the assault on the policeman petitioned the Watch Committee on his behalf. To begin with the committee refused to reverse its decision, and it was only after a campaign lasting three months that it agreed to reinstate both the policeman and the bridewell-keeper, but this was done very quietly and without any formal reference in the order book. As the *Porcupine* commented at the time, this case clearly demonstrated that there was, 'so far as the shame and publicity of conviction are concerned, one law for the rich and another for the poor'.[39] One wonders how many other cases of drunkenness involving well-connected middle-class people were hushed up in this way to save the culprits' faces.

Second, there was sex. On race days the roads out to Aintree were crowded with 'coaches filled with harlots'. Shimmin gave a graphic descrip-tion of the scene:

> At every coach you see well-dressed men dancing attendance on these women...Cards have been distributed amongst the fash-ionable and sporting gentlemen during the morning, and in imitation of the cards of the horses these ladies' cards have writ-ten on them the colours in which their owners will appear, and are in this style – 'Matilda, primrose and pale blue', 'Fanny, pink and French white', 'Sarah, white and green', 'Jemima, pink and blue', &c., &c., the colours corresponding with the bonnets and dresses. The great event being over, lazy-looking and fashionably attired

men cross the course and enter the ploughed gallop, drawing from their pockets the cards they have received in order that they may more easily distinguish their favourites. The girls, flushed with wine, waited on by bullies and pimps, watched keenly by their keepers, who are hovering about, are thus decorated to captivate the turfites.

Nearer the grandstand was a tent with 'a very aristocratic title' over the entrance, which was specifically intended for 'respectable people', yet here too the behaviour was less than respectable: 'Young girls and women are here – their faces daubed with paint, their persons profusely adorned with highly coloured dresses. They pass the time in drinking, laughing and giggling with men – with merchants who on the Exchange and at home pass for gentlemen.' This tent was run by a 'notorious brothel-keeper'. Shimmin watched a young man sip wine with this 'bloated and brazen-faced hussey', and commented: 'active as this young man may be on the Exchange in the morning, when cotton is on the carpet, leering and simpering as he is now, he will in all probability meet his mother and sisters in the evening without a blush'.[40]

Third, of course, there was betting, which to many people seemed to be an even greater sin than drink or prostitution. It was, however, one of the principal reasons for going racing: 'it cannot be anything else, for the throng is so great that the racing cannot be seen by one in twenty of those upon the course, and thousands do not take the trouble to clear out [of] the tents to witness the running'. At Aintree the main betting ring was situated in front of the grandstand, and one needed stand tickets to gain entry to it. Here were situated the 'professional betting men of the higher class',[41] who serviced the 'crowd of well-dressed men in the ring'.[42] Lower-class bookmakers who served the poorer sections of the crowd were situated in a double row outside this privileged enclosure.

Nor was horse-racing the only medium for betting at Aintree. There were also cock-fighting, pugilism, archery and a whole host of sideshows offering gambling games of all descriptions. Many of these survived on the racecourse long after they had been made illegal. Cock-fighting, for instance, was outlawed in 1849, but it continued to take place at Aintree for many years afterwards. In 1875 the police raided a building on the course where they found 'a large number of dead fowls', about 30 live ones, and sets of weights and scales. In all about 100 people were thought to have been present, including some who occupied 'high positions in society', and the fact that the owners were said to have bet as much as £3,000 on the match

Figure 3.3. The betting ring. Source: *The Sportsman's Magazine, c.* 1845, author's collection

suggests that it was supported from a wider cross-section of society than the list of defendants implies.[43] Pugilism too survived at Aintree, and elsewhere in the city; on one occasion in 1879 it was stated that 'a number of our merchant princes, more than one of whom has been Mayor of Liverpool', were patrons of the sport.[44]

Women, and especially middle-class women, are even less visible in the sources than middle-class men, and to read some accounts one might think that the only women to attend the races were 'loose' women or prostitutes. At the Summer meeting in 1862 it was even reported that 'the will to be riotous displayed itself more on the part of the women than the men'.[45] This comment was probably directed at young working-class women, who, like their male counterparts, were well-known for their uninhibited behaviour at the fair that accompanied the race meeting.[46] Yet there is considerable evidence to show that many middle-class women did attend the races at Aintree and that they were encouraged to do so by the racecourse's management. When Aintree opened in 1829, for example, the new grandstand included a spacious withdrawing room specifically designed 'for the accommodation of ladies',[47] and at the inaugural meeting that July it was noted that the balcony was crowded with 'ladies, attired in all the dazzling variety of the present fashions'.[48] Similarly, when the first steeplechase was run at Aintree, seven years later, it was again reported that 'ladies and gentlemen appeared in great numbers from various parts of the country', the lower part of the grandstand being filled with 'elegantly dressed females'.[49] Later in the century, when 'Wizard' Topham was clerk of the course, he expressed a desire to attract more 'Liverpool ladies' to attend the races.[50] From 1878 onwards Albert Edward, Prince of Wales, was a regular visitor to Aintree and in 1881 the Empress Elizabeth of Austria–Hungary came to watch the Grand National. This royal and imperial patronage may have encouraged more women to attend; for example, Mrs Maybrick (see below) and her friends were keen to see the Prince when they attended the Grand National in 1889.

What proportion of the crowd was composed of women is virtually impossible to say, although there are some clues to be found in the various engravings that were published of early Grand Nationals. Some of these depict sections of the crowd in quite considerable detail and from these a few tentative conclusions can be drawn. F.C. Turner's view of the grand-stand at the Grand National of 1839, for example, shows 14 women and 56 men standing at the front of the balcony. This can be compared to a similar view by G.H. Laporte, done at the Grand National of 1853, which shows 11 women and 138 men on the same balcony. A rather different view taken at the Grand National of 1845 and published in the *Sportsman's Magazine* shows a section of the crowd in the centre of the course opposite the winning post: here there are two women in a coach who, judging from their dress, can be identified as prostitutes, but there are also eight soberly dressed women in plain bonnets and 17 men. This picture is also interesting because it shows two well-dressed and clearly middle-class children. Another view of the same race shows 16 women in a crowd of rather more than 100 men. Clearly it would be unwise to be too dogmatic in the conclusions one draws from so small a sample as this, but I think it is not unreasonable to state that these pictures reinforce the view that middle-class women did attend Aintree, and that they may have formed something between 10 per cent and 20 per cent of the crowd; or, as the *Liverpool Daily Post*'s reporter at the Croxteth Hunt meeting put it, there was 'always . . . a sociable representation of the fair sex'.[51]

Not surprisingly, many of the ladies used the races as an opportunity for flirtation, and sometimes much more than flirtation took place. A little-known ballad, entitled *The Liverpool Races*, and written at the time of the first meeting at Maghull in 1827, ends as follows:

> And a thousand or more I could name,
> Who are all in the like kind of cases.
> They've started and think it no shame,
> To catch sweethearts at Liverpool Races.

And when next April comes round,
What lots of sweet innocent faces
Will then come to light and be found
Three months old at next Liverpool Races.[52]

Did women bet at the races? In 1872 Topham planned to move the betting ring so that the 'Liverpool ladies' whom he planned to attract to the course would be less offended by the 'noisy Welchers', as he privately termed the bookmakers.[53] However, there is also some evidence that women were less offended by the presence of the bookmakers than he may have thought, for at the Grand National of 1871 it was noted that the women in the crowd, as much as the men, were 'all bent upon pocketing the odds and becoming rich at a bound'.[54] Of course, they may have asked their husbands or chaperons to put their bets on for them, but it seems equally likely that they did bet directly. They were certainly known to speculate on the Cotton Exchange on their own account, as a further extract from *The Lays of Cotton Broking* shows:

That lady there, so neatly dressed,
To embonpoint inclined,
Let us follow her in, she has lots of tin,
And hear a bit of her mind.

Having seated herself by the Broker,
At the subject she went with a dash,
I have come for a fresh spec in Cotton,
I'm expecting a little spare cash: . . .

The Broker was sadly distressed,
What was the poor beggar to do?
It must be confessed she was charmingly dressed,
So he booked her a hundred or two![55]

The Maybrick case, discussed below, presents convincing evidence of middle-class women betting on horses as well as cotton. Women were also known to frequent the betting area around Houghton Street, where they were observed 'paying or receiving with the greatest composure'[56], and to belong to some of the gambling clubs in the city, including a Jewish gaming club 'in a highly respectable street' where 'it was worth a whole Sunday stroll to hear a certain Hebrew lady pile up blasphemy in a foreign tongue'.[57] Occasionally, there is also evidence from the courts of women betting, as in this instance from the Liverpool County Sessions House, which occurred after the Grand National of 1897:

> a very determined-looking female charged a stylishly dressed young man with swindling her out of 1s 6d [one shilling and sixpence], to which extent she had backed Manifesto in the Grand National. After apologising for the insignificance of the bet, the lady went on to relate that, after Manifesto came in, the prisoner gave strong indications of a desire to 'go out'. 'Then', said the witness, 'he ran away. I went with him. He asked me to mind the board. 'No', says I, 'I'll mind you, where you go I go'. The prisoner stoutly denied the charge, and accused the witness of a want of veracity, but this nineteenth-century Ruth only smiled, and winked a knowing wink at the policeman standing by. The prisoner was sent to gaol for a month.[58]

Given the connection between many of Liverpool's trades and gambling, it should not come as a surprise to learn that on the floor of the Exchange 'the odds on sporting events are quoted quite as often as the prices of produce'.[59] On another occasion it was noted that among the papers subscribed to in the Exchange's newsroom were the *Sporting and Dramatic News* and *Sport*, and it was asked 'How can any man attend to his business unless...he spends half his time reading the "pink 'un"?'.[60]

There was a considerable amount of off-course betting in Liverpool. Hugh Shimmin wrote in 1857 that 'Betting houses in Liverpool are more numerous than is generally supposed, and less respectable than the proprietors would wish the public to believe.'[61] Shimmin's writings provide a vivid description of some of these establishments and make it clear that people from 'every class in life' could be found in them, including, on a typical day, 'broken-down merchants, clerks, foundrymen, one convicted dog-stealer, a "gent" said to be worth a "plum", in the shape of £20,000, cartowners, brewers and their draymen, counter-skippers, billiard players, [and] the fellow who "does the music on his cheeks" for coppers in the low houses about the docks'.[62]

Betting off course became illegal with the passing of the Act for the Suppression of Betting Houses in 1853, but despite this there is ample evidence that in Liverpool the magistrates and the Watch Committee were reluctant to use their new powers, and that betting houses continued to exist for many years afterwards. Tobacconists' and stationery shops often served as fronts for the bookmakers.[63] At least one music hall (a 'free and easy') was also used as a 'betting meet', being frequented by gentlemen 'of education and intelligence'.[64] Pubs and hotels also continued to offer facilities for betting. In 1860, for example, around 40 of 'the chief sporting characters of the town' were arrested in a raid on the Albion Hotel in Ranelagh Street, and this was followed by a similar raid on the Talbot Hotel in neighbouring Great Charlotte Street, where between 15 and 20 'gentlemen of the turf' were picked up. Significantly, however, when the case came to court all the defendants were discharged, only the landlady of the Albion being fined the maximum £100.[65]

By the 1870s, however, most off-course betting was taking place on the streets, at least during the daytime. The centre for this activity was the area around Houghton Street and Williamson Square known as 'the Lane'. Ten years later it was remembered as:

> a betting man's exchange, where the public houses of the neighbourhood were doing a roaring trade all day and late at night with bookmakers and 'sporting gents'; when the 'champions of the ring' loafed about the bars 'got up' in a manner usually described as regardless of expense. There was a bookmaker of Semitic aspect who used to be a well-known figure; a man who dressed loudly, smoked cigars eternally and had a jaunty way of wearing his shiney [*sic*] hat on 'three hairs'. There were seedy men who never had any money but were a kind of brokers...who were always on the look-out for people with money...; and above all barbers who had commissions from customers.[66]

This area was 'crowded daily with the betting rabble of the town'. These included 'several young men, sons of highly respected parents'. Middle-class involvement in off-course betting was shown even more clearly by the fact that 'regular messengers are despatched almost daily during the season from select coteries around "the Flags" to "put the money on" in and around "the Square"'. So important was this trade to the bookmakers that some of them even set up stalls on the Exchange flags themselves, without fear of being molested by the police or the magistrates, who seem to have turned a blind eye to their activities in the city's commercial heartland.[67] It was reported of the Watch Committee that 'if any ugly subjects, such as this, occasionally crop up, they are quietly and speedily smothered or ushered out by certain eminently respectable officials' and 'strangled with red tape'.[68]

Nevertheless, there were a number of attempts to clear the area.[69] These appear to have been ineffectual, but in November 1877 a number of the bookmakers were prosecuted for obstructing the streets around Williamson Square. The case was heard before Liverpool's stipendiary magistrate, Thomas Stamford Raffles, who found against the bookmakers, but made the helpful suggestion that 'If they took a club belonging to themselves it would be all right enough . . . that would be better than this mischief outside.'[70] The bookmakers took the hint. By 1887 more than 20 'sporting clubs' had been established in the city.[71] The first of these was the Top Club, which was opened by a bookmaker called Ben Hughes, but by 1879 this had been forced out of business by the Waterloo. The Waterloo's premises were in Brooks Alley, off Church Street, and it seems always to have been the busiest of the clubs, as well as appealing to 'sporting gentlemen' of all classes. It had a 'congenial and aristocratic' atmosphere, and it was said that, if a raid was made on it by the police, 'the extent and variety of the capture would considerably astound the public; and many men well-known in Liverpool society would certainly be in the haul'.[72] By 1893 it was regarded as 'a well-managed Liverpool racing centre'.[73] It seems to have survived until the First World War.[74]

Of the other clubs, some, such as the Camden, were mainly for 'mechanics and working men', but others aimed at a higher class of member. St Thomas's Club, which was situated in the business district, was frequented by men who had a 'character for respectability to maintain'. It was 'better-furnished than the ordinary betting clubs' and food as well as drink was provided. This club had about 300 members, who each paid a subscription of five shillings a year. They included ship brokers, corn merchants and 'people in business for themselves', as well as clerks, and it was noted that 'the members keep going coming in and going out, evidently devoting to the club all the precious moments they can steal from the absorbing cares of business'. The Grosvenor Club in Williamson Square was also regarded as respectable and exclusive, with a membership of between 200 and 300. Here bets could be made with any one of three resident bookmakers, and in the evening there was gambling on cards.[75] At least one of the clubs, the Pelican, which masqueraded as the Pembroke Musical Social Club, was run by a woman, Elizabeth Jones.[76]

The clubs had the desired effect of removing betting from the streets, although betting men were said still said to 'linger around' on Houghton Street 'as the aroma of tobacco clings to an empty pipe'.[77] They were generally left alone by the police and the magistrates. By 1884 the *Liverpool Review*, which had long run a campaign against them, felt obliged to report that 'betting seems rapidly to be increasing, and from the immunity, and, we might say, protection that the clubs are receiving from the police authorities, it is beginning to be thought a trifle respectable to belong to a betting club'. In the same article the *Review* noted that it was 'from the respectable class of backers that the bookmakers extract their money'.[78]

The bookmakers who ran the clubs generally received a hostile press, but it is worth reiterating the point that 'money commands position' and that the biggest bookmakers could themselves be regarded as respectable. Consider this description of R.H. Fry, perhaps the biggest of the Liverpool book-makers in the last quarter of the nineteenth century, published in the ultra-respectable *Liverpool Daily Post* in 1899: he was 'as straight as the proverbial gun barrel' and was 'a keen business man, quick to see both sides of a bargain and on the alert to seize any legitimate advantage'. These words could have been used of any of Liverpool's merchant princes. Significantly too, the *Post* stressed the 'immense sums' that Fry had given to charity, although since these were given anonymously it is impossible to substanti-ate this claim. Fry was 'known to the aristocracy of racing as no other bookmaker was known' and, despite the fact that towards the end of his life he suffered 'serious financial difficulty', he was still worth more than £31,000 (about £1 million in today's values) when he died in 1902.[79]

There were occasional police raids on some of the clubs, as in 1891, when six premises, 'all...being in the neighbourhood of the Exchange', were raided and 80 people were arrested, although only some of the betting-house keepers were subsequently taken to court.[80] Similarly, attempts to suppress the clubs in the courts tended to be dismissed on technicalities, the sympathies of Mr Raffles, the stipendiary magistrate, towards the bookmakers being commented on more than once.[81]

The Registration of Clubs Act, passed in 1893, gave encouragement to those who wanted to close down what were referred to as the 'bogus' clubs The *Liver*, for example, commented that 'it will undoubtedly crush out of existence many of those dens which, with their alluring surroundings, have so often ruined youth and indiscreet young men'.[82] The evidence of the Liverpool directories suggests that it was at least partially successful, as the number of clubs listed declined substantially after that year, although some, such as the Waterloo, survived. Betting, however, continued unabated, merely moving once again to new premises. Nor was it surprising that some of these were in the heart of the business district, one such being a hatter's, C.E. Saunders, in Exchange Street East, where 'those who crowded the shop were mostly men "on 'Change"'.[83] Initially, at least, the authorities contin-ued to turn a blind eye to much of the betting going on: in 1894 there were only 12 convictions for betting and gaming.[84]

Nor was it just on matters connected with betting that the magistrates showed their partiality to horse-racing. In 1870 there was a very close finish to the Grand National, and subsequently the Royal Society for the Prevention of Cruelty to Animals (RSPCA) prosecuted George Holman, the jockey on The Doctor, which had come second, on grounds of cruelty. This was one of the first cases of its kind and attracted considerable press attention. The evidence for the prosecution seems convincing: the *Daily Telegraph*'s racing correspondent had written that 'The Doctor's sides were fairly ripped up with the spurs'; a policeman who was present said that 'he had never before seen a horse with so much blood on his side after a race'; and, perhaps most tellingly, a cab driver said that if one of his horses had been in a similar condition he would certainly have been summonsed. Yet, after hearing the evidence from the defence, which largely comprised people who had bet on The Doctor saying that if he had been punished a little more he would have won the race, the magistrates dismissed the case and awarded costs against the RSPCA. This verdict was greeted with a 'wild cheer' from the public gallery. The *Porcupine*'s apparently rather sour comment on these proceedings was that:

> the gentlemen on the bench had a great deal more sympathy with sporting institutions than with the attempt to reduce cruelty on the race-course to an endurable limit. It is no wonder that the Houghton Street patrons of the turf were quite unable to confine their demonstrations of satisfaction within decent bounds. It is not every day that they are gratified with such proof of magisterial feeling.[85]

Many of the themes addressed in this essay come together in the lives of James Maybrick, a Liverpool cotton merchant born in 1838, who had offices in Tithebarn Street, and his US-born wife Florence. This couple were to achieve notoriety in 1889, after James Maybrick died of arsenic poisoning in suspicious circumstances and, following a manifestly unfair trial, Florence Maybrick was convicted of his murder and sentenced to death. After a considerable public outcry the Home Secretary commuted the sentence to penal servitude for life, on the grounds that Mrs Maybrick had administered and attempted to administer arsenic to her husband 'with intent to murder', a crime with which she had not been charged. In the event she spent 15 years in prison before being released in 1904, after which she returned to the United States, where she died in 1941. This remarkable case hit the headlines again in 1993 when a document came to light that, it has been claimed, is the 'diary' of James Maybrick, containing his admission that he was Jack the Ripper. Not surprisingly, this claim has been hotly

Figure 3.4. 'The trial and sentence of Mrs Maybrick'. Source: author's collection

contested and the genuineness of the 'diary', let alone the reliability of the supposed admission, remains unproven.[86]

The sensational nature of the Maybrick case has led to considerable research being carried out on the Maybricks, with the result that we now know a good deal about their lifestyle. Fortunately, perhaps, one does not need to pronounce on whether Mrs Maybrick was guilty of murder, or whether James Maybrick was Jack the Ripper, or even whether the so-called 'Ripper diary' is entirely genuine, to accept that in many respects they can be taken as representative of at least a segment of Liverpool middle-class society of their time. The picture that emerges confirms the view that respectability was often only a surface veneer, behind which lay a pleasure-seeking involvement in a range of unrespectable activities, among which horse-racing and betting were prominent.

John Aunspaugh, another member of Liverpool's business community, once said of James Maybrick that he was 'one of the straightest, most upright and honourable men in a business transaction I have ever known'.[87] Despite this, Maybrick was a womaniser and a drug addict, and both the inquest on his death and his widow's trial helped to pull back the veil on 'a form of existence in the social sphere to which he belonged that is distressing to contemplate'[88] – a turn of phrase (from the *Liverpool Echo*, commenting at the time) that in itself suggests that his lifestyle was not uncommon among the Liverpool business class. Like many merchants, Maybrick was a gambler: John Aunspaugh's daughter Florence recalled that 'he bet on the races and played stud-poker';[89] and this is echoed by one line in the 'Ripper diary' that at least has a ring of truth to it: 'tomorrow I will make a substantial wager'.[90] He was a regular racegoer, not just at Aintree and on the Wirral, but at the fashionable southern meetings such as Ascot and Goodwood, and was also fond of hunting; after his marriage he kept six horses, two of them saddle horses for riding.[91]

Maybrick's love of horses and racing was something that he shared with his wife. Indeed, this shared interest may even have contributed to their whirlwind romance on board the SS *Baltic* in March 1880, for Florence had already attended the Grand National at least once, and she recalled later that her special pastime during her childhood had been riding.[92] Certainly after their marriage they 'both played whist and danced the polka, but most of all they followed the horses on whatever track they were running'.[93] Although Florence was regarded as 'good-natured and pretty',[94] she was far from innocent and, like her husband, led a far from 'respectable' life. Recent research suggests that she almost certainly had an illegitimate child when she was still in her teens, and after her marriage she is known to have had at least three affairs: one with a man called Williams, about whom nothing else is known; another with her brother in law, Edwin Maybrick; and a third with Alfred Brierley, another cotton merchant.

This affair came out into the open at the Grand National in 1889. James Maybrick had invited a number of his friends and business associates, including Brierley, and Charles and Christina Samuelson, to join him on a hired omnibus to go to Aintree, but Mrs Maybrick travelled to the course separately, accompanied by another woman friend. No-one appears to have thought this unusual, nor does anyone seem to have been surprised that Maybrick's party included 'both ladies and gentlemen'. However, during the afternoon Maybrick observed his wife flirting with Brierley. Husband and wife quarrelled, and Mrs Maybrick was overheard to say 'I will give it him hot and heavy for speaking to me like that in public', a remark that was to count against her at the subsequent inquest and at her trial.[95]

It was Mrs Maybrick's affair with Brierley that provided the prosecution with a motive for murder and destroyed her reputation in Liverpool, but her love of the turf was also held against her by 'respectable' society. As the *Liverpool Courier* put it, seemingly somewhat disingenuously:

> It has been a matter of some surprise that Mrs Maybrick should have been so desirous of attending race meetings. She was present not only at those in Cheshire and at Aintree, but at others, and some of those acquainted with the family say that it came to her husband's knowledge that, like many other ladies who take an interest in matters of sport, she sometimes risked a little on the result of races.[96]

Mrs Maybrick's love of racing clearly survived her 15 years in prison. Although her later years in the United States were spent in impoverished obscurity, in 1927 she managed to find the money for one last visit to Britain, during which she revisited some of her old haunts, 'not forgetting the Grand National', which had played so important a part in her tragedy.[97]

The lives of other members of the Maybricks' party at the Grand National of 1889 are also instructive. Alfred Brierley was 38 years old at the time of the Maybrick affair. Described by the *Liverpool Echo* at the time as having 'an irreproachable commercial standing',[98] he was the senior partner in Brierley & Wood, cotton merchants, which had its offices on Old Hall Street, and he lived at 60, Huskisson Street. Somewhat 'dashing', like the Maybricks he too was a keen racegoer and went to many meetings with them before the fateful encounter at Aintree.[99] The exposure of this outwardly respectable merchant as being far from respectable was devastating, as was recognised at the time, the *Liverpool Echo* commenting that 'to a Liverpool merchant placed in his unenviable position, the exposé must have been peculiarly painful'.[100] Although he was never called to give evidence at the trial, his business was dissolved and he emigrated to the United States.[101]

Two other members of the party at the Grand National, Charles and Christina Samuelson, got off more lightly. Although Mrs Samuelson gave evidence at the inquest, she and her husband then disappeared, and neither of them was called to give evidence at the trial. It seems reasonable to infer that they realised that they had to protect their own reputations, for Charles Samuelson was a partner in the firm of Edward Samuelson & Co., tobacco brokers, and his father, the head of the firm, was Alderman Edward Samuelson, who had been Mayor of Liverpool in 1872–73.[102]

There is one final, rather gruesome connection between the Maybrick case and the racing world. On the day the verdict was announced some race-goers at Brighton races wanted to bet on the outcome, but, rather to their credit, the bookmakers refused to accept bets on 'such a terrible subject'; even so, after the result came in 'there was a general offer to lay long odds that the sentence was never carried out'.[103]

There is thus abundant evidence that the majority of the Liverpudlian middle classes, like those in other sections of society, were keen supporters of horse-racing, as owners, as spectators and, especially, as punters, while simultaneously posing as upright figures in society. Their attitude could easily be dismissed as an example of stereotypical Victorian hypocrisy, yet this seems too simplistic an explanation. Rather, it seems that the concept of 'respectability' was a fluid one, and that what was acceptable in one location was not acceptable in another. The racecourse was one place where 'conventionality' could be safely left behind; although perhaps on a lesser scale, this seems to have applied to women as much as to men. It also seems, as the Maybrick case demonstrates, that a great deal of unrespectable behaviour was accepted by society at large, but only as long as it could be kept out of the public domain. As always, money and influence mattered. In a leading article on betting, published in 1888, the *Liverpool Citizen* contrasted 'the open and flagrant encouragement of it in the highest quarters, the passive winking at it in others, and the stern and pseudo-virtuous putting of it down as an unmitigated severity in other and less blameworthy quarters'.[104] It is surely not coincidental that it was the betting clubs catering for the less well-off that were raided by the police and not the 'aristocratic' Waterloo, which survived long after the others had been closed down or driven underground.

The contrast between the rich and the poor in Victorian Britain was nowhere more obvious than in Liverpool, as was often remarked at the time. Yet the commercial nature of the city, and the dependence of almost all its business on the port, either directly or indirectly, meant that that there was also a certain commonality among the classes. Writing in 1907, W. Dixon Scott expressed this well when he said that it 'interweaves class with class, [and] provides merchant, clerk, seamen and dock-labourers with a common unifying interest'.[105] Perhaps, therefore, it is not so surprising that they should also have shared an interest in horse-racing and in betting, and that those who were used to taking risks in their business life should have been willing to take risks in their leisure time too, secure in the knowledge that the close-knit business community could generally use its influence to prevent any unfortunate misdemeanours from becoming public knowledge.

Part 2:

The power of print: the media and respectability

Popular Sunday newspapers, respectability and working-class culture in late Victorian Britain

DAVID SCOTT KAMPER

By the end of the nineteenth century the press critic Henry Sell could confidently declare that 'Sunday papers have established a precedent that no opposition can break down.'[1] Numbers alone proved his assertion: in 1890 some two million copies of popular Sunday papers such as *Lloyd's Weekly Newspaper*, the *People* or the *Weekly Dispatch* were being sold every week. Their coverage of sensational news, sport and crime was highly appealing. Sunday penny papers were the leading cultural products of late Victorian Britain, eclipsing music halls, cheap novels and football in size, if not necessarily in influence.

Size, however, did not guarantee cultural acceptance. Sunday newspapers had shed their reputation as mouthpieces of revolutionary anarchism, which had been prevalent in the 1840s and 1850s,[2] but even in the later years of the Victorian era it 'was not considered respectable to read a Sunday journal'.[3] Sunday newspapers were either ignored by their contemporaries, or, at best, disparaged and belittled as unworthy counterparts of the *Daily News* or the *Standard*. Why were popular Sunday newspapers, so commercially successful, unable to attain the same status as their daily counterparts?

One important reason was that the 'respectability' of Sunday newspapers was inextricably linked with questions of class. Respectability was not the same thing as social class; there could be respectable labourers just as there were dissolute noblemen. However, in the case of Sunday newspapers respectability was defined by its relation to class. There was a general feeling, best expressed by an anonymous journalist for a Sunday newspaper, that they were 'low-class papers'.[4] The ambiguous meaning of 'low-class' helps illuminate the position of Sunday papers. Not only did they fall below the horizontal dividing lines of social class, they, and by extension their readers, also faced challenges along the vertical line of respectability.

This chapter examines how the cultural position of Sunday newspapers was influenced by these links between class and respectability. While

Sunday newspapers were not simply working-class organs, they were *perceived* as being so. If many historians today are no longer entirely comfortable about acknowledging an autonomous 'working-class culture', Victorian Britain had no problems in doing so, and Sunday newspapers were a part of it. This identification with the working class challenged the precarious respectability of Sunday newspapers in middle-class cultural contexts, but also allowed them opportunities to define respectability for their readers.

Sunday papers were challenged in two ways. First, they were on the wrong side of a powerful discourse on how the respectable working classes were supposed to spend their Sundays. Second, they fell prey to existing stereotypes about the sensational nature of working-class reading habits. This chapter examines how the interaction between class and respectability affected one group's relationship with Sunday newspapers: the newsagents. In the 1890s retail newsagents across Britain organised themselves to improve not only their working conditions, but also their status in society. Their ambiguous attitudes to Sunday newspapers demonstrate how class language was used by many in society to articulate claims to respectability.

Despite this lack of respectability, however, Sunday newspapers were still purchased by millions every week. These readers, too, were not immune to the desire for status in society and Sunday papers had to respond to this perceived need. They did so by helping to create a cultural context that reinforced the beliefs of their readers. In essence, Sunday newspapers tried to make their readers feel respectable, and they did so, like their opponents, by using class language. This chapter concludes by looking at one example of how Sunday newspapers did this, in relation to working-class betting on sport. While many in Victorian society were solidly opposed to betting in general, and working-class betting in particular, the Sunday newspapers articulated a different view. Sunday papers sought to reassure their readers that sports betting, within reasonable limits, was a harmless form of recreation whose only dangers came from the efforts of 'unrespectable' elements, often at the top of society, to prey upon those lower down the social scale.

This chapter touches upon several important aspects of Victorian social and cultural history. Many historians have examined the development of popular and working-class cultures in late Victorian Britain, but so far empirical studies have tended to focus on specific locales and small populations. As Sunday papers reached much of the country and millions of people, a study of them might offer a new perspective on class, culture and politics.[5] This chapter is also intended to contribute to the literature on the construction of working-class and lower-middle-class respectability in Victorian Britain, which is in need of further case studies.[6] Finally, I hope that this chapter can encourage a renewed look at the role of Sunday newspapers in the development of the Victorian popular press, a role often marginalised by modern historians.[7]

Who read Sunday newspapers? They had enormous circulations in the later years of the Victorian era. *Lloyd's Weekly Newspaper* was in every respect at the head of the pack. In 1870 it was already claiming a circulation above 500,000, and in 1896, under the editorship of Thomas Catling, it became the first paper in Britain to reach sales of more than one million.[8] The *People*, founded in 1881 as the only major Conservative-supporting Sunday paper, reached 360,000 by 1890.[9] Four others – the *News of the World*, the *Weekly Dispatch*, the *Weekly Times and Echo*, and *Reynolds's Newspaper* – were smaller, but at least one of them 'guaranteed' advertisers a circulation of 150,000 a week in 1895.[10]

With so many copies being sold, therefore, it would be foolish to assume that their readership was drawn exclusively from the working class. Yet this is precisely what Victorian commentators did whenever they deigned to discuss Sunday newspapers at all, which was rare. J.F. Stephen's opinion, published in 1856, that the readers of Sunday papers included a 'man who has passed six days in the week on carting parcels from one railway station to another, in unloading ships, in watching the wheels of the machine', was echoed by that of a newsagent, published in 1899, who characterised them as 'carpenters, bricklayers, plumbers, smiths, navvies, labourers, carters, gardeners and so forth'.[11]

This impression was reinforced by the rigid dividing line set up between readers of daily papers and readers of Sunday newspapers. They were seen as two distinct sets of people. Robert Donald, Managing Editor of the *Daily Chronicle* (also owned by the Lloyd family), was certain that Sunday papers were for 'the multitude ... a class who do not buy a daily paper regularly'.[12] According to the Rev. H.R. Haweis, 'there are daily papers that are not Sundays, and there should continue to be Sunday papers that are not dailies'.[13] When T.P. O'Connor started the *Sunday Sun*, in 1891, he made a deliberate effort to disassociate his venture from the existing Sunday papers. 'Our Journal will be', he claimed, 'to use a conscious contradiction, a daily paper published once a week.'[14] Even with his energetic effort at rhetorical distancing, however, he soon felt it necessary to change the name of the paper to the *Weekly Sun*.

This dividing line was never more accurately demonstrated than in the uproar over 'seven-day journalism', which erupted in 1889 and again in 1899.[15] In 1889 the London edition of the *New York Herald* began, promising a paper every day of the week, including Sundays. In 1899 the two London dailies with the largest circulations, the *Daily Telegraph* and the *Daily Mail*, decided to introduce Sunday editions. Massive protests took place on both occasions, the first being led by William Thomas Stead, editor of the *Pall Mall Gazette*, and Edward Benson, Archbishop of Canterbury, and those in 1899 involving almost every bishop of the Church of England, prominent labour leaders such as John Burns and more than 50 members of Parliament. Both protests were successful: the London edition of the *New York Herald* survived for less than two years, and the Sunday editions of the *Mail* and *Telegraph* lasted for just seven weeks each.

While the controversies were primarily about seven days' labour, there was a strong feeling that daily papers had no business alongside Sunday papers. When the *New York Herald* defensively pointed to the existing Sunday papers, it was told by the Rev. Newman Hall that 'it is not the same', because the existing Sunday papers 'do not distract the mind by... the ordinary contents of a newspaper'.[16] In 1899, meeting a deputation, the Home Secretary, Sir Matthew Ridley, acknowledged that 'it is quite true that at the present moment there are a very large number of papers distributed throughout the metropolis on Sunday... but those papers [e.g., *Lloyd's*] are not, as I understand it... *pari passu* with the new issues (Hear, hear).'[17] *Pari passu* means 'equally' or 'side by side': there was a consensus among opponents of 'seven-day journalism' that a Sunday edition of a daily paper was fundamentally different from the existing Sunday papers. They were culturally segregated; there was not a popular press, but, rather, there were popular presses.

In short, while the *News of the World* could claim in advertisements that 'its general news and information fits it alike for the aristocracy and middle classes, as well as mechanics', Sunday newspapers were seen as papers for the lower-middle and working classes.[18] How did this identification affect their status? Respectability was, as Brian Harrison puts it, 'always a process, a dialogue... never a fixed position', but it had tremendous normative power.[19] Respectability was contested precisely because being respectable was so desirable. Victorians asserted their respectability not only by participating in respectable culture, but also by opposing unrespectable culture. The close link between Sunday newspapers and the working class allowed Victorians to take both of these routes. While many sought to become respectable by opposing Sunday papers, others looked to popular Sundays to support their own views of respectable behaviour.

Let us first look at the way in which Sunday newspapers were opposed by much of Victorian society. Two significant discourses of respectability were used to challenge Sunday newspapers specifically because they were identified with the working classes. The first was Sunday observance. 'The weekly holiday', observed one future bishop, H.H. Henson, 'must be kept under lock and key until the working classes have learned how to use it.'[20]

Late Victorian discussions of the proper place for Sunday frequently treated it primarily as a question of what to do about the working classes.[21] The middle classes and the elites, it was assumed, did not need protection from Sunday labour. The lower orders, however, were lost souls in need of special attention; they could not be trusted to look after their own best interests. 'The working classes are not awake to the value of Sunday', wrote one commentator during the seven-day journalism protests in 1889; 'they see that there is no foundation for its theoretical sanction, but they do not see what an intensely human value it possesses'.[22] The support of existing legislation, therefore, was vital in the eyes of Sabbatarians. The most relevant statute was the Lord's Day Observance Act, which dated back to the reign of Charles II, although it had been amended in 1871. In the latter year the seventh Earl of Shaftesbury, who presided over the Working Men's Lord's Day Rest Association (WMLDRA), had described the Act as 'the working-man's charter, securing to him the right to a suspension of toil for one day in seven'.[23]

While it is true that, in the eyes of some, such as the Radical P.A. Taylor, Sabbatarians 'seemed to think that they could never serve God unless they were prosecuting men', we should not assume that only extreme Sabbatarians held strong views on Sunday observance.[24] Few Victorians were vociferous on the issue, but most seem to have felt that Sunday was a special day and that infringement of its status as such was tolerable at best. John Burns, still describing himself as a 'Socialist' in 1889, felt that Sunday labour was 'a desire of the capitalists' vanguard to extend the period of labour's exploitation'.[25] In 1884 the WMLDRA claimed the support of 2,412 'working-class societies', totalling 501,705 members, in its fight against Sunday opening of the British Museum.[26] Even the Sunday League and other groups pushing for the relaxation of Sabbath restrictions felt the need to qualify their positions, stressing utility and necessity, instead of insisting openly on a free Sunday. The evidence suggests that support for the traditional status of the Sabbath was the respectable position to take, both for the elites, and for members of the lower-middle and working classes.

The second challenge to Sunday newspapers arose from the prevalence of stereotypes about working-class reading habits. These stereotypes were by no means universal. In 1856 J.F. Stephen (already quoted above) had written: 'It is certain that there is a general impression abroad that they [Sunday papers] are unfailing sources of furious political incendiarism, and pander to all kinds of prurient curiosity...nothing can be more unlike the impressions which we get from the papers themselves than the expectations.'[27] Few, however, followed Stephen's lead and examined Sunday newspapers before condemning them.

The main charge was that the Sunday papers printed indecent or sensational material. While Thomas Catling maintained that a 'murder mystery has always been of great service to every newspaper', Sundays were singled out for special attention.[28] The *Saturday Review*, which had been complimentary in 1856, could hardly be too critical of Sunday papers by 1870. While railing against 'indecent' advertisements in the daily press, it nevertheless did 'not propose to attempt the reformation of the weekly press. The newspapers that lay themselves out for the work of public corruption – the *Reynolds* and the *Lloyds* – the buzzflies of dirt who stink and sting – are beyond indignation.'[29] An article reprinted with evident approval in the *Newspaper Press* called Sunday papers 'a catalogue of all the villainies of the week'.[30] It mocked *Lloyd's* with a fake table of contents: 'Trial of a Burglar and a Murderer – Shocking Suicide of a Girl and Her Betrayal – A Woman Murders Her Five Children – Brutal Treatment of a Pauper – An MP Garotted in the Seven Dials – Thrilling Death of a Drunkard'.[31]

This general pattern continued throughout the Victorian era. Mr White of the retail giant W.H. Smith & Son thought that the 'majority' of Sunday papers were 'simply summaries of the week's accidents, murders, police-court cases and that sort of thing; and are read by servants, or those whom you see sitting at their windows in their shirt sleeves, with pipes in their mouths, instead of going to church'.[32] At the height of the controversy over seven-day newspapers in 1899, the *Sun*, forgetting its own foray into Sunday journalism a few years before, published a cartoon entitled 'Going to Church in the Near Future'.[33] It showed a respectably dressed couple surrounded by a score of handbills for fictitious Sunday newspapers, all advertising vicious murders, horrible scandals and indecent revelations. 'There is a special charm about the Sunday morning's paper', wrote a newsagent, 'because special attention is devoted to the collection of sensational news on Saturday, and this class of thing suits the taste of the majority of working men.'[34]

Few critics paid close attention to the content of Sunday newspapers, such as their regular dramatic and literary reviews. Few noted the political news that they carried, even though Ashton Dilke, a brother of the politician Charles Dilke, owned the *Weekly Dispatch*. One of T.P. O'Connor's first jobs was as parliamentary reporter for *Lloyd's*.[35] The Sunday papers did undoubtedly print a lot of police news. Indeed, the memoirs of Thomas Catling, an editor of *Lloyd's*, show that he was proud of the quality of his paper's crime reporting. The point, however, is that the *perception* of Sunday newspapers was that their content was sensational and scandalous. Sunday newspapers were less respectable not only because their content was suspect, but because the content so neatly accorded with stereotypes about working-class reading habits.

From at least two angles, then, Sabbath-breaking and sensationalism, the respectability of Sunday newspapers was attacked using discourses of class. It is not enough, however, to lay out Victorians' broad, generic views of Sunday papers and leave matters to rest. Rather, it is important to descend to the particular, to see not what supposedly respectable Victorians *thought* about Sunday newspapers, but how they *acted* when confronted with the uncertain status of purportedly working-class newspapers. Let us explore the tensions between the commercial success of Sunday newspapers and their shaky respectability as experienced by one important segment of the Victorian mass media network: newsagents.

While W.H. Smith & Son had a near-monopoly on the railway station trade, independent newsagents still supplied the majority of newspapers throughout the country. The Retail Newsagents and Booksellers Union (RN&BU) was founded at the beginning of the 1890s to unite independent newsagents and to address their many grievances. Its first General Secretary, E.C. Gowing-Scopes, was, it appears, a very active organiser, and soon the RN&BU had branches across the country. The official organ of the RN&BU was the *Newsagent and Bookseller's Review*, which claimed a weekly circulation of more than 10,000.[36] It published minutes of the meetings of the RN&BU's executive committee, its quarterly council and its annual conferences, as well as those of branch meetings across the country. It is, therefore, an excellent public record of the activities and thoughts of the organised section of the newsagents' business in the 1890s.[37]

The RN&BU's main activity was putting pressure on newspaper publishers over practical grievances. Thus, we read about the folding of newspapers, payment for inserts and postal rates. A great deal of this activity was focused on relatively narrow business concerns, but what is noteworthy is how often the RN&BU employed the language of respectability. Responding to the charge that newsagents formed an 'illiterate class', for example, the *Newsagent and Bookseller's Review* was quick to reply that 'retailers of newspapers are, without exception, far above the average in both knowledge and intelligence'.[38] One of the RN&BU's campaigns was aimed at securing regulation of independent news hawkers, who worked irregularly but cut into the income of newsagents' shops, by licensing them all to work with 'established' newsagents. Far from pleading fear of competition, however, the newsagents made the scheme sound like benevolence on their part: 'The idea was to secure respectable lads...to make them responsible to and employed by a respectable tradesman, to have them respectably dressed;...and to pay them a respectable wage, and if possible, to see that they spent it respectably'.[39] The RN&BU, like almost all other Victorian business associations and trade unions, saw collective organising and bargaining, not as a form of class conflict, but as part of the process of improving the status of its members. Such a move required not just money, but also respectability.

Sunday newspapers proved a challenge not only to respectability, but also to increased incomes. In the opinion of E.W. Hickox, President of the North London branch of the RN&BU, 'Sunday trade has done more than anything else to bring the news vending trade into disrepute'.[40] The Executive Committee, whose members presumably knew what they were talking about, claimed that perhaps one quarter of the country's 20,000 newsagents traded on Sundays.[41] They were quite aware of their predicament: many newsagents 'derive the better part of their weekly income' from Sunday sales, yet 'the feeling of even those who are Sunday sellers is entirely opposed to the system'.[42] In their efforts to salvage both respectability and profits, newsagents went to great lengths to distance themselves rhetorically from Sunday newspapers, but never went far enough to threaten their business.

Their first challenge was to justify their existing Sunday trading. One technique was to blame the readers. One newsagent wrote in the *Newsagent and Bookseller's Review* that he supported 'Sunday as a day of rest for the workers', but wondered 'how these same workers show their gratitude for our consideration', and contended that:

> The fact remains that those who cater for these classes are compelled to work on Sunday, and the 'hardly treated' working man, who . . . will not work a minute after half-past five at night without being paid one and a half times his usual rate of wage, is responsible for practically every scrap of the Sunday opening of shops.[43]

A regular stream of letters in the following weeks supported him. According to one, the working-class buyers of Sunday papers were 'the greatest tyrants under the sun, and make the worst masters. I believe they are patted on the back as the poor, suffering working man too much.'[44] According to another, 'When the toiler opens his paper on Sunday morning it must be piping hot from the press.'[45] Even those who were not so disparaging agreed with Mr Pratt of the Executive Committee that 'the Sunday paper was an institution in the land. The working man had always been used to it', and would not easily abandon it.[46]

The problem with blaming Sunday papers on the readers, however, was it did not explain why newsagents could not close their shops on Sundays.

Newsagents made it clear that the alternatives to Sunday trading were worse: a stream of undesirables would swarm the streets if they closed. 'Under present conditions', said J.W. Miller, another member of the Executive Committee and a staunch opponent of Sunday trading, the Sunday trade 'must be turned over to street loafers unless the retailers worked seven days a week (Applause)'.[47] Closing on Sunday would 'create a street sale by a class of people who can and will make themselves so obnoxious that the respectable inhabitants of each town will petition to have the [Lord's Day Observance] Act repealed'.[48] Street sellers, Mr Jones of the Executive Committee declared, 'did not as a rule want [need] money, and [he] instanced cases of men in regular work, earning good money, going out in this way'.[49] One newsagent asked, concerning street sellers, 'are they Jews ... or is it possible he is too idle to work on other days and would rather do his bit on Sunday?'[50] All agreed with Mr Curtice that 'all the scum went into the trade on Sunday ... much to the annoyance of the respectable trade'.[51]

As if that was not enough, it was also claimed that Sunday sales would corrupt wayward youth. An alderman in Southampton contacted the RN&BU, concerned that children were playing truant from Sunday School and selling papers instead; he urged the newsagents to stay open on Sundays so that the newsboys would have no trade.[52] One of the regular columnists of the *Newsagent and Bookseller's Review*, writing from Southsea, marvelled at the 'pack of boys and lads of all ages, from about ten years old to 20', who 'were scrambling like hungry wolves over a carcass' to sell their papers. He added that 'I will only say ... that the newsagents' shops are open on Sunday ... and ought to be able to do this trade in a respectable manner.'[53]

Justifying Sunday trading was not enough for many newsagents; they wanted to find a solution to the burden of selling Sunday newspapers. However, they could not accomplish this without upsetting those who depended on Sunday newspapers for their livelihood. A letter from 'Newsman' asked:

> if I were to go to my opposite neighbour, whom [*sic*] I know depends on his Sunday business ... and try to persuade him to join the Union, telling him that the Union is going to compel him to close on Sunday ... what would he think of me? He would think I was a lunatic.[54]

The RN&BU, unable to reconcile the demands of profit with those of respectability, ended up allowing the opponents of Sunday newspapers to claim the moral high ground, but never gave them enough support for success.

The newsagents most actively opposed to Sunday newspapers were not all rigid Sabbatarians. The two members of the Executive Committee who led the first push in 1893 to end Sunday newspapers, T. Chismon and J.W. Miller (one looks in vain for first names in the RN&BU's papers), were ardent trade unionists and political Radicals. Miller, who had become a newsagent in part to sell newspapers 'of an advanced character', and had been interested in trades unionism 'from boyhood', insisted that the way to end Sunday papers was to mount collective action to secure one day's rest in seven.[55] Chismon warned that

> there is a mighty struggle in the paper trade coming... in a very little while, in which trade unionists will have all the advantage on their side, and the rich publisher, with all his wealth, will be powerless... They will find themselves face to face with a power they have not had to face before... then, perhaps, they will see that the shekels they are so eager to scrape in on Sunday [are not worth the price of a labour struggle].[56]

The first concrete proposal, made by Miller at a meeting of the Executive Committee in January, 1893, was to ask the publishers of Sunday newspaper to print late Saturday editions that could be sold late on Saturday evenings, thus allowing newsagents to close on Sundays. The proposal was enthusiastically received and was passed unanimously. The RN&BU's Chairman, Charles Roberts, said 'I don't think any resolution put before the Executive has ever given me greater pleasure (Applause).'[57] Almost immediately, however, differences appeared. When the Stepney branch endorsed the scheme on the proviso that there be no Sunday editions whatever, the General Secretary, E.C. Gowing-Scopes, urged the branches not to tack on 'impossible conditions'.[58] Yet, two weeks later, Gowing-Scopes suggested in an open letter that an Act of Parliament against Sunday selling 'would prove an immense blessing to the newsagent'.[59] Another two weeks later, in response to a stream of letters from members opposed to the scheme, he backtracked again, claiming that 'it is quite useless to think of stopping Sunday papers – we could never do it if we wanted to (Applause)'.[60] In his report to the annual meeting of the RN&BU in April he sought to clear everything up: the Sunday issue was a 'bone of contention' between members; 'we have had to approach the subject very delicately'.[61] 'Delicately' may have meant 'not at all', because, while Gowing-Scopes wrote to the publishers asking them to print late Saturday editions, no further action was taken once he had received their unsupportive replies.

The members of the Executive Committee found themselves shifting back and forth, unable to avoid contradictions. When Chismon announced at a meeting in May 1893 that he had persuaded nearly all his customers to sign a petition opposing Sunday papers, he was greeted with applause. A few minutes later, however, Mr Legg, who had supported the original proposal for late Saturday papers, was also applauded when he argued that 'their agitation on the question showed a great deal of the dog-in-the-manger business. Those who wished to give up Sunday papers should do so and not try to make others follow suit.'[62] At the same meeting Chismon urged the Executive Committee to pass a resolution commending the cities of Birmingham and Southampton for restricting Sunday selling, but by a majority of 10–7 the Committee refused to do so. At the next meeting, however, in a purely symbolic gesture, it voted to expurgate that vote from the minutes, on the grounds that it looked bad to refuse to congratulate others whose actions supported their cause.[63]

This went on for more than a year. In 1894 Chismon persuaded the general secretary to ask every branch for its opinion on Sunday newspapers, but it took a month for the Executive Committee to agree on the wording of the letter. All but two of the branches supported a ban of some sort. Acting on that information, Chismon arranged for Archbishop Benson to receive a deputation from the RN&BU on the subject of Sunday newspapers. However, a few days before the meeting the Chairman of the Executive Committee suddenly decided that 'it was deemed inadvisable to continue the matter, as it was a question of considerable difference of opinion'.[64] A serious debate ensued, as many members of the committee expressed fears that a deputation to the archbishop would give the appearance of a unanimity that did not exist. Yet Diprose added that 'we should keep in touch with the question and not appear to want to shelve it'.[65] In the end Miller, Chismon and a third member of the Committee went to see the archbishop, but said that they were doing so in a private capacity: they received a lukewarm reception.[66]

When the controversy over seven-day journalism erupted in 1899, once again the newsagents showed themselves desirous of respectability but unwilling to make the financial sacrifices to obtain it. The RN&BU quickly joined the protests against the *Sunday Daily Telegraph* and the *Daily Mail (Sunday Edition)*. Unity was maintained during the seven weeks' struggle and Gowing-Scopes became Secretary of the National Protest Committee, alongside bishops and MPs. A petition circulated through the pages of the *Newsagent and Bookseller's Review* received nearly 250,000 signatures. A great many newsagents boycotted all publications affiliated with either of the seven-day papers. The attempt to mix respectable daily and unrespectable Sunday newspapers crossed a strong cultural dividing line. When that dividing line was restored after the withdrawal of the seven-day editions, the newsagents' unanimity collapsed. At the annual meeting of the RN&BU, in Liverpool, just weeks after the defeat of seven-day journalism, there was, it appeared, a strong anti-Sunday mood. Mr Fletcher's speech declaring that 'he wished to see them band together in such a way as it could be said "the newsagents are altogether opposed to Sunday trading"' drew loud applause from the assembled newsagents.[67] Speaker after speaker followed, agreeing with Fletcher, and with Chismon's characteristically aggressive cry that 'the time had arrived for whipping away the thing at once'.[68] One member even urged that those who sold Sunday papers should be expelled from the RN&BU. However, despite apparent unity, the newsagents found reasons to avoid action. They agreed that 'the working man could not be aroused to take action...he was a bit selfish'. Others warned that their allies in Parliament and the churches might not support a step this far. Having thus excused themselves from taking any substantive steps, a face-saving motion was introduced, seconded by Chismon, the most ardent opponent of Sunday newspapers among them, to direct the Executive Committee to 'carry the matter out to the best of their [*sic*] ability'.[69] The Executive Committee never discussed the subject again.

It is not surprising that newsagents were unwilling to deprive themselves of the profits from the sale of thousands of Sunday newspapers. What is surprising is the lengths to which they went to give the appearance of wanting to do so. In all the records of the RN&BU examined while preparing this chapter, no newsagent admitted to *reading* a Sunday newspaper, very few claimed to like doing Sunday business and even those who favoured Sunday trading were careful to present it as a necessary evil, to keep the trade in respectable hands. Being seen to oppose Sunday newspapers was perceived as a necessary step to achieving respectability.

If Sunday newspapers failed to achieve respectability, and if respectability was highly sought after, then how were Sunday papers able not only to survive but to thrive in late Victorian Britain? The 1880s and 1890s saw sales of Sunday newspapers rise faster than at any other time in the century. By the time of the seven-day journalism controversy in 1899 *Lloyd's* alone was selling 1,100,000 copies a week. How can these facts be reconciled? Were the readers of Sunday papers not desirous of respectability, or were other factors at work?

Certainly, some of the reasons why people read Sunday papers were purely economic and logistical. A Sunday paper was a tremendous bargain.

Sunday papers were as cheap as daily papers, but they were usually twice their size, carried about half their number of advertisements and contained news from throughout the preceding week.[70] As Virginia Berridge has demonstrated, the advertisements in Sunday papers were targeted especially at the lower-middle class and the working class, and thus probably provided a resource unavailable elsewhere for many readers. In addition, Sunday was, for many Victorians, the one day of the week when they had the leisure and, in ill-lit homes, the daylight to read and digest fully a newspaper's contents.

These reasons may be sufficient to explain why Sunday papers were read, but they do not address a major problem: that, by buying and reading Sundays, readers were seemingly participating in an unrespectable activity. However, the struggle for respectability always takes place in cultural contexts, and the readers of Sunday newspapers had access to texts and context that those who shunned *Lloyd's* and *Reynolds's* did not have: the Sunday papers themselves. Unlike clergymen, politicians or newsagents, who condemned Sunday papers without reading them or, at least, admitting to reading them, those who paid for them were exposed to their ideas and their language. While popular Sunday papers rarely got a fair hearing from the broader public, they probably had a sympathetic reception from their readers, who had almost as much reason as the proprietors of the papers to want to think them respectable.

However unpopular they were in much of Victorian society, Sunday newspapers proudly donned the mantle of respectability within their own pages. They drew their own boundary lines between respectable and unrespectable behaviour. At times, these discourses served a pedagogical purpose, to instruct readers how to behave respectably in society. More often, however, Sunday papers sought to reassure their readers that they already had a claim to respectable status, by justifying and supporting their cultural and social practices.

What is notable about Sunday newspapers' attempts to make their readers feel respectable is that they also employed the language of class in the process. Sunday newspapers did not dispute the prevailing wisdom that their readership was drawn from the lower-middle class and the working class. On the contrary, most embraced the label, and sought to make the most of it by challenging conventional thinking about working-class habits and morals, notably on sport and gambling.

According to the historian Richard Holt, 'By 1900 the scale of working-class involvement in organised sport was astounding.'[71] Millions paid to see football and cricket, and hundreds of thousands more became players in amateur leagues of one sort or another. Annual attendance at First Division football matches tripled between 1888/89 and 1895/96.[72] As real wages for many in the lower-middle class and the working class rose in the last third of the century, so more was available for expenditure on sporting events. Mr Hobbs of the RN&BU claimed that '99 out of 100' people bought a Sunday newspaper primarily for the sporting news.[73]

While there was nothing inherently unrespectable about sport in general, there was a strong stigma attached to gambling on sports. While people were willing to bet on almost anything, until 1914 horse-racing was the main focus of gambling activity. With so many factors – jockeys, training, condition of the turf – in play, betting on horses, when done with care, 'constituted a whole system of knowledge ... open to all working men'.[74] Gambling was very much an activity with class overtones. While all social classes, albeit largely the men in all social classes, engaged in gambling on sport, mass betting was a 'proletarian institution' that 'bore all the characteristics of the British working class'.[75] Lower-middle-class and working-class communities developed important social structures to accommodate gambling, and made use of other, more traditional cultural venues, such as pubs, as well. Entire publications, such as the *Sporting Chronicle* or the *Sportsman*, sprang into existence for the main purpose of supplying would-be gamblers with all the latest intelligence necessary for placing a winning bet.

Not surprisingly, the growth of popular gambling raised no small amount of concern among those Victorians who concerned themselves with the habits of the working classes. They worried that gambling prevented people from participating in the kinds of rational recreation that reformers thought best for the urban working classes.[76] More importantly, gambling was seen, along with drink, as 'twin evils feeding off each other in a culture of misery and sloth that dragged decent men into crime and vice'.[77] What is significant about the cultural challenges to gambling was the class character of the rhetoric. In many ways gambling was more a 'popular' than a 'working-class' activity, but, in the language of the opponents of gambling, the class connotation received the most attention. The same cultural processes that made Sunday newspapers unrespectable – linking them with unacceptable and dangerous forms of working-class behaviour – made gambling not just an unrespectable activity, but an unrespectable *working-class* activity.

Sunday newspapers, therefore, faced considerable cultural challenges when it came to reporting sport and gambling, in addition to the financial challenges posed by the *Sportsman* and other sport-only papers. Gambling on sports, especially betting on horses, was fully integrated into the lives of many of their readers, and the communities that they belonged to, but it was also an activity that was rhetorically condemned, or at least frowned upon, by mainstream opinion. Mainstream opinion was not a monolith, however: if Sunday papers were unable to gain respectability in one context, they were not compelled to accept that judgement within their own pages. Instead, they chose to follow the sentiments of their readers.

Joan Neuberger indirectly illuminates this process in her study of the 'boulevard press' in St Petersburg, the Russian imperial capital, before the First World War.[78] In order to appeal to the public, Neuberger contends, papers have to rely on 'cultural clues' that are 'comprehensible to a large number of people'.[79] Within the discursive and rhetorical languages of any newspaper there are 'symbols that represented and reflected readers' cultural values and expectations'.[80] If Sunday newspapers wanted to cover matters where respectability was contested, such as gambling, they had to do so in ways that reinforced the beliefs of their readers.

This is exactly what they did. Sunday newspapers rarely attacked the respectability of betting, even when they took on gambling in general. Instead, they accepted working-class gambling as a fact of life. When Sunday papers did attack gambling, they did so using a class language that was an inversion of the language of middle-class reformers, attacking not the vices of the poor but the depredations of the rich for the troubles caused by gambling. Far from simply apologising for, or defending, working-class gamblers, Sunday newspapers, with remarkable unanimity, made them seem more virtuous than rich 'speculators'. All would have agreed with *Reynolds's* that '[i]nfinitely more damage is done by dabbling and gambling in stock and shares than in betting. The only difference is that one is held to be respectable, and the other is not.'[81]

The types of sports covered in Sunday newspapers exemplified this support of working-class cultural habits. While they paid attention to myriad sporting activities, from cycling to chess, from billiards to angling, the sport that Sunday newspapers covered in the most detail was horse-racing (see Table 4.1).

Table 4.1 Sports coverage in three Sunday newspapers, March, June and September, 1890

Paper	Percentage of sports coverage devoted to:					Sport coverage as % of total paper
	Racing	Football	Cricket	Rugby	Other	
The People	49	4	5	5	37	3.4
Weekly Dispatch	49	1	34	1	15	2.8
Reynolds's Newspaper	42	6	28	6	18	1.4

While E. Gowing-Scopes, the General Secretary of the RN&BU, asserted that people would be willing to buy 'anything at any time providing it is the latest out and contains the last sporting result,' sports coverage was clearly not as significant in Sunday papers as contemporaries seemed to believe.[82] Sundays had to compete with dedicated sporting papers, which, being smaller and devoted only to sport, could quickly produce special editions after important matches or races. Of the sports covered by the Sunday papers, however, horse-racing was clearly the most important. It was not only the sole non-seasonal sport, it was also the most heavily covered at each point in the year.[83] Even in the summer cricket season horse-racing was more prominent in two of the three papers cited in Table 4.1.

Horse-racing may have received more attention because most coverage involved tips and predictions of future races, which were less time-sensitive than match results and therefore could be more reliably inserted into a Sunday newspaper.[84] The reporting of football, rugby and cricket generally consisted solely of scores and brief accounts of games. For horse-racing, in contrast, there were regular advice columns. In the *People* 'Larry Lynx' devoted most of the space in his column 'Turf, Field and River' to predictions on coming races and commentary on those recently run, only occasionally switching to cricket or football, although special events such as the Oxford–Cambridge Boat Race always received a fair amount of attention. The *Weekly Dispatch* had 'Sporting Notes' by 'Mordred', which fulfilled the same function as Lynx's column: racing tips and commentary dominated throughout the year. *Reynolds's* was the only Sunday paper that did not run a regular sporting column, but its coverage often included a digest of predictions made by other newspapers.

The Sunday newspapers were well aware that gambling on horses was a culturally contested activity. As the *Weekly Dispatch* once put it, 'The patrons of the turf would never look at a racehorse if it were not for the "book".'[85] All the papers reported public meetings against gambling, and their police columns included reports of gambling dens raided by the police, and of fraudulent bookmakers arraigned in court. Nevertheless, the constant refrain of Sunday newspapers was that working-class gambling was a largely innocent and safe enterprise. According to the *People*, 'This excessive tenderness for the morals of the working classes is quite out of place. Gambling does them no more harm than it does to the better endowed.'[86] One of its writers concluded that 'Gambling will live in England, I predict, long after the league ... formed for its suppression is forgotten.'[87] Sunday newspapers contended that gambling was a product of human nature and therefore unchangeable. *Reynolds's* declared: 'Certain it is, however, that men will bet, and if they do not bet on horse-racing or running, they will bet on two ships crossing the sea, two flies settling on a piece of sugar...and even on such a ghastly subject as whether Mrs Maybrick would be hanged or not.'[88] (On Mrs Maybrick, see Chapter 3 of the present volume.) The *People* agreed: 'The speculative instinct is extraordinarily keen in most Britons...You cannot expel nature with a fork.'[89]

Working-class gambling, in particular, was entirely defensible in the eyes of Sunday newspapers, largely because it was a form of relaxation and recreation. They consistently drew parallels with respectable forms of recreation that were confined to the wealthy in society. 'The public house is the poor man's club,' wrote the *People* of attempts to stop bookmaking in pubs, 'the profit made [on drinks and bets] representing his subscriptions.'[90] In this context, working-class gambling became less and less about money, and more and more about socialising, fraternising and intellectual challenges.

Gambling became a problem for Sunday papers when it was manipulated by the rich or by criminals. The *Weekly Dispatch* regularly ran stories on the National Anti-Gambling League alongside its racing columns; one story to show the evils of fraudulent touts, the other to sanction honest betting.[91] Working-class betting was an open, honest affair, where all, supposedly, had an equal chance to win. Gambling intended to swindle or cheat, which was mostly undertaken by the wealthy, was very different. *Reynolds's* exhorted its readers: 'Look at the gambling which takes place in our corn markets, fruit markets, hop markets, and even in our fish markets. The money lost on betting...is mere child's play in comparison with that lost in card-playing in West-end [*sic*] clubs and on the Stock Exchange.'[92]

What is perhaps most surprising about these condemnations of dishonest gambling by the rich is how universal they were in Sunday papers. The *People* was the most conservative Sunday paper, while *Reynolds's* was easily the most radical, but they saw eye to eye in their contempt for excessive speculation by the rich. During the preparations preceding Queen Victoria's Diamond Jubilee in 1897, for example, all the Sunday papers excoriated the speculators who forced up the price of seats along the London parade route. A regular columnist wrote: 'I wish, sir, to place it on record, for the benefit of future readers who may turn up files of *Reynolds's Newspaper* in the British Museum, that in this year of the Diamond Jubilee we are a nation of gamblers.'[93] The *Weekly Dispatch* reported that a 'slump at length in the Diamond Jubilee window-letting department' seemed likely to leave some 'speculators' out in the cold.[94] In the language of Sunday newspapers, speculation for profit, in financial markets, gambling or the price of seats, was far worse, and far less respectable, than working-class betting on horses.

Even when Sunday newspapers did attack sports gambling, they did so using class rhetoric. The most prominent example was the decision taken by the *Weekly Times and Echo* in 1890 to stop printing its column, 'Sporting Notes' by 'The Baron', which ran the paper's racing tips and predictions. It made this decision, it claimed in a front-page leader, because 'we do not see that we can...any longer pander to the vile and dishonest gambling instincts,' and 'hold up a standard of life in these columns which the world may profit by'.[95] Letters to the *Weekly Times* congratulated the paper for taking such a courageous stand against gambling, 'a curse upon the healthy, moral and social existence of a people...an accursed mania'.[96] One reader wrote from Northampton: 'The evil is assuming such large proportions that it is running a neck-and-neck race with drink in the injury that it inflicts upon its victims.'[97]

The attack by the *Weekly Times*, however, was not simply a blanket assault on working-class gambling. The true targets were those who preyed upon the working classes, 'the vast organised conspiracy into the hand of which they [working-class gamblers] so blindly play, and which they enrich with their losses'.[98] The conspiracy was 'between "sportsmen" and many of their hirelings who prostitute the Press, to transfer half-crowns and shillings of the public...into their own pockets, by tricks which are so transparently and abominably dishonest'.[99] Betting on sports became a problem when a gambler 'wastes his substance on bets,' not when it was only a leisure activity.[100]

What is perhaps most surprising about the *Weekly Times*'s attempt to make itself 'known to respectable readers as *the* non-sporting weekly penny paper' is how little the paper's sports coverage changed.[101] Racing continued to be the most prominent sport covered, and the paper still listed odds and prizes of past and upcoming races as it had before. Only the tips and predictions went missing. Its explanation, which seems highly disingenuous, was that: 'We must, of course, still continue to give the results of races. A newspaper cannot pick and choose its news; it is obliged to record a race as it does an execution, or any other disagreeable or disreputable occurrence.'[102] Perhaps, then, the paper's apparently quixotic stand against gambling was little more than a publicity stunt, or even a measure of cost-cutting, as it no longer had to pay 'The Baron' for his sporting column. For all the sound and fury, the *Weekly Times* never printed anything that would have seriously challenged the legitimacy of working-class sports betting.

Sunday newspapers knew that many of their readers engaged in sports betting of one kind or another, and geared their sports coverage towards that activity. By doing so they helped to create a cultural space in which popular gambling could be seen as a respectable recreation. This recreation only became disreputable or dangerous when working-class people were victimised by the rich or criminals. Within their pages the Sunday papers articulated a language of respectability that was designed to appeal specifically to a working-class readership, even though gambling was not respectable in mainstream middle-class circles.

We can conclude, therefore, by suggesting that the Sunday newspapers' struggle for respectability was neither an empty intellectual debate nor a pitched battle for survival, but something more subtle and further-reaching. Because they were seen as 'low-class' publications, Sunday newspapers opened themselves up to criticism from Sabbatarians and cultural critics. The existence of popular Sunday newspapers was never in doubt in late Victorian Britain, but endurance is not the same as respectability. Even if they could not be eliminated, *Lloyd's*, the *People*, *Reynolds's* and the others were able, by association, to challenge the respectability of working-class and lower-middle-class society. The case of the newsagents shows how far some in that society were willing to go to be seen as respectable. Britain's lower-middle-class newsagents may have found Sunday newspapers unrespectable, but without them they would scarcely have had the opportunity to claim respectability for themselves.

While they lost the battle for middle-class respectability, however, Sunday newspapers had greater success at carving out a space in late Victorian Britain's expanding popular culture. In order to do so they had to find ways to overcome their critics and appeal to a broader market. They did this, in part, by articulating ideas and beliefs that allowed their lower-middle-class and working-class readers to feel respectable. As the example of working-class sports gambling shows, Sunday newspapers, like middle-class cultural critics, adopted the language of class as a way to bind together their readers. Being among the few cultural products that were available across the country in almost exactly the same form, Sunday newspapers had the ability to lend legitimacy to highly contested forms of leisure.

The history of Sunday newspapers in the late nineteenth century needs to be more closely integrated into the history of popular culture and working-class respectability. Sunday newspapers helped to define the terms of the class-based cultural debate in which claims to respectability could be articulated and accepted. This debate operated on at least two different levels, affecting both those who wanted to gain respectability by shunning Sunday newspapers *and* those who read Sunday newspapers to confirm that they were respectable. In both cases, respectability was closely tied to class rhetoric. This dynamic seems to confirm David Cannadine's contention that class, while not widely accepted as a fixed social category, retains its usefulness as a means by which people engage in 'social description'.[103] If class identification prevented Sunday newspapers from attaining respectability in some circles, it also allowed them to define what was respectable in others.

Acknowledgements

I would like to thank Professor Walter L. Arnstein for his unceasing support, the US/UK Fulbright Commission for sponsoring my doctoral research, Professor Roland Quinault for his service as my mentor in Britain, Mike Huggins for encouraging me to undertake this piece, and the staff of the British Library's Newspaper Library, who were unfailingly helpful and polite.

Parts of this chapter were previously published as 'Popular Sunday Newspapers, Class, and the Struggle for Respectability in Late Victorian Britain' in Martin Hewitt (ed.), *Leeds Centre Working Papers in Victorian Studies*, Vol. 4: *Unrespectable Recreations* (Leeds: Leeds Centre for Victorian Studies, 2001), pp. 81–94.

Disreputable adolescent reading: low-life, women-in-peril and school sport 'penny dreadfuls' from the 1860s to the 1890s

JOHN SPRINGHALL

It has become a truism that 'respectability', as a desirable indicator of social position, was a quality much sought after by a large proportion of Victorians, apart from those at the highest and lowest levels of the social hierarchy. Even so, from a cultural standpoint respectability periodically came under threat, given the scandalous British taste for 'sensational' gothic melodrama in theatrical and literary entertainment. Great literary gothic horrors, ranging from Matthew Lewis's *The Monk* and Ann Radcliffe's *Mysteries of Udolpho* in the 1790s, through Mary Shelley's post-Napoleonic *Frankenstein*, to the late-Victorian climax of R.L. Stevenson's *Dr Jekyll and Mr Hyde* and Bram Stoker's *Dracula*, have exerted among the most resonant and pervasive British literary influences on global culture and mass entertainment. Yet sanctimonious early-Victorian literary critics were convinced that the popularisation, by the cheap publisher Edward Lloyd and others, of gothic's sado-masochistic and horrific elements, coupled with the criminality of Newgate fiction, could well corrupt the morally innocent young, or infect the 'dangerous' lower orders.[1]

The expansion of a mass market for cheap reading matter, created in the 1830s through weekly or monthly serial publication, had been accelerated by the new rotary printing presses, cheap manufactured paper, improved transport and rising literacy. Yet by the 1860s, with adult readers having forsaken Lloyd's 'penny bloods' for cheap Sunday newspapers and illustrated weekly magazines now carrying serialised novels, a more accessible version of gothic melodrama was required for a new replacement juvenile audience (according to the census returns for 1861, some 45 per cent of the total population of England and Wales were under the age of 20). Penny-a-line authors seeking work from the small publishing offices in and around Fleet Street that tried to reach this expanding youth market soon learned that macabre and 'sensational' fare could be cast just as successfully in contemporary as in historical dress. Hence a fascinating source for historians anxious to explore the less respectable and more private side of mid-to-late-Victorian recreation is those 'penny dreadful' serials that can be broadly categorised as low-life London, women-in-peril and boarding-school stories. Other popular variations that space does not permit examination of here include tales of highwaymen, pirates, historical adventure, rags to riches and island exile (*robinsonnades*). These cheap and exciting instalment tales were almost certainly read by those young men and women in the upper-working and lower-middle-classes who might well have adopted, in less relaxed circumstances, the conventional earnest, improving and puritanical Victorian positions.[2]

Middle-class moral panic

The enduring appeal of neo-gothic melodrama in the ephemeral penny fiction that appealed so widely to the young, such as *Tales of Highwaymen; or, Life on the Road* (1865–66) was a particular target of those evangelical and high-minded Victorian critics who abhorred its 'sensationalism', its supposed incitement to delinquency and its generally disreputable reputation. One literary critic, Francis Hitchman, expressed his anguish thus: 'When it is remembered that this foul and filthy trash circulates by thousands and tens of thousands week by week amongst lads who are at the most impressionable period of their lives, it is not surprising that the authorities have to lament the prevalence of juvenile crime.' Charles Knight, a former editor of the self-improving but didactic *Penny Magazine* (1832–45), also routinely denigrated popular tastes in reading, only to be admonished in 1854 by Charles Dickens, in a tone that some might regard as self-righteous: 'The English are, so far as I know, the hardest-worked people on whom the sun shines. Be content, if, in their wretched intervals of pleasure, they read for amusement and do no worse. They are born at the oar, and they live and die at it. Good God, what would we have of them!' Young readers living in a rule-bound school or office environment also needed a therapeutic release from adult control 'in their wretched intervals of pleasure' and the 'penny dreadful' provided this, both cheaply and amusingly.[3]

Evidence for the precise readership of 'penny dreadfuls' from the 1860s onwards is difficult to assess because generalised speculation by unsympathetic contemporaries is not the most reliable way to gauge the potential audience. According to a hostile report published by the Society for the Diffusion of Useful Knowledge in 1872, they were read, as a rule, 'by ignorant shop and office-boys, young apprentices and factory hands, and by, perhaps, a small number of school lads'. Other sources suggest that working-class boys, compelled from 1870 onwards to attend the new English state elementary schools, were among the most avid readers of penny serials and secular juvenile periodicals (also labelled 'dreadfuls'). On the other hand, much of the 'moral panic' that cheap fiction intended for adolescents aroused in middle-class people seems to have derived from anxiety that their own sons and daughters were as much at risk from contamination by 'pernicious' reading as the children of the urban poor were.

The seventh Earl of Shaftesbury, the Tory evangelical and factory reformer, warned in 1878 that penny fiction 'is creeping not only into the houses of the poor, neglected and untaught, but into the largest mansions; penetrating into religious families and astounding careful parents by its frightful issues'.[4] Shaftesbury was, coincidentally, addressing the Religious Tract Society in the year before it launched the eminently respectable and 'manly' *Boy's Own Paper* (*BOP*, 1879–1967) as a virile Christian alternative to the 'penny dreadfuls'. Earlier, a crusading journalist, James Greenwood, had startled middle-class magazine readers in 1869 by depicting the voracious 'penny dreadful' as having, like the 'fabled vampire', already 'bitten your little rosy-cheeked son Jack. He may be lurking at this very moment in that young gentleman's private chamber, little as you suspect it, polluting his mind and smoothing the way that leads to swift destruction.' Yet authors of popular serial fiction for the urban young were convinced of their own rectitude, because usually their story lines saw vice punished and virtue rewarded. According to a self-confessed author of 'penny dreadfuls', writing to the *Daily News* in 1895, they did not corrupt their readers with 'the foul sexual problems that disgrace so many of the society novels of today'; indeed, 'The masses, partially educated, vulgar perhaps, but certainly clean-minded, read the "penny dreadful" for its fare is strong, satisfying and healthy. The people love melodrama, but society prefers the immoral play [and] detective stories, dealing with gruesome crimes, unlawful love, the triumph of evil over good.'[5]

It is likely that what offended pious middle-class adults about 'penny dreadfuls' was, in many cases, the precocious independence and potency of their boy heroes, together with their implicit challenge to the generational status quo. In 1874 one agitated London headmaster, Lewis W. Potts, citing the Anglican catechism, claimed:

The hero in these periodicals, read openly in the streets, devoured, I should say, by thousands of errand and work boys, is he who defies his 'governors, teachers, spiritual pastors and masters', and is the leader of the most outrageous acts. It is, I believe, the universal testimony of the Governors and Chaplains of prisons, that a large proportion of juvenile crime can be traced to the reading of such literature.

Regardless of Potts's naïve cause-and-effect logic, there is indeed a virtual absence in 'dreadfuls' of adolescent heroes embodying the public-school (G.A. Henty) or Christian (R.M. Ballantyne) manliness so beloved of authors writing for a more bourgeois youth market, with the partial exception of a few of the school stories published by Edwin Brett (see below). It seems plausible, then, that 'penny dreadfuls' appealed to those mid-to-late Victorian adolescents who demanded a vicarious escape from the uneventfulness of their everyday lives through participation in the cheerfully amoral yet exciting fictional escapades of heroic nonconformists. According to Marjory Lang, a specialist in mid-Victorian children's periodicals: 'Middleclass Victorians found in these adolescent rebels an uncomfortable contradiction to their romantic and nostalgic images of childhood purity and innocence, inseparable from a state of weakness and dependence. Literature exalting the cheeky, capable juvenile hero they felt to be especially dangerous to their own well-protected children.'[6]

Low-life dreadfuls

The notoriety attracted by the best-selling serial *Charley Wag: The New Jack Sheppard* (1860–61) can probably be explained by the antisocial and mischievous character of its eponymous young burglar hero. The indispensable subtitle alludes to a boyish eighteenth-century prison-escaper who had become, through dramatised versions of W. Harrison Ainsworth's middlebrow novel *Jack Sheppard* (1839), the most renowned figure in popular Victorian youth culture. Arguably, this may have signified a reassertion of the trickster figure from the more festive rural and oral tradition, setting out to mock the restraining disciplines of an urban, industrial, class-bound society. The sixth number of *Charley Wag* features a provocative cover engraving depicting the grinning boy burglar fleeing confidently down the Strand in London with a stolen goose and two bottles of rum, hotly pursued by a policeman brandishing a truncheon and urged on by a smiling crowd. A dog scampering alongside Charley is also in possession of a stolen goose, while a notice on a wall nearby offers £500 for the delinquent's capture.

Figure 5.1. Front page illustration by Robert Prowse for No. 6 of 'George Savage', *Charley Wag: The New Jack Sheppard* (London: William Grant, 1860–1). Source: by kind permission of the Hess Collection, Children's Literature Research Collections, University of Minnesota Libraries, Minneapolis, Minnesota, USA.

'Pugnacious, great at punching heads and bunging up eyes', a cigar smoker at 13 and a 'regular rascal' where a pretty girl is concerned, Charley rescues the beautiful Lucinda from the debauchery of the Prime Minister, the Duke of Heatherland, 'who is always scheming to oppress and grind down the already over-oppressed and ground-down working classes'. From small-scale burglaries Charley works his way up to become the most successful thief in London, breaking into the Bank of England and, after numerous plot twists, being wrongfully arrested for murder.[7]

The fashion for setting serial novels such as *Charley Wag* in disreputable parts of contemporary London emerged out of a literary formula pioneered by Pierce Egan's *Life in London* (1820–21), with its colourful account of the exploits of an innocent rustic, Jerry Hawthorn, who is taken on a guided tour of the capital's sporting low life by two urban sophisticates, Corinthian Tom and Bob Logic, their wanderings brilliantly engraved by the meticulous Cruikshank brothers. The flood of English serial publications that took the urban low-life theme and adapted it extensively for a largely juvenile audience were chiefly inspired, however, by the extraordinary success of the long-running serial *The Mysteries of London* (1845–50), an anglicised version of Eugène Sue's exciting *feuilleton* bestseller *Les Mystères de Paris* (1842–43). *The Mysteries of London*, the most successful English penny-issue work of its time, selling nearly 40,000 weekly copies, was written by George William MacArthur Reynolds (1814–79), a jobbing author and journalist steeped in French literary culture, in a commercial style that juxtaposed the pseudo-radical with the thrilling. After the first series was continued without his consent, using other authors, Reynolds put out an even lengthier work, *The Mysteries of the Court of London* (1848–56), making this late-Chartist activist, serial-novelist and editor of *Reynolds's Newspaper* arguably the most widely read nineteenth-century English author. He updated the gothic novel by casting it in modern dress and setting it with great precision in familiar, everyday London locales that highlighted his shock effects, 'unveiling lurid criminal conspiracies which took place just behind the scenes', exchanging 'city houses for gothic castles, slum cellars for dungeons, and financial extortioners [*sic*] for the evil count or monk'.[8]

'Penny dreadfuls' that placed youthful heroes to whom readers could relate among sordid and criminal milieus in the lower reaches of metropolitan society were extensively circulated in the 1860s by the much-reviled Newsagents' Publishing Company (NPC). Low-life serials such as *The Poor Boys of London; or, Driven to Crime* (1866), *The Boy Detective; or, The Crimes of London* (1865–66), *The Work Girls of London: Their Trials and Temptations* (1865) or *The Jolly Dogs of London; or, The Two Roads of Life* (1866) suffused the commonplace with dramatic encounters, conveying

THE

WILD BOYS OF LONDON;

OR,

THE CHILDREN OF NIGHT.

Figure 5.2. Front page illustration by Harry Maguire for No. 3 of Anon., *The Wild Boys of London: or, The Children of Night* (London: Newsagents' Publishing Company, 1864–6). Source: by kind permission of the Hess Collection, Children's Literature Research Collections, University of Minnesota Libraries, Minneapolis, Minnesota, USA.

extremes of emotion and fortune through concrete details of everyday urban life. The first edition of *The Wild Boys of London: or, The Children of Night. A Story of the Present Day* (1864–66), which achieved a notoriety exceeding that of any other NPC 'dreadful', was published in 103 weekly parts of

80 double-columned pages each, making a combined total of about 800,000 words, or ten times the length of the average modern thriller. It depicts, with some grasp of urban vernacular, the often violent and lurid adventures of a gang of Cockney street urchins who run the gamut of delinquencies from piracy to lynching. The Society for the Suppression of Vice, which opened a prosecution of a reprint late in 1877 under the Obscene Publications Act, probably feared the seditious effects that the representation of homeless boys 'cocking a snook' at authority might have upon impressionable young working-class readers. The 'street arabs' of the title hatch their mischief 'round a fire in their haunt beneath the sewers of London', somewhere near London Bridge Pier; they fight off ruffians, salvage corpses and traffic in stolen goods. Above ground they come to grips with thieves, murderers, kidnappers, incompetent policemen and grave-robbers, not to mention child-stealers. 'At times', E.S. Turner wittily reported in 1948, 'the scene shifted to a mutinous convict ship, or to the Australian bush, but sooner or later the writer would return, nostalgically, to the sewers of London.'[9]

There are occasional radical sentiments in *The Wild Boys*, which make it reminiscent of the work of Reynolds, but these are subverted by the melodramatic plot elements and the reader-identification figure of Dick Lane, the fastidious boy-hero. Better educated than his scavenging companions, Dick is driven to make a living on the streets because his father, a previously sober and industrious Lambeth bricklayer, has taken to drink after being led astray when his corrupt union called an unnecessary strike. Meanwhile, Dick's *alter ego*, Arthur Grattan, has been brought up by a poor schoolmaster but is in reality the kidnapped son of Lord Wintermerle and heir to a vast fortune. The anonymous author could not conceal an ultimate reliance upon the hackneyed plot device (also used by Dickens in *Oliver Twist*) of the stolen child, reared in obscurity, fallen among young street thieves and beggars, while in the background a mysterious stranger plots his downfall. The likelihood is that consumption of such penny serials reached adolescents closer to Dick Lane, the well-spoken protagonist of *The Wild Boys*, than to the homeless and ill-educated orphans of the title. Thus sons and daughters of skilled working men, shop-keepers and clerks, seeking a romantic release from their repetitive daily lives, could enjoy the adventures of boy thieves, pirates, detectives, actresses and even heroes not unlike themselves in the comfort of outwardly respectable, semi-suburban homes. Whether at school, in offices, in warehouses or in workshops, these mid-to-late Victorian youngsters could participate in the criminal yet thrilling adventures of vagrant ragamuffins such as Charley Wag or the Wild Boys without having their own lifestyles radically altered in the process.[10]

Women-in-peril dreadfuls

In contrast to the focus on Dick Lane at the outset of *The Wild Boys*, the opening chapters of *The Young Ladies of London; or, The Mysteries of Midnight* (1867–68) introduce the sinister Count Lewiski, a man about town who entraps rich gentlemen visitors to the wicked metropolis, using as bait the beautiful Emma Langton, his mistress, once a happy farmer's daughter. The serial's engraved frontispiece depicts fashionably dressed women importuning male clients wearing top hats in the Haymarket district of central London, then notorious for its prostitution. Once near Petticoat Lane, Lewiski is transformed into Edward Lewis, 'the keeper of several lodging-houses and brothels in the east-end [*sic*] of London; a shrewd fellow, who had amassed a considerable sum of money by his dishonest and filthy calling'. Great play is made with the vulnerability of exploited seamstresses in the area as a means of sketching in local colour: poor, pale, weak girls with half a dozen shirts to finish, paid only ninepence for 18 hours of toil to support children or a dying mother. By the time that this novel was published victimised East End seamstresses had become elements in a safe and sentimental iconography, their usage being evident since the radical journalism of the 1830s. The real conditions of East London's huge casualised labour force, characterised by low wages, irregular employment and foreign immigration, appear never to have been directly confronted in penny fiction. Any radical sentiment in *The Young Ladies of London* is both subordinated to, and subverted by, the melodramatic plot. Hence Count Lewiski employs one Ghastly Gaskill to drug and then kidnap unsuspecting girls who are soon put to work in his Haymarket *seraglio* – 'another poor wretch doomed to fall a victim to your accursed toils' cries Emma, unavailingly.[11]

In the absence of publishers' records (aside from lists of shareholders), we can only speculate as to which age group such *risqué* but otherwise inoffensive tales were intended for. The schoolboys who avidly read tales of highwaymen and historical adventure may also have perused titillating fare such as the above. Attempts to gauge the intended market are muddied because several puzzling serials that masquerade as boys' nautical adventure stories, such as *The Boy Rover; or, The Smuggler of the South Seas* (1866) or *The Boy Pirate; or, Life on the Ocean* (1865), turn out, on closer inspection, to be extended narratives of imminent female seduction. The Boy Rover, a murderous villain who robs and kills shipwrecked sailors in an underground smuggler's cavern, rescues the attractive Ellen only because 'there was a demon in his heart, urging on his base passions to more unholy deeds'. The Boy Pirate comes ashore and roughly seizes Lilia, the hero's fiancée, with rape on his mind. Later she is viciously flogged, as shown by an illustration of her half-naked, her back torn and bleeding. Such unexpectedly prurient serials put out by a small Fleet Street firm such as the NPC, well-known for its youth-oriented tales, confirm the view that the vast undergrowth of Victorian erotic literature was not confined to pornographic fare such as the obsessive 'Walter's' *My Secret Life* (1888–94). Equally, the NPC and its Fleet Street rivals sought to appeal not only to boys and young men, their primary audience, but also to factory girls, shop assistants, milliners and domestic servants.[12]

Many young women were reached through the popular appeal of women-in-peril stories, or the cheap literature of aristocratic seduction, arguably a metaphor for the exploitation of the poor by the upper classes. 'No, no! A long and glorious career of profligacy and dissipation is still in store for me!' Count Lerno reassures himself, following a threat to his reputation, in the NPC or London Romance Company's *Rose Mortimer; or, The Ballet-Girl's Revenge* (1865?). This was judged by an anonymous reviewer in the *Bookseller* to be 'a sensational tale of love and intrigue, illustrated with suggestive woodcuts, representing the abduction of the heroine at the stage-door of the theatre, and similarly exciting subjects'. Hence, after Rose's successful performance as the Queen of Beauty in a Boxing Day pantomime, the Count carries her, resisting and still in ballet costume, to his carriage. The kidnapped heroine is taken to a large house in that part of Fulham lying west of Walham Green that was supposedly known as 'Dead Man's Land'. The sinister aristocrat confesses that he is master of the house and seeks to make Rose its mistress: '"Count Lerno", said Rose, drawing herself up to her full height – "Count Lerno, sooner than agree to your degrading proposals I would kill myself."'[13]

The wicked and lecherous aristocratic villain typified by Count Lerno was a stereotype from early-Victorian 'penny bloods' resuscitated in the 1860s by the authors of women-in-peril stories. Lord Dundreary in *The Work Girls of London, Their Trials and Temptations* (1865) also represents the type:

> 'Tut,' was the cruel answer, 'do you think I have nothing to do but
> to marry every girl who wishes to father a child on me? I tell you
> all I will do for you is to give you some money, but I never want
> to see you again: as for the brat, never let me hear of it!'

The overheated and hyperbolic opening chapters of *The Outsiders of Society; or, The Wild Beauties of London* (1866) are devoted to the unscrupulous and licentious Lord Vineyard: 'a proud name in *Burke's Peerage* sounded well in the eyes of the world; but if people only knew the infamy attached to it!' This stage villain adopts the tragically orphaned but 'well-proportioned' Lydia Wilson and lavishes money on her in order to satisfy his evil designs, leading the ruined girl to attempt suicide by throwing herself off Westminster Bridge.[14]

In the unattributed *Fanny White and Her Friend Jack Rawlings: A Romance of a Young Lady Thief and a Boy Burglar* (1865?), published by George Vickers, great play is made with the attempted seduction of the sedated Fanny, a music-hall dancer, by an old Palmerston-like *roué*, Lord Crokerton, in yet another isolated house somewhere in Fulham. Ingredients of sex and violence have always been a commonplace in popular culture, no less in prudish mid-Victorian England than in any other era. Miss Fanny is 'a spanking, bouncing young wench – beautiful enough, in all conscience, to excite the desires of the most cold-blooded', yet also 'as strong as a young bull. Voluptuous, graceful, pliant, and muscular. She could love and languish; but, when her blood was up, she could scratch and bite.' Thus the redoubtable yet erotic heroine, recovering from the effects of a soporific drug, makes short work of the 'horrible old rascal' who had set out to seduce her: 'Then, as he strove once more to seize her, she doubled up that pretty fist of hers... and dealt my Lord Crokerton such a terrific right-hander on the nose, that it spread him out flat upon the floor, where he lay, bleeding and gasping, a sight pitiful to behold.'[15]

Women-in-peril and low-life stories appear to have inherited an earlier London-based radical-populist demonology, exemplified by G.W.M. Reynolds, which cast titled landlords living off their rents and property, rather than the new entrepreneurial middle class, as the chief exploiters of the labouring poor. Given the current historiographical emphasis on the continuing hegemonic importance of the aristocracy throughout the nineteenth century, Reynolds should perhaps be reclaimed as someone who was trying to define the real nature of the Victorian state. In penny fiction it is usually the rich aristocrat, hardly ever the grasping capitalist, who sets out to assail the virtue of the modest heroine. The editor of the *Bookseller* commented astutely during the passage of the Second Reform Act in 1867 that it was 'as though temptation and immorality were only to be found in wealthy neighbourhoods, and lewd thoughts were the special and particular property of noblemen and "swells", with rent rolls of ten thousand a year'.[16]

Such assumptions were, of course, as much part of the ideological baggage of thrusting, upwardly mobile middle-class businessmen, with their Manchester-bred intolerance for aristocratic privilege and unearned wealth, as of the outlook of downwardly mobile penny novelists. Yet the popular literature of seduction evaded the reality of sexual assault among and within the working classes in the mid-Victorian years. Very few unmarried mothers or victims of rape fell prey to genuine aristocratic villains. Violent

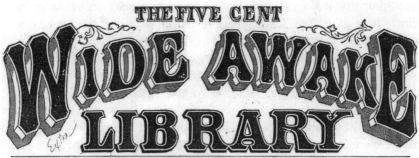

Mr. Mole redoubled his exertions. A low sob, and then another, which he could not repress, broke from Jack. It seemed as if the tension of the rope was dragging his arms out of their sockets.

Figure 5.3. Front page illustration for reprint of Samuel Bracebridge Hemyng's 'Jack Harkaway's Schooldays' in the American half-dime *Wide Awake Library*, nearly 25 years after its original English publication. Source: by kind permission of the Hess Collection, Children's Literature Research Collections, University of Minnesota Libraries, Minneapolis, Minnesota, USA.

assaults against working women were largely committed by drunken males with whom they were already familiar. Perhaps the theft of poor men's daughters by profligate aristocrats such as Count Lerno symbolised the betrayal of the English working classes by their elite rulers, investing the public rhetoric of class struggle with personal and emotive images of women's sexual oppression. Women-in-peril writing also contributed to a wider rhetoric of the poor as weak and passive victims who needed to be protected by kindly middle-class paternalists.[17]

School stories with added sport

The mould-breaking serial 'Boys of Bircham School' (1867–70), started in the *Young Englishman's Journal* on 8 June 1867, and written by the author, editor and proprietor George Emmett, appears to have been the first genuine school story to be written for a boys' weekly periodical, ten years after *Tom Brown's Schooldays* but 12 years before the first issue of the *BOP*. Along with his brothers Robert, Henry Charlton, and William Laurence, George Emmett ran Hogarth House, an underfunded publishing firm based near *Punch*'s offices in Bouverie Street, off Fleet Street. Here George, who commuted in from Peckham Rye, acted as the editor and proprietor of several cheap secular and 'sensational' boys' periodicals, to which he and his versatile brothers contributed weekly serials. The small publishing offices in the City of London were crowded with 'bohemian' writers, underpaid journalists, eccentric well-bred scribblers, improvident artists and despised plagiarists, who together made up a fascinating literary subculture. Fleet Street reminiscences portray George as a bluff, heavily bearded, drink-sodden gentleman who claimed to have been present as a cavalry officer at the siege of Lucknow during the Indian Mutiny and to have been wounded in the charge of the Light Brigade at Balaclava. Yet George's account of the latter, in 'Captain Jack; or, One of the Light Brigade' (1868), written to increase sales of the *Young Englishman's Journal*, owed as much to Alfred, Lord Tennyson as to personal experience. Details of the famous charge also varied in the telling at the Cheshire Cheese and other Fleet Street watering holes.[18]

The archetypal 'Boys of Bircham School' takes place entirely in a small private boarding school where the aptly named Dr Bircham is the judge, mentor and friend of his pupils, albeit with a pronounced enthusiasm for flogging bullies and rule-breakers. The minimal plot focuses on a highly unpopular French language master, Monsieur Jean Gailland or 'Frenchy', who attempts to supplant the young school usher, Philip Randall, in the affections of Eleanor, the daughter of an old wooden-legged seadog, Captain

Figure 5.4. Back page advertisement for the Hogarth House publications, edited by the Emmett brothers, when their office was in St Bride's Avenue, London, EC. Source: by kind permission of the Hess Collection, Children's Literature Research Collections, University of Minnesota Libraries, Minneapolis, Minnesota, USA.

Oakplank, who lives at Woodbine Cottage near the school. The school's pupils, determined to prevent the Frenchman's courtship from being successful, make him the butt of a series of sadistic practical jokes that escalate in outrageousness and have as their repeated outcome the comic foreigner's total humiliation. Emmett's serial bears all the insular hallmarks of mid-Victorian English (or, arguably, British) xenophobia, snobbishness and jocose humour, accentuated by their employment in a 'penny dreadful' periodical.[19]

Edwin Harcourt Burrage (1839–1916), a neglected master of comic plotting and characterisation, was invited to take over the writing of George Emmett's successor serial, 'Tom Wildrake's Schooldays' (1871–72), which ran in the Emmett brothers' *Sons of Britannia* (1870–77). From August 1872 onwards, after George had apparently found himself out of his imaginative depth, Burrage turned this mediocre school story into a best-seller by dispatching Tom Wildrake and his stereotypical companions overseas, 'to a field of adventure less limited than the circumscribed area of a school', where they participated in various comic, violent and ethnocentric adventures. Burrage, who for a while helped to secure the Emmett brothers' fortunes, thereby set down an enduring template for other writers for boys to adopt, and went on to become one of the most prolific and popular of all authors of boys' stories in 'low-class' periodicals. His best-known creation was the wily Oriental hero Ching-Ching, a sort of juvenile Charlie Chan, who was eventually featured in *Ching-Ching's Own* (1888–93), for which Burrage wrote practically all the major stories. Ching-Ching became the only serious rival to Jack Harkaway, the most famous schoolboy hero since Tom Brown (see below). By this time Burrage was no longer a bibulous *habitué* of Grub Street and had even written a pseudonymous total abstinence tract, *The Ruin of Fleet Street* (1885), exposing the pitfalls of drink and the literary life. Semi-retired by the first decade of the twentieth century, he became a valued resident of Redhill in Surrey and was elected to the local council. Burrage churned out countless weekly serials and millions of words in a hack-writing career of more than 25 years, meriting the accolade of 'the boys' Charles Dickens' for quantity, if not quality, of output: the British Library catalogue lists 56 stories and this overlooks many unattributed titles.[20]

The Emmett brothers faced severe competition from another editor–proprietor, Edwin John Brett (1828–95), ultimately their more successful rival in the field of boys' periodicals, whose titles they slavishly imitated until they got into financial difficulties in the late 1870s. Brett, a disillusioned former Chartist and a mediocre engraver, remained dubious about the sales potential of unvarnished school stories, yet W. Thompson Townsend's well-liked serial 'The Captain of the School' started its run on

20 July 1867 in number 35 of Brett's long-running *Boys of England* (1866–99), less than six weeks after 'Boys of Bircham School' first appeared. This was followed by a hiatus of another 50 numbers before the publication of the same (unacknowledged) author's 'Unlucky Bob; or, Our Boys at School', which divides its storyline between startling melodrama and an inconsequential string of jocose classroom incidents reminiscent of George Emmett at his most uninspired. 'The Captain of the School', conversely, opens with a tense cricket match played between two rival schools in the town of Riverdale, testifying to the centrality of school sports as a plot device in periodical fiction, long before Talbot Baines Reed featured school stories in the *BOP*. Dr Placid's well-behaved school eleven, the Hearts of Oak, is pitted for the championship against the Rev. Dr Rodwell's more aristocratic and conceited team, the Nil Desperandums. The snobbish members of the latter team, led by its villainous trainer, the local poacher Abel Slinker, are not above resorting to foul play to assure victory. School bullies manage to injure the bowling arm of the opposing team's captain, Rupert Ingleby, 'a fine-spirited, noble lad', who nonetheless wins through for the Hearts of Oak eleven in the crucial match.[21]

The vital cricket match whose outcome is delayed by skulduggery, already present in the disreputable 'penny dreadful' serials, was to become a stock ingredient of subsequent public-school fiction. Betraying its origins, Dr Placid's school features among its pupils a curious French boy, Adolph Levasse, endearingly known among his playmates as 'the Dancing Frog' for his 'admirable dancing, his buoyant spirit, and that elasticity of mind so characteristic of his great and gallant country'. Adolph appears, performing somersaults all over the place, in some memorably strange accompanying illustrations. The author makes great play with false imprisonment in asylums and stolen-will plot mechanisms, both here and in 'Unlucky Bob', being apparently more at ease with the traditional historical-adventure serial than with the broad comic brush-strokes of the new-fangled school life and sports story. Eventually, Townsend's favourite missing-heir plot emerges, with suitably gothic touches, and the school becomes a mere resting place between increasingly mysterious escapades. Significantly, George Emmett (or E.H. Burrage) made malicious fun of such melodramatic plot lines as having been 'written by putty-heads for putty-heads'.[22]

Edwin Brett's shrewd response to the unprecedented success of George Emmett's 'Tom Wildrake's Schooldays' was to commission a proficient all-round author, Samuel Bracebridge Hemyng (1841–1901), to write a rival serial, 'Jack Harkaway's Schooldays', which also started in 1871. Sales of *Boys of England* leapt as a result from 150,000 to 250,000 copies, most of which were probably shared among several readers. Hemyng took over what had already become the traditional stock figures of 'penny dreadful' school stories: the stupid and hypocritical headmaster, the ridiculous French master, the school bully, the devoted friend, the schoolboy sweetheart, the snobbish young aristocrat and so on. All these hackneyed characters, with the exception of the headmaster, were to be transported overseas to exotic destinations as Jack's companions in countless sequels.

In this first Harkaway serial there occurs a curious sado-erotic episode, a reminder of Hemyng's apprenticeship writing quasi-pornographic novels purporting to tell the life stories of the most notorious 'fast' women about London.[23] Hence, in Chapter 9 the school headmaster's mysterious wife, the 'beautiful pythoness' Mrs Crawcour, has young Jack severely whipped for flinging stones in the direction of her carriage. He takes his punishment from a flunkey, standing upright in his shirt-sleeves, arms drawn up over his head: "'Cane the little wretch as severely as you can, and go on until I tell you to leave off. It will be some satisfaction to me to see him suffer what he so well deserves."' Mrs Crawcour then abjectly apologises for this flagellation by offering to have her pretty maid rub Jack's back with liniment: "'I have come to ask your forgiveness for my passionate and cruel conduct to you this afternoon. Oh! If you only knew what a dreadful curse my temper has been to me all my life. Had it not been for my temper, I should not now be the wife of a schoolmaster in a country town."' Jack sustains an ambivalent relationship with the headmaster's vivacious and 'strangely contradictory' wife – until she was abruptly dropped from the serial, perhaps at the editor's request.[24]

The career of Bracebridge Hemyng, the eldest son of the Registrar of the Supreme Court in Calcutta, and himself an Eton-and-Oxford-educated barrister (without briefs), well exemplifies the lower stratum of the literary life in Victorian London. By the age of 30 this versatile and prolific author had already produced some tortuous three-volume novels, such as *The Curate of Inveresk* (1860) or *Gasper Trenchard* (1864); first-person 'edited' narratives exposing various criminal practices, such as *Secrets of the Turf, or How I Won the Derby* (1868); reputedly licentious stories about London's 'fast' women, such as *Skittles* (1864) for the 'Anonyma series' put out by George Vickers; semi-autobiographical two-shilling 'yellowback' novels to be sold at railway bookstalls, such as *Eton School Days* (1864) or *Called to the Bar* (1867); and the well-informed section on 'Prostitution in London' for the fourth volume of Henry Mayhew's *London Labour and the London Poor* (1864). Yet Hemyng, like many other decayed gentleman scribblers, discovered his true vocation only late in his career, when he turned to popular juvenile fiction and created Jack Harkaway, his most commercially successful character. Having gone to the United States to write for the expatriate

Frank Leslie's periodicals, Hemyng lived for some years on Staten Island in New York. A stout figure in middle age, sporting 'Dundreary' sideburns and a monocle, he continued to write novels, serials and magazine articles for pressing financial reasons. Hemyng ended his life at 60, practically penniless, in a dreary apartment in Fulham, then an unfashionable area of London, familiar as the location for attempted seduction in several women-in-peril serials, of which Hemyng may even have been the author.[25]

Returning to a sporting theme, the elderly Brett put out the up-to-date but moralistic *Bicycle Bob; or, Who Will Win?* (*c.* 1895), which features the young engineering apprentice Bob Ready. He is in love with his employer's niece, Polly Warner, who proves 'as difficult to manage as a bicycle at first start'. Bob brings welcome employment to old John Stout's smithy by making a successful prototype bicycle from a Paris drawing. He tests this penny-farthing along the Kennington Road in London while his rival for Polly's hand, the disgraced former apprentice Luke Croft, is lured into burglary by 'evil companions' at the beerhouse. Bob subsequently pursues the foolish Luke on his unwieldy machine and, after various escapades, the gang of miscreants, whose leader is a member of the Shakers, is brought to justice. Polly exclaims: 'Who would think that boys could be so audacious? If the girls did half as much there would be an end to the world.' To his mother's shame, Luke confesses his guilt, for 'such is the punishment of a person who once takes a false step from the path of honesty and industry'.[26]

Another novel from the same firm, *The Oxford and Cambridge Eights; or, The Young Coxswain's Career* (*c.* 1890), originally serialised in *Boys of England* in 1875, opens on the day before the Oxford–Cambridge Boat Race. Cecil Barrington, the young coxswain of the Oxford boat, discovers an anonymous note at the riverside: 'Private and v. confidential. Drug the C's; I have a heavy bet on the O's. If you fail I can hedge at the last moment.' This incriminating missive was intended for the haggard-looking Shuffling Jemmy, otherwise known as the dishonoured ruffian Harold Mainwaring, 'evidently a long way down in the social scale', who attempts to garrotte and then drown young Cecil. '"He'll pay for this Quixotic interference", Mainwaring muttered; "curse him, he belongs to a family I hate. His mother jilted me; in desperation I took to horse racing, gambling – worse. I'll be even with her yet though, through him."' Harold, a vicious and unmanly gambler, makes a neat contrast with the gentlemanly hero Cecil, who recovers sufficiently to warn the Cambridge crew of the dastardly plot. Further melodramatic developments take place before and after the famous boat race, revealing a certain familiarity with gaming vocabulary, until wicked cousin Harold is finally exposed and brought to his just deserts by the young coxswain.[27]

Brett's firm also continued to churn out and reprint school stories, such as John Cecil Stagg's *The King of the School; or, Who Will Win?* (*c.* 1895) or the anonymous *The Rival Schools: Their Fun, Feud and Frolics* (*c.* 1875), but with *Tom Floremall's Schooldays* (*c.* 1878), serialised in *Boys of England* in 1876, the 'penny dreadful' school story had already become formulaic. Tom becomes resident at Lashem School, a former convent that abounds in secret passages, where he encounters an unjustly accused boy, a missing heir, comic French and German masters (Monsieur Bricabrac and Herr Phule), a comic fat boy, a bully, a flash swindler, and even a sadistic headmaster who uses a cat-o'-nine-tails until the blood runs. The anonymous author races through the narrative, throwing away story ideas and stock characters with a splendid insouciance, and even introduces the formula prop of a ventriloquist–impersonator who causes havoc among the masters. Rituals of inversion and charivari combine to give endless release to the forces of misrule.

'Penny dreadful' school stories seem to have catered to ordinary boys' desire to see adults in authority being made to suffer pain and appear ridiculous, discomfited through the superior cunning of their adolescent charges. Reading about the deflation of pompous schoolmasters by anarchic boarding-school pupils may have provided a much-needed safety valve for circumscribed and regimented state-school pupils. As the *Leeds Mercury* lamented in 1884, 'the schoolboy is regaled with a record of tricks and pranks which disguise, under the seductive name of humour, dishonesty and disobedience and indecency'.[28]

Conclusion

'I wish I know'd as much as you, Dick. How did you manage to pick it up?' one of the eponymous Wild Boys of London asks the well-mannered young hero in the first chapter:

> 'Mother taught me most, and I read all the books I can get.' ...
> 'So do I; sich rattling tales, too – *The Black Phantom; or, The White Spectre of the Pink Rock*. It's fine it is; somebody's killed every week, and it's only a penny.'
> 'That is not the sort of book I mean. Mother does not like me to read them.'
> 'Why?'
> 'She says they have a bad influence.'

'Who's he?'
'That means a bad effect.'
'Don't know him, neither.'
'You would, if you read proper books.'

As this presumably self-parodying dialogue suggests, many adults among the aspiring lower-middle and educated middle classes believed that 'penny dreadfuls' were dangerous and corrupting because they did not lead the newly literate working classes towards the high ideal of self-improvement but were 'merely' entertaining. Neither did they endorse, despite their racism and xenophobia, the public-school notions of manliness and Protestantism that fed more generally into British imperial culture, and came, in particular, to be defined against both 'effeminate' Catholicism and continental revolution.[29]

What the more hostile commentators generally chose to overlook was the likelihood that 'penny dreadfuls' were read equally by the sons and daughters of the middle, lower-middle and skilled working classes, especially in periodical form, as well as by less discriminating and poorer semi-literate readers. This commercially produced and genuinely popular fiction for the young was generally harmless, if stodgy and melodramatic, yet by the early 1870s it was being constructed as disreputable or 'dreadful' in order to incite a middle-class 'moral panic'. The campaign against 'penny dreadfuls' endorsed censorship of *The Wild Boys of London* late in 1877, and the scapegoating of periodicals published by Brett and the Emmetts by using their possession as evidence of guilt in criminal trials of juveniles. This escalation of the perceived threat coincided with a late-Victorian increase in the conscious regulation of working-class boys, encapsulated in compulsory state elementary schooling; the opening of reformatory and industrial schools for vagrant or delinquent youths; a fixation on uncontrolled, high-earning 'boy labour'; and the rise of adult-organised and well-drilled youth organisations such as the army cadet corps or the Boys' Brigade.[30]

Equally, the wider consequences of age discrimination, by which certain tastes, values and hierarchies were established as culturally adult, 'respectable' or preferable, and others not, was that aesthetic distinctions became a symbolic weapon in the struggle between classes and generations for ideological domination. Consequently, late-Victorian middle-class idealists and literary critics came to exaggerate or distort the nature of cheap popular fiction as 'sensational' and 'dreadful', in order to nurture due chagrin at the disappointingly escapist fruits of a youthful working-class literacy that they had themselves helped to nourish. Labelling thus represents a way for cultural authorities to construct taste hierarchies and to amplify anxiety or rejection over products of the mass culture, such as cheap fiction, which threaten established adult taste. The invention of labels such as 'horror comic', 'video nasty' or 'penny dreadful' signifies the continuous modern struggle between the perceived need to socialise children into the norms of adult middle-class society, commercial provision of mass popular entertainment and youthful market demand for the disreputable.[31]

Cartoons and comic periodicals, 1841–1901: a satirical sociology of Victorian sporting life

MIKE HUGGINS

By the mid-nineteenth century, as advances in technology allowed cheap, high-quality engravings to be both easily created and distributed, the illustrated London press had become a main medium of modernity, one which attracted a mass following. In the past 20 years there has been increasing exploitation of this visual evidence of the Victorian and Edwardian periods to shed new light on conventional topics, and this important 'visual turn' has allowed images to take their place alongside literary and oral texts as key sources for cultural historians.[1] More recently Lynda Nead and Peter Burke have both shown the central role that visual images and the consumption of visual culture played in cultural life.[2]

As part of the wider process of Victorian illustration, the power of visually appealing comic periodicals and comic art became a recognised feature of Victorian visual and verbal culture, seized upon and read by peers, politicians and the proletariat alike. They communicated complex ideas and influenced perceptions. Dozens of comic journals can be identified in both early and late Victorian England, all trying to capture a market with varying degrees of success, pricking pomposity, satirising the superior and ridiculing the respectable. The metropolitan press, for example, ranged from the knowing allusions of up-market periodicals such as *Punch* (from 1841) to the more popular, and not just working-class, pages of the late Victorian *Ally Sloper's Half Holiday* (1884–1916: referred to as *ASHH* from now on). Even the more juvenile-oriented comics, such as the *Joker* (1892–93), *Nuggets* (1893) or *Fun* (1861–1901), assume a 'knowing' understanding of cartoons relating to racing life, drink and variety girls. In part the popularity of these important and entertaining distorting mirrors of the more 'respectable' press were a measure of a newspaper's financial success, and, more indirectly, the prosperity of its audience. London papers offered the largest number of cartoons, although local and regional papers also contained cartoons in the later nineteenth century.

Political historians have always been alert to the potentialities of cartoons, drawing on them for evidence about topics ranging from German right-wing propaganda against the Versailles settlement, or Low's ridicule of Hitler and Mussolini, to the reign of George IV.[3] Likewise, mainstream social historians have exploited cartoons to explore the political and social attitudes, values and cultural life of the Victorians, or to look at such topics as shop-floor relationships between the wars.[4]

Despite this 'visual turn' and the move towards the analysis of verbal humour in wider cultural history, sports historians in both Britain and the United States have tended to be 'conservative in their explorations of mediums and primary sources', so that the role of humour has been largely ignored and 'relatively little scholarship has focused on media representation of sport'.[5] Nuanced analyses of evocative cultural constructs such as films, photographs, sporting fiction or cartoons have been relatively neglected, although some significant areas covered recently include twentieth-century football fiction, dialect humour and sporting television advertisements.[6] Recent work on Victorian sport has often eschewed any use of cartoon material, despite its direct, populist style, and the ways in which associated captions and commentary provide evidence for attitudes to sport, its respectability or unrespectability, and for sporting preoccupations. Comics are, after all, themselves not entirely respectable. The few exceptions to such neglect are largely to be found in wider historical scholarship where sport is covered in passing, as, for example, in the work of the literary historian Richard Altick or the cultural historian Peter Bailey.[7] The most common use of cartoons in books on the history of sport and leisure has been as simple illustrations for textbooks, with little evidence of any in-depth reading. J.A Mangan provided a relatively early example of the use of visual images as illustrative of critical comment in sport and as ideological artefacts, but the practice of most historians has been variable, depending on the author's personal predilection for visual material and the breadth of sources consulted.[8]

Victorian sporting cartoons provide an impressive, highly compressed, visual and verbal narrative of leisure experiences either directly familiar to audiences, or linked to their lives. For their readers they provided key interpretative frameworks for the construction of meaning, and for historians they shed light both on aspects of sporting experience that were often so much taken for granted that they were not referred to in journalistic texts, and on attitudes shown to those aspects of 'respectable' sport seen as more disreputable, less approved of or less enjoyed by the cartoonists and editorial boards. Cartoons and texts mediated between sports and audience, and revealed relationships of power and meaning in terms of respectability. Their humour reflected changes in social and cultural values.

There is insufficient space to fully explore the problems and possibilities of the genre, and so the focus here is on two of the major London-based comic journals, *Punch* and *ASHH*, selected because of their circulations and their public notoriety. The chapter begins with a discussion of methodology and the general potentialities of the genre; this is followed by an introductory overview of the ways in which cartoons shed light on Victorian attitudes to sporting respectability and disreputability. The next four sections focus on *Punch*, exploring the patterns, themes and narratives that framed its sports coverage. The second section examines the varied nature of its sporting cartoons and the breadth of sports coverage that it provided, or failed to provide. The third section discusses male sporting social relationships and attitudes, while the fourth section shows how *Punch* responded to male concerns over women's growing participation and the fifth section briefly explores its disapproval of the cult of athleticism. The sixth section provides a comparative analysis of the late nineteenth-century coverage of sport in *ASHH*. The final section shows that, although a beginning has now been made, a great deal more empirical research will be needed before our understanding of the visual evidence for Victorian sport can be considered satisfactory.

Methodology and overview

Use of Victorian sporting cartoons creates problems of decipherment, reliability and interpretation. They should be approached with caution and the application of normal historical scepticism, and a basic methodology needs to be established. Although cartoons are accompanied by texts their interpretation is problematical and meanings cannot be absolute, since they adopt a variety of codes, incorporating playfulness, satire, irony, parody and paradox. In order to fully understand them as a cultural product it is vital to fully understand and be able to place cartoons historically in the social and cultural context in which they were created, and they need to be read alongside more conventional sources such as the press, diaries, or memoirs.

Discussion of medium and methodology forces a recognition of the centrality of the intended audience. Cartoons rely on instant responses and rarely challenge the stereotypes that contemporary readers carry with them in relation to the language and visual appearance of characters. Thus, the texts and pictures in the nineteenth-century cartoons under consideration here largely confirmed the 'way things were' in Victorian society: the upper middle classes usually speak in standard English; effete London swells lisp; working-class cockneys drop their Hs or introduce them unnecessarily and speak with non-standard grammar forms ('yer was'), as may the newly rich, signifying to readers their lack of education and social background. Clothing and appearance largely indicate class background too. Young women engaged in sporting activity were drawn in ways that provided contradictory messages. Sometimes they are slim, attractive and well-dressed, perhaps intended to appeal to the voyeuristic fantasies of male readers, young and old, while others are portrayed as thickset and more 'manly'. Muscular male athletes might have appealed in different ways too, depending on the predilections of the audience.[9]

The question of who was being mocked and by whom in any single cartoon sums up the challenge of this material, yet the visual and verbal messages of most cartoons were created with elements of almost certainly deliberate ambiguity, and were capable simultaneously of a range of read- ings and multiple identifications that reflected the breadth of young and old, male and female audiences to whom they had to appeal. Cartoons could be read differently, and more or less knowingly, by different sections of the readership. To provide just one textual example, a hunting cartoon of 1894 apparently signals its basic double entendre unambiguously with the title 'LIABLE TO MISINTERPRETATION':

> Awful Young Brother (son of MFH, to his sister, 'who in course of a slight flirtation has wandered too far forward down Covert- side with the Captain'): 'Here, I say, Maude, the Governor's just sent me on to say you're getting a dashed lot too forward with Captain Sparks, and you ought to know better.'

Some double meanings here would have been clear to most readers, since in sexual terms female 'forwardness' and girls who 'ought to know better', or were 'no better than they ought to be', were never compatible with Victorian respectability. However, visual/textual material also relies on readers' iden- tification with characters, and here different readers could identify with different characters in the story, and so would see the narrative of events and dialogue in different ways, since the cartoonist leaves the reasons lying behind the actions of each character similarly ambiguous. In what sense and to whom is the young brother 'awful'? Is the paterfamilias, the MFH, call- ing his daughter back, in the moral sense of feeling that she is being 'too forward' sexually, or are his priorities more for his hunting and a positional disturbance, so that being too far forward would deter the fox from making its run? What would the sister and the moustachioed captain each under- stand by 'a slight flirtation'? Has the wandering too far forward been

LIABLE TO MISINTERPRETATION.

Awful Young Brother (Son of M.F.H.—to Sister, who, in course of a slight flirtation, has wandered too far forward down Covert-side with the Captain). "HERE, I SAY, MAUDE, THE GOVERNOR'S JUST SENT ME ON TO SAY YOU'RE GETTING A DASHED LOT TOO FORWARD WITH CAPTAIN SPARKS, AND YOU OUGHT TO KNOW BETTER!"

Figure 6.1. 'Liable to misinterpretation'. Source: *Punch*, 24 March 1894.

intentional or accidental, or intentional on the part of one of the couple and not of the other? Is the word 'covert', meaning both 'a thicket sheltering game', and 'secret or disguised', while 'to cover' was also what a stallion did to a mare, equally 'liable to misinterpretation' in this context? The possibility of the latter reading is perhaps reinforced by the visual evidence provided by the position of the woman's mare, to which the captain's much larger stallion is adopting the standard pre-mounting position adopted in thoroughbred breeding.

Although cartoons are by no means realistic representations, a check against more conventional sources suggests that much of the supporting detail has substantial elements of accurate reportage. This suggests that we may also see cartoons as very useful visual sources to deepen our understanding of sporting clothing, practices and behaviour. Despite their light-hearted tone, they provide vivid detail of how the Victorians practised, watched and made meaning from their outdoor sports. For example, Richard Doyle's cartoon 'A view of Epsom Downes on ye Derbye Daye' (1847) is filled with a lively, eating, drinking, convivial gathering bent more on enjoying sociability and a menu of commercial amusements, from pugilism to thimblerigging and musical entertainments, than on watching the races.[10]

Doyle's picture is an early precursor of Frith's much better-known panorama painting, *Derby Day* (1858). Many of its details are confirmed in journalists' accounts such as Charles Dickens's piece, 'Epsom', written with W.H.Wills, or in descriptions by foreign visitors.[11]

Recognising the work of individual cartoonists is relatively easy in the case of *ASHH*, which used only two artists, first Baxter and then Thomas, for its Sloper portrayals, but is often difficult in the case of *Punch*, since many of its cartoons are unsigned. Many cartoonists contributed to *Punch*, including such regular artists as Doyle, John Leech, John Tenniel or Charles Keene, and more occasional artists such as W.M. Thackeray. Each cartoonist touched on sport only rarely, perhaps finding a different source of humour in sport each time. Tenniel, for example, had a political thrust, with some 58 cartoons on horse-racing alone. In his Derby cartoons political leaders are portrayed in unrespectable contexts, as jockeys, welshers of bets, thimblerig operators, blackface minstrels or Gypsy queens.[12] Yet here too, as we shall see, an overall editorial perspective does emerge alongside some differences in style and subject among the cartoonists. The men who produced *Punch* often shared the habits and biases of their predominantly middle-class readers, and often exploited them. Overall, therefore, it is clear that the source problems can be overcome. We can now turn to an examination of what the cartoons reveal.

At best sporting cartoons offer an opportunity to look through the eyes of their Victorian readers, capturing their attitudes, foibles and prejudices, and their beliefs about the 'respectability' of behaviour. Many Victorians themselves were, as we might expect, well-aware of this. For example, in 1872 James Fraser, Bishop of Manchester, described *Punch* as illustrating 'the foibles of the age' and 'the general tone of that fast fashionable life...whose follies they so often admirably expose'.[13] Reading the caption, and trying to explain the issue at stake, the cartoonist's probable point of view and the probable audience, all help to open up the stakes that made sport so important in Victorian Britain.

For the Victorians themselves respectability was a psychic as much as a social phenomenon. What was 'respectable' and hence acceptable differed from person to person and from context to context. This crossed over into speech, writing and visual forms. The values of respectability shaped the ways in which recreations regarded as unrespectable were represented, while sometimes 'unrespectable' recreations could be found in the lives of even the more respectable. The meanings that Victorians attached to sporting activities shared such problems of definition. They could be seen in ambiguous ways. Sporting activities that were 'respectable' when indulged in by 'respectable' middle-class and upper-class men might become less acceptable and more disreputable when participated in by women, or by lower-middle-class or working-class males. A reactive tension was always generated when systems of power were threatened or rearranged, and despite, or even because of, the prejudices and stereotyped attitudes they display cartoons are especially valuable as evidence of the history of such Victorian mentalities.

Cartoons provide us with a deeper and subtler understanding of the meanings attached to sport by readers and cartoonists during the Victorian period. Satirical cartoons were in part a distorted comic mirror of respectability. They provide a running commentary on the general expansion of sport, and open up a window to indicate the specific pleasures, problems and possibilities of Victorian sporting culture. The carefully nuanced meanings and rich symbolism often lying behind these often satirical commentaries provide historians with a rich source of evidence about Victorian sporting attitudes and values. Visual comic media interacted with readers and their expectations, playing with them and helping to structure and restructure class and gender relations. They can carry multiple and complex meanings, and are often capable of being read simultaneously as either radical or conservative, as satirically mocking the new sporting aspirations of the Victorians or sympathetically endorsing them. They also show the Victorian love of satire and self-deflating humour, a challenge both to contemporary foreign beliefs that the Victorians took their pleasures sadly and to later generations' stereotypes of solemn Victorians.

Such material operated dialectically both as a central indicator of the broader transformation of sport, and as itself one of the agents of change, through its challenge to taken-for-granted attitudes, and showing how particular behaviours in sport were socially 'respectable' or less acceptable. Study of the complex nexus of discourse and ideology shown by visual humour in the second half of the nineteenth century thus helps to document an evolving, complex and shifting picture of such key issues relating to the respectability of sport as masculine identity, the complex relationships between classes and sexes, and the evolving metropolitan and provincial attitudes to sporting ideologies such as athleticism.

An important aspect of such analysis is that of the relationship between disreputability, social class and gender. Disreputability in the sense served by satirical sporting cartoons is often a matter of failure to preserve male social status and reputation in the eyes of the middle-class world. The sporting 'revolution' of the Victorian period, and most especially the more complex class interactions that it entailed, threw up new problems about the way in which social sporting encounters had to be negotiated. Middle-class status anxiety, and consequent worries over the language, dress and look that were necessary to reputably pass oneself off in this more sophisticated social world at national events such as the Derby, Ascot, the Boat Race, Henley or the Eton and Harrow match without embarrassment or rejection, were a rich source of plunder for comic satirists. As revealed by cartoons, middle-class attitudes were clearly somewhat mixed, with those firmly ensconced in their sporting positions in the hunting, shooting and fishing fraternity enjoying cartoons reflecting worries about invasion both from below and by women, and despising their supposedly less respectable social inferiors. The 'respectability' of such readers was confirmed through their snobbish glee at ridiculing selected aspects of the 'disreputable' behaviour of classes below them, and this was another staple feature of comic cartoons. Such snobbery reflected concerns about losing public status, reputation and respect. More recently arrived members of the middle class were flattered and comforted, and may well have felt smug. Other readers, however, from the lower end of the middle class, enjoyed cartoons that attacked barriers in the way of sporting aspirations, pricked pretensions and yet confirmed their own status. At different times cartoons and cartoonists pointed up such divisions in complex combinations of self-mockery, petty-bourgeois mockery of upper-middle class pretensions and *vice versa*. Cartoons also shed new light on gender relationships in sport. Historians interested in the fascinating and still somewhat unresearched attitudes of men to female involvement in both the older and newer forms of Victorian sport can certainly find a rich source of evidence here. Cartoons play on or undermine stereotypical roles and expectations, explore male–female relationships in sport, and address questions of empowerment, hegemony and control within these. Yet here again cartoons offer ambiguous readings. There were women among the cartoonist's readers too. Some cartoons were aimed more at a misogynist male audience and anti-sporting females, yet another cartoon in the same magazine might mock the social and intellectual inadequacies of a male athlete trying to strike up a conversation with an Oxbridge bluestocking.

Punch and sport

Punch was the most famous of the Victorian comic papers, even though its actual circulation was lower than some others'. It combined verbal and visual wit in a way that appealed to upper-class and middle-class readers, who ranged from Queen Victoria, Emily Brontë or Thomas Carlyle around the middle of the nineteenth century to the Marquess of Salisbury at its end. Parliamentarians may have enjoyed those cartoons that employed sporting metaphors and images to satirise inter- and intra-party disputes and contests.[14] Others enjoyed *Punch*'s ridicule of middle-class pretensions, social ceremonies and vanities. In the most recent and most thorough of the many books published about *Punch* and its contributors, Richard Altick argues convincingly that the periodical commonly used the device of satirical vulgarisation to take a prejudice or practice conventionally associated with the upper classes and apply it to the lower classes, opening up the mores of fashionable life to burlesque, while simultaneously dwelling on the humorous shortcomings of the working classes, and ridiculing the snobbery, foibles and follies of the middle class itself, the very class from whom it largely drew its readers.[15]

At the same time *Punch*, on the surface, appeared to be a major agent for the transmission of English 'respectability', with an apparent absence of abuse or bawdy. As Hippolyte Taine curiously pointed out, unlike similar French periodicals it had 'not a single drawing dealing with prostitutes of any kind' or 'on marital infidelity'. Its focus was on 'legitimate love' and largely on 'decent, respectable people'.[16] Yet Taine was a foreigner and thus, presumably, less able to decode any sexual or social subtext. In fact, double meanings are by no means improbable and are more likely in cartoons, where a reader might well *expect* puns or metaphorical slang. Indeed, recent research has begun to suggest that sexualised popular discourse can be found even in Dickens's apparently respectable work.[17] Likewise, Steven Marcus has pointed out the elaborate, genteel and periphrastic nature of sexual puns in the mid-nineteenth century, implying that many writers enjoyed the masculine discourse of subversive and raffish linguistic jokes.[18]

A search for editorial attitudes and coverage of sport through a longitudinal survey of issues over the period indicates some changes in social attitudes. *Punch* was at its most radical in its approach to sport in the 1840s, a period of political upheaval and class tensions reflected both in its sports coverage, and in its critiques of bourgeois sporting pretensions, sporting excesses and middle-class disreputability, perhaps largely because many of the early contributors were relatively young. Thereafter, despite the growth of new sporting habits in the later part of the century, its radicalism become attenuated, and it became more conservative, limited and middle-class in its approach to, and coverage of, sport.

There was a fairly consistent pattern in *Punch*'s coverage of sports. Even in the 1840s sport, and most especially the more aristocratic field sports, which received numerous new aspirant recruits during mid-century, provided a fruitful target for its jibes.[19] Although the cartoons show a broad approval of blood-sports, growing concerns about cruelty to animals meant that the suffering or capture of the quarry was not pictured graphically. Thus, although pictures relating to the hunting field and dangerous riding to hounds were almost always the most common, there was special emphasis,

PRACTISING FOR A MATCH.

Leonora. "Dear! Dear! How the Arrow sticks!"
Capt. Blank. (with a sigh of the deepest). "It does, indeed!"

Figure 6.2. 'Practising for a match'. Source: *Punch*, 19 July 1862.

ENCOURAGEMENT.

Professional Golfer (in answer to anxious question). "Weel, no, Sir, at your Time o' Life, ye can never hope to become a *Player*; but if ye practise hard for Three Years, ye may be able to tell Good Play from Bad when ye see it!".

Figure 6.3. 'Encouragement'. Source: *Punch*, 14 February 1891.

in a Surteesian vein, on misadventures, mishaps, incidents and socially inappropriate remarks by the hunters. Constant visual fun was made of timid or clumsy horsemen, or those who hesitated at a jump, but the sport itself was seen as unproblematic. The qualities of a rider to hounds were part of 'manliness' and a poor horseman was a man of poor reputation. Boys and girls, slim young men and women, and stout parents of both sexes were all regularly depicted hunting. Between 1850 and 1901 there was little change: in most years between 30 and 40 per cent of *Punch*'s sporting cartoons had a hunting theme.

The next most common subject in most years was shooting, sometimes linked to sporting tourism in the Highlands, and so contributing to the myth of the Highlands as a 'natural' sporting playground in which to enjoy salmon-fishing, deer-stalking and grouse-shooting, although fishing was rarely covered in much more than two cartoons in a year.[20]

Horse-racing was usually featured only during the Derby week, which was seen as an annual London carnival, with a much more occasional cartoon relating to the highly select meetings at Ascot, and even more rarely Goodwood. This suggests that generally horse-racing was not 'respectable'.[21]

In the 1860s activities that were seen as 'respectable' and yet potentially problematic enough to be covered in perhaps an average of one cartoon each year included archery, billiards, cycling, cricket, croquet, fencing, skating, rowing and yachting. By the 1890s hunting, shooting and fishing had been joined by golf as a major participant sport, and cricket was receiving more attention, while the rest of the list from the 1860s had survived, except for archery, which had become unfashionable, and was joined by casual swimming, mainly as a women's sport, and by women's hockey. A few scattered references to middle-class betting suggest a now slightly more tolerant attitude to its acceptability. By contrast the total absence of sports such as pedestrianism, dog-racing or coursing, association football or, perhaps more surprisingly, rugby football, whether professional or amateur, all suggest that these were assumed to be of less interest and less acceptable to the readers.

Cartoons relating to the newly fashionable London sporting calendar represent one of the key ways in which new and 'respectable' key national sporting 'traditions' such as the Boat Race, the Derby, Henley or the Eton and Harrow match were created and disseminated. These cartoons often provide an alternative narrative to that of the national daily newspapers, and perhaps a more disreputable one, concentrating on the spectators and crowd rather than on the contestants, the range of leisure activities rather than the result, and the social interaction rather than the competition. *Punch* was an early user of the mode of the comic strip, extending an initial comic idea over space and time.

Doyle's 'Pleasure Trips of Brown, Jones and Robinson' (1849) satirises the comic adventures of the naïve and inexperienced middle classes out for a sporting spree at Epsom or taking riding lessons. His Derby Day kaleidoscope of such disreputable events resembles stock accounts in the less reputable sporting press, and includes Robinson falling off the coach; Jones upsetting the coach and four en route; Brown gaming and losing five pounds at thimb-lerig, like many mug punters before him; Robinson being arrested by the police for crossing the course; Robinson falling off the back of the coach, clutching a bottle as he makes his way home; and Brown being unable to find his horse when he wishes to return. Another example, 'Blossom at the Boat Race', drawn in 1872, likewise portrays the comic misadventures of a young swell as he tries, unsuccessfully, to get to the Thames to meet his Clara and see the race at a physical, financial and emotional cost that includes a hansom cab, first-class train fare and two boat trips, tar-ruined lavender gloves, heavily mud-stained clothing, and a scolding.[22]

Male sporting relationships and attitudes

Reading cartoons helped the audience to negotiate the complex and chang-ing social relationships and expectations of Victorian sport. Sporting cartoons of the period often demonstrate a deep upper-middle-class status anxiety, and a consequent condescending derision towards, and ridiculing of, particular groups when members of those groups showed ignorance of the 'correct' way to behave. Such groups include the more *arriviste* members of the upper middle class itself, as well as the young and, more rarely, visiting foreigners. Names of characters are often used to locate such characteristics, while cartoons themselves satirise and so soften such moments of potential tension. Sometimes such ridicule is levelled directly, as in a cartoon showing a woollen draper, out for a day's shooting, who does not know how to hold his gun correctly; or another, where Perkins, who has 'paid a mint for his shooting and had bad luck all the season' finally sees something and fires, only to find that 'it turns out to be a cow'; or others in which a grouse or a fish is purchased at a local shop in order to avoid arriv-ing home empty-handed.[23] In another cartoon 'Young Finsbury', an effete Londoner ignorant of country sports who has shared a day's rabbit shooting with his 'country cousins', indicates a small dog standing nearby and lisps: 'Hullo Wichard, does this little Quadwuped belong to you, because...?' Richard replies 'Yes, she's a clever little thing; so I generally take her...' Young Finsbury completes his sentence: 'Because, stwikes me, I've been shooting at it all the morning.'[24]

"Beg pardon, Sir! But if you was to aim *at* His Lordship the next time, I think he'd feel more comfortable, Sir!"

Figure 6.4. 'Beg pardon, sir! But if you was to aim *at* his lordship the next time, I think he'd feel more comfortable, sir!' Source: *Punch*, 18 October 1890.

At other times gleeful joy in others' incompetence is displaced onto certain groups within the working class, the often more expert caddies, ghillies or keepers who were expected to serve and support their *arriviste* sporting masters in a deferential way. One key characteristic of membership of the Victorian middle class was servant-keeping: as newly rich men rose in status, these outside staff had to support their often limited sporting skills. This could be problematical. Such employees must often have had to find the words to apparently praise, or tactfully find excuses for, sporting incompetence. Showing this happening presumably gave more expert sportsmen, who might well also have had to find such words, opportunities for a quiet smile of recognition and a savouring of their own superiority. It might also, however, have struck a chord in the less skilled, forcing them to come to terms with their own abilities. 'Harmless Amusement' (1875) shows Muckleston, who has missed his bird for the twentieth time, saying to his keeper: 'I say, Gaskins, I do believe the birds are frightened at me!' Gaskins 'blandly' replies: 'They didn't ought to be, sir.' A cartoon entitled 'Making Things Smooth' (1894) depicts a shooting party featuring a group of sportsmen each of whom has just fired all four barrels without touching a single bird's feather. The keeper remarks: 'Deary me, uncommon strong on the wing birds is gentlemen! 'Stonishing amount o' shot they carries away with 'em to be sure.'[25]

Sometimes gamekeepers are shown playing a more active supporting role. In a cartoon published in 1864 'Little Chickmouse' (a name suggesting shyness, fearfulness, lack of size and hence unmanliness), who has rashly accepted the offer of a day's partridge shooting, has kicked up a hare; the game-keeper encourages him with: 'Now for it sir', but Chickmouse finds himself unable to 'get over his horror of firearms' and says: 'Look 'ere, you 'old the gun, and I'll pull the thingummy.'[26] The carefully drawn expressions of the two characters, and the difference between the more standard, respectful language of the gamekeeper and the less 'respectable' language of Chickmouse, who does not even know the word 'trigger', makes the point for the readers.

At other times such support and guidance from members of the servant class are shown to be lost on the ignorant. A cartoon entitled 'Politeness' (1866) shows a gamekeeper, keener on preserving his master's pheasants in the preserves than on allowing a hunter to cut though them in pursuit of a fox, who tells 'Young Topboots' that there is 'No road that way sir', only to be told, much less politely, 'Quite good enough for me, thank you.'[27]

Punch, women and athleticism

Historians are agreed that the Victorian revolution in sport was predomi-nantly a male phenomenon and that participation by middle-class women was on a modest scale.[28] In the pages of *Punch* women's respectability is narrowly defined: all middle-class women are expected to be respectable, modest and feminine. The magazine often seems laden with disapproving references to the challenge of 'disreputable' sporting female behaviour, especially in the form of attacks on 'new women' and their increasing appearance in a sporting context (a field now attracting significant academic attention).[29] *Punch*'s cartoonists generally shared a belief that males and females should fulfil broadly different roles and functions. The incursion of women into sport posed a threat to this ideology. Cartoons were used to present their view of women's social place, to reinforce traditional gender ideas and maintain prevailing ideologies. Their male fears meant that sport-ing women were consistently denigrated. Visually many cartoons reinforce male superiority by showing women playing a more passive role as specta-tors, looking admiringly at male athletes or playing more gentle, 'respectable', 'ladylike' games such as croquet. The pictures appear to have been drawn largely with the 'male gaze' in mind: many portray 'conspicu-ous sporting women' as young attractive, slim, 'the wifely ornament of

beauty... inhibited and imbued by convention'.[30] Their pictured clothing –
their decorative and flamboyant wasp-waisted dresses, long heavy skirts,
numerous petticoats, high heels and tight corsetry – looks as if it might have
been calculated to confirm their restriction.[31]

Sometimes *Punch* cartoons suggest that most women are dizzy creatures,
whose ignorance of all sport is abysmal and marks them as inferior. When
women spurn such stereotypes by taking part as participants and spectators
a consistent claim of the cartoons is that this is only for the sake of flirting
and finding prospective partners, women being assumed to be subordinate,
not ascendant, restrained, maidenly and genteel. Yet they also show women
who clearly do enjoy sport. A common strategy here is to suggest that these
are over-keen, pseudo-masculine 'hearties', with more 'masculine' bodies.
Cartoons that indicate that there were women whose skills were better than
those of some men are rare indeed.

Although the most common pictures of female sporting interest in *Punch*
are those of attendance at race meetings and participation in the hunt, regular cartoon attention to female sporting participation had already widened by
the 1860s to include archery, croquet and yachting.[32] Such evidence suggests
that increases in time and opportunity, as well as in interest in more elite
female sporting recreation, occurred somewhat before the supposed beginning of what John Lowerson calls 'the Great Sports Craze' of the 1870s.[33]
Women had been riding to hounds, for example, long before the 1870s and
did so increasingly, but their involvement did not meet with universal
approval. At the same time it is quite clear that such participation, while
problematic, was accepted, largely because these activities were predominantly social and recreational, had limited competitiveness, and allowed
both men and women to play and watch together. Nevertheless, the columns
of *Punch* continued to contain expressions of opposition to such involvement. In general, *Punch*'s view was more that of the aged uncle in a cartoon
of 1875, dedicated 'to girls who walk with the guns'. Ethel: 'Aren't you
going to shoot today uncle?' Uncle: 'Not if you are. When I was young the
man shot the birds and the women stayed at home to cook them!'[34]

One anti-feminist subtext regularly employed invoked the Victorian
feminine ideal by portraying women's supposed concern for appearance,
flirting and finding a partner.[35] In many of the cartoons sexual attraction
makes the disguised running, with banter and badinage from the women,
and flattery and flirtation from the men. By the 1870s, according to *Punch*,
the ambitious young girl wanting to marry into luxury would not consider a
suitor without 'a house in town', 'a moor in Scotland' and 'a hunting box at
Melton'.[36] *Punch* applied such criticism to all female involvement in sport
from as early as the 1860s, at a point when demureness and propriety were

already beginning to fall out of favour among at least some young women. In croquet, for example, women appear delicate and refined, yet more bent on finding male partners, not always to some other women's entire pleasure. In one cartoon of 1863 a couple in the background have abandoned their game to engage in more intimate conversation, while a foregrounded 'chorus of offended maidens' exclaims: 'Well!! If Clara and Captain are going on in that ridiculous manner – we may as well leave off playing'.

This last cartoon arguably shows the irritation of more sporting females at what they may well have seen as 'betrayal'. *Punch* cartoons often attempt to marginalise sporting females, to imply that their interest in sport is a disreputable, almost unnatural madness or obsession, and to suggest that all women are really only out to find partners through sport. Such views come out very clearly in a cartoon of 1864, in which an 'energetic' mixed party meet to prepare the lawn for croquet by the use of rollers. In the background a well-dressed man, Major Mallet, is standing talking to a demurely seated lady, Ellen.[37] In the foreground two other women are rolling the lawn. The caption reads: 'Croquet Maniac (a trifle jealous perhaps): "Well, if Ellen does not mean to help us, she need not make Major Mallet idle, too!".'[38] Here sexual jealousy seems to provide an added strand to the madness ('maniac') narrative, a strand also, perhaps, implied in the previous cartoon.

In depicting hunting too, conventional cartoons show predominantly slim, attractive young women wearing hats set at a slightly rakish angle and tight-waisted riding jackets, often in pursuit of prospective partners, and not the fox. The caption to a cartoon of 1875 shows a young lady who has missed the hunt asking: 'Do you know where the hounds are, Robins?' The old keeper replies, 'compassionately': 'Y'are just too late, miss, the gentlemen are all gone.'

In the 1860s and 1870s women were only playing at playing games, constrained by costume and custom, but by the 1880s sporting women and 'new women' in general were seeking more liberty and more strenuous games. By the 1890s women are shown playing golf and cricket, and even, much to *Punch*'s disgust, climbing in the Alps, as well as taking part in hunting and other field sports. One way in which *Punch* responded was by placing an increased emphasis on the portrayal of women who challenge male boundaries as masculine, and thus unfeminine, freakish, over-muscular and over-active in their relations with men. A cartoon entitled 'The Course of True Love' (1894) shows a scene of a young couple, a curate named the Rev. Spooner and Miss Di, on the bank of a small stream, watching the hounds on the drag of an otter. Miss Di, 'six feet in her stockings, to deeply enamoured curate, five feet three in his, whom she has inveigled out

Otter-hunting', says: 'Oh, do just pick me up and carry me across. It's rather deep, don't you know.' In parentheses the writer states that 'The Rev. Spooner's sensations are somewhat mixed.' For male readers there is humour in Miss Di's expectation that her suitor will fulfil the traditionally expected male role, while she fails to fulfil hers. It may also be the case that, for readers steeped in classical mythology, anyone named Diana would be recognisable as the Roman goddess of the hunt, suggesting, perhaps, that it is not just the otter that is being hunted. The cartoonist neatly locates the context still further by the (probably quite careful) choice of the name 'Spooner', 'spooning' being the usual term used in Victorian times for the early stages of a romantic entanglement, while 'spoonerisms' allowed the creation of *double entendres*. The apparent romantic turbulence on the face of the lovelorn curate, given the choice between carrying Miss Di and getting totally soaked, or refusing and thus risking future rejection, was presumably a further source of amusement.[39] The world of female cycling brought out further *Punch* cartoons employing euphemisms and puns to criticise the sport by linking cycling and immorality, and attacking the immodesty of 'rational' dress.[40]

A further reason why *Punch*'s cartoonists opposed competitive women in sport was the possibility that bookmakers, who were well beyond the boundaries of the respectable, might actually become interested and find a source of revenue in female sporting contests. The thought provided the basis for an attack on women's tennis. A cartoon entitled 'Caution to Lady Championesses' (1887) shows a tennis match between Miss Harriet de Vere Talboys and the Hon. Emily Vavasour, with a 'chorus' of bookmakers shouting 'Go it 'Arriet! Three to one on Hemily etc. etc.'[41] It is even possible that the word 'chorus' was chosen to indicate that such incidents resemble Greek tragedy.

However, by the end of the century, with the increased emphasis on women's suffrage and emancipation, there was, perhaps, a panicked sense that there were a few 'new women' whose enthusiasm and intensity in action might be equal to those of men. Hockey was an early target for *Punch*'s attacks. Following the first women's inter-university hockey match, it sarcastically warned that the Cambridge triumph rendered 'insignificant' all men's team victories in other sports.[42] Another of the dominant images of this period, found in a number of comics, is represented by *Punch*'s picture of 'Our Ladies' Hockey Club' (1899), showing a highly active set of female players with their sticks thrusting at the ball while a man, with his cap just falling off, unavailingly tries to avoid them. The heavily ironic caption announces that 'one of the inferior sex who volunteered to umpire soon discovered his office was no sinecure'.[43]

Punch and the cult of athleticism

While it might be expected that a periodical as (relatively) conservative as *Punch* would show hostility to the incursion of women into sport, it may seem at first sight more surprising that its cartoons also ridicule the highly powerful, popular and increasingly pervasive cult of athleticism that first emerged in the mid-nineteenth century in the English public schools. By the late nineteenth century compulsory games had been enthusiastically adopted in the majority of British public schools. Its consolidation can be seen through the evolving provision of games facilities, the anti-intellectual contempt for academic learning on the part of many boys and some masters, and the growing number of robust public school pedagogues who loved games.[44] Yet while athleticism was undoubtedly a dominant ideology in most schools, it was not all-pervasive, and *Punch* was a constant critic of the values, attitudes and practices associated with it, holding up to ridicule many of its manifest preoccupations. Here again *Punch*'s sporting cartoons chart the ground for a battle over activities that could be seen as respectable by some, unrespectable by others.

The powerful forces of ideological rhetoric that created the athletic heroes, 'bloods' and 'hearties' who were to make such an impact on national and global sporting culture failed to impress *Punch*'s cartoonists, who were largely men of an older generation, perhaps more bookish and certainly more resistant to sporting culture. In their view, it appears, schools were there to provide an appropriate and more intellectual education, and athleticism was seen as unrespectable part of an anti-intellectual approach. A cartoon of 1873, for example, ridicules the 'seasonable athletics' honeymoon of two former public school pupils who take their new wives on a 30-miles-a-day walking tour.[45] By 1889 a picture of a stern, firm-chested, muscular housemaster looming over a small, timorous pupil named Fitzmilksoppe is captioned 'The New Tyranny', a title that perfectly summarises *Punch*'s view of the extent to which compulsory games had come to dominate the curriculum and the thinking of staff. As the master in question tells the boy: 'Of course you needn't *work*, Fitzmilksoppe, but *play* you *must*, and *shall*!'

Public school athletes increasingly carried their sporting preoccupations from school to university. In the 1870s *Punch* began to ridicule the evolution of muscularity at the universities (by which it generally meant only the two 'ancient' universities of Oxford and Cambridge), where brawn increasingly dominated brains, especially in those colleges where there were supportive dons with sporting enthusiasms.[46] An early example, from 1872, shows a university rowing club room overlooking the river, with wine glasses and a bottle, and undergraduates in rowing kit. An 'unsuccessful oar' asks his trainer: 'I say, Muscles, how do you account for my breaking down?' The trainer, who, judging by his deference and his dialect, is work-ing-class, explains reproachfully: 'Wery easily, sir. Yer would read while yer wos in course o' trainin' and I always told yer that books and literatoor and them things spiled the 'ands, and wos death to a good education.'[47] By the end of the nineteenth century, when athleticism had become a legitimised and solidly sustained feature of university life, *Punch* showed how games-playing and anti-literary prejudices could also help to demonstrate male students' masculinity to prospective female partners.[48] A cartoon of 1897 shows a 'muscular undergraduate' walking in the country with a parasol-twirling young lady, 'Miss Girton' (Girton, established in 1873, was the first women's college in Cambridge). She asks him if he likes Browning. The undergraduate, clearly feeling that he can confide in his companion, replies: 'Well, to tell the truth, I'd as soon read a timetable!'

Cartoons about sport in *Ally Sloper's Half Holiday*

The cartoons from the other periodical to be discussed here, *Ally Sloper's Half Holiday* (1884–1916), cover a somewhat later period and seem more in tune with the new world of popular leisure than *Punch* was. *ASHH* boasted the largest circulation of any British illustrated paper of the period, some 340,000 copies.[49] It had a readership that, if the evidence of competition winners is reliable, was largely a mixture of members of the lower middle class and the working class, and mainly between 16 and 30 years old, while just under one fifth of its competition winners were women, including some who used pseudonyms, such as a 'a saucy young girl of 19', which hints at 'boldness' and attempts to shock. Although about half of the competition winners had addresses in London or elsewhere in southeastern England, the readership of *ASHH* covered the whole of the United Kingdom, with regu-lar winners from the Midlands and the North of England, and occasional winners from Scotland and Ireland. The paper's pictures of the eponymous Ally Sloper, an *arriviste* at such major metropolitan events as the Derby, Ascot, the Henley Regatta, the Oxford and Cambridge Boat Race or the Eton and Harrow cricket match, both flattered and encouraged aspirants to 'fashionable' life, while simultaneously amusing and comforting their social superiors.

Some of the cartoons also reveal the need that many in the middle class felt to maintain appearances and a front, to create the image of respectabil-ity or membership of the 'fast set', rather than the reality, as well as the related social aspirations of the spurious 'gent', often demonstrated by medical students, clerks and other related groups among the readers of *ASHH*. Ally Sloper gives life to such pretensions. The Victorian admirers of Sloper – the impostor and confidence trickster *par excellence*, the fake *flaneur* in pursuit of 'adventure', who moves among and regularly adopts the manners, style or dress of the 'fast' upper and middle classes – knew that Sloper regularly claimed expertise. He describes himself as 'the eminent *litterateur*'. He constantly claims to be able to steer, row, shoot, referee or bat, but, to the delight of his readers, he nearly always comes to grief. In comic reality his achievements are limited to being 'Stroke of the Battersea Bounders Rowing Club eight'; 'perpetual long slip' of the Mildew Court CC'; 'colonel of that crack Volunteer corps, the 1st Shoe Lane Shifters'; captain of the 'gallant craft, the *Tootsie Belle*'; and rider of a run-down race-horse, The Skunk.[50] Sloper not only claims skills that he lacks, but at times concocts a spurious background, or even sometimes impersonates others for gain. The Sloper family regularly attend the annual Eton and Harrow match, for example, which had become a key annual event, followed enthusiastically by thousands, and attracting former pupils, the relatives of those playing and a wider spectatorship that showed the increasing importance of the code of public school athleticism in wider middle-class society. In 1885 we find Sloper among the spectators, dressed in an Eton collar, jacket and other appropriate accoutrements, telling a group of admiring young women 'that he well remembered being at Eton as a boy', although he is somewhat let down by his more proletarian wife, clutching her packet of ham sand-wiches and her bottle of Bass beer.[51] In 1895, the year when a national shilling testimonial was organised for W.G. Grace by the *Daily Telegraph*, Sloper puts on a false bushy beard and promptly passes himself off down at Clacton as the one and only Dr Grace in an attempt to raise money, although his assumed identity soon collapses and he has to make a 'hasty and undig-nified' exit.[52] Yet the same time Ally is popular and is made welcome in wealthy sporting society. His friends include the impecunious and less 'respectable' aristocrats, Dook Snook, Lord Bob and the Hon. Billy, and he has tea with the Queen. Evidently, for Sloper respectability means having the confidence, appearance and front to carry off the charade.

The captions on the Sloper cartoons often purport to be extracts from his daughter Tootsie Sloper's correspondence. Tootsie is an actress at the 'Friv' (the Frivolity Theatre) and therefore a participant in the glamorous, highly charged and purportedly permissive world of popular entertainment. Her by-line, 'The Well-Regulated Girl', suggests a calculated, retained and restrained sense of sexuality, while her sense of maintaining appearances is well-illustrated by the way in which, when her fiancé Lord Bob takes a villa

Figure 6.5. 'Eton and Harrow: the weather-beaten Fabric a boy again'. Source: *Ally Sloper's Half Holiday*, vol. II, no. 63, 11 July 1885.

at Epsom for Derby week to share with his friends and invites six girls from the Friv, Tootsie makes sure to tell the readers both that the girls 'brought their mas, of course, for propriety's sake', but also that when she sets off for the Downs 'we pack them in a waggonette and tell the man to take care and lose them somewhere a long way off us on the other side of the course'.[53]

The captions often show Tootsie's embarrassment at her 'Pa' when he arrives uninvited to join her and the other 'girls from the Friv', who are regularly taken by their escorts to sporting events. A picture illustrating the 'Terrible Scene at Henley Regatta' is accompanied by Tootsie's statement that:

> I don't mind saying it was a terrible shock to all of us on the 'Friv' launch to find Poor Pa was on board as nobody had invited him. Some said 'Put him ashore' and others 'Put him overboard' for it really was too bad of him! But Pa settled it himself by falling backwards over the side, singing 'The Last Rose of Summer'. Then there was a scene if you like. And the brandies and whiskies it did take to bring him round. Then he went to sleep, and at first we thought, when he began snoring, that something was wrong with the engine.[54]

ASHH also provides a clear picture of the life of the 'fast' set at such major events, a life that encompasses all the disreputable pleasures that were disapproved of when found among the working class: copious drinking of alcohol, philandering and betting. The cartoons conflate such pleasures in the person of Ally, who is simultaneously plebeian and 'fast'. A cartoon of Ally at the Derby shows him dominating the scene, sharing a carriage with three glamorous women and drinking champagne, which is spurting orgiastically out of his bottle, while well-dressed aristocrats below the carriage pay court to all four and a bookmaker offers them odds on the race. The link between betting and the ambiguously 'respectable' moral culture of the comic is reinforced by the caption: 'THE FIRST FAVOURITE EVERY-WHERE' and the bookmaker announcing: 'Now my Sportive Noblemen and Festive Dames! Plank down the plebeian penny! Beg, borrow or steal, or even work for it – but get it, anyway, and plank it down. A moral certainty: – Sloper . . . . . 1st. THE REST NOWHERE.'[55] Sloper was also, in true rhyming slang, a 'toper', with a great love of the bottle, yet he unfailingly chooses the appropriate drink for the various events – champagne at Epsom and Ascot, Chablis on the River Thames, or gin when hunting.

As the paper's circulation indicates, despite, or perhaps because of, his being an over-the-top, womanising, heavy-drinking impostor, Sloper was a sympathetic comic character, close enough to reality to be understood and recognised, yet somehow inoffensive, so that readers could laugh at him without mocking themselves. At the same time, it may be argued, he shows up the limitations of any respectable reading of late Victorian society, since his is a character capable of multiple readings. He could epitomise the falseness and hypocrisy of some middle-class behaviour to some working-class readers. To some middle-class readers he perhaps pointed up the poor taste

Figure 6.6. 'The first favourite everywhere'. Source: *Ally Sloper's Half Holiday*, vol. II, no. 58, 6 June 1885.

and incompetence of the impostor and social climber, a person who often gets his comeuppance. To still others his drinking and randiness could well have offered a social model.

Women's sport was also covered by *ASHH*. While *Punch* was largely opposed to the idea that women should take part in sport, and showed predominantly individualistic forms of sport throughout the second half of the nineteenth century, *ASHH* by contrast signalled the participation of women in sports that required a greater degree of competitiveness, more rigorous physical exertion and team collaboration. This suggests that such participation was becoming more respectable, although *ASHH* still gently mocked female participation. Tootsie Sloper, referring to the matches for the Ladies' Lawn Tennis Championship, argues that 'all well-regulated girls ... should play at lawn tennis and develop their muscles. Muscles come in handy if you get married – when he gets tiresome, you can let him have one proper, straight from the shoulder.' A little later she says that 'every well-regulated girl might as well know how to play tennis, but very few look at all graceful when playing it'. She claims to be 'among the cracks' of the Chiswick Park Club, where her dress 'was the talk of the whole place, the men delighted and the women spiteful'.[56] Here readings about male concern with over-muscularity and the affront that it potentially posed to traditional roles in marriage are coupled, it seems, with a more emancipated reading about female independence, while older themes about female concern with appearance and attracting men resurface in new forms.

In the 1890s, when Thomas took over from Baxter as cartoonist, a more modernistic theme was introduced in which Sloper was occasionally used as an incompetent sporting foil to suggest that some young women might play sports better than many older men. This technique was carried out through the enhanced foregrounding given to Tootsie and the 'girls from the Friv' as in some way sporting participants at the various sporting events that Ally attended. This, perhaps, reflects the sporting and social freedoms to which some young women readers aspired.

The first reference to women's football comes in October 1885, when Tootsie tries to recruit her own club. Her advertisement asks prospective members to send in their names and addresses, 'accompanied by their age, height and fighting weight'. She is anxious, she claims, to 'get up a thoroughly strong team and so prove once more the utter uselessness of men'.[57] In March 1895 the 'Friv' girls are shown as having recently formed a Ladies' Football Club, and 'profess their ability to knock corners of any team composed of men male things in the United Kingdom'.[58] Ally is pressed into service as referee, but finds it a 'ticklish job', since he is expected to rule in accord with the girls' wishes, while the girls are portrayed arguing among themselves over the appropriate decision. Some of the older *Punch* subtext survives here too, not only in the girls' lack of clarity about the rules, but in a picture of a girl tidying her hair while waiting for a decision, and the knee-length attire, slimness and general attractiveness of the girls pictured, a parasexual dimension that is found in almost all cartoons of sporting females at this period and can be paralleled by pictures of barmaids.[59] An *ASHH* text later the same year draws this out further,

his Copy of "ALLY SLOPER" is a **Railway Accident Life Policy for £150.** (Nine Claims already Paid.)

ally Sloper's Half Holiday

FOUNDED AND CONDUCTED BY GILBERT DALZIEL.

Vol. XII.—No. 567.] SATURDAY, MARCH 9, 1895. [ONE PENNY.

A TICKLISH JOB.

*" That football is a charming pastime no one can possibly deny. The 'Friv.' girls, who have recently formed themselves into a Ladies' Football Club, are enraptured with the game, and profess their ability to knock corners off any team composed of men nale things in the United Kingdom. Poor Pa, who has been pressed into their ranks as referee, is not quite so enthusiastic over the game: probably this is to be accounted for by the fact that his ruling is not always in accord with the girls' wishes. In time, doubtless, Dad will get used to his new vocation. At present he finds refereeing anything but an enviable task."—*TOOTSIE.

Figure 6.7. 'A ticklish job'. Source: *Ally Sloper's Half Holiday*, vol. XII, no. 567, 9 March 1895.

commenting that 'the members of the club are pleasing to gaze upon, and moreover possess exquisite taste in costume. They will no doubt prove a big attraction wherever they exhibit their *incompetency* and charms' (emphasis added).[60]

An early *Punch* cartoon of 1866 had depicted 'The Boat Race of the Future' with an all-girl crew. *ASHH* took up the same theme in 1895, showing the 'Friv' Girl Eight, coxed by Ally, who is hoping to 'assist and cheer up' the rival Oxford and Cambridge crews, being moved over by a police launch, thanks to Ally's incompetent steering. By June Ally has turned to cricket, with as little success. Tootsie reports that:

> Although perhaps not a second Grace, Papa, nevertheless, flatters himself that he knows just a little bit about cricket. He was there-fore, naturally, considerably offended that his claims were discarded in the selection of an English Eleven to meet Surrey last week. I am rather afraid, though, that those who witnessed his match against eleven 'Arriets on Hampstead Heath, on Monday last, were rather taken aback at his astonishing display. It will be a long time, I fear, before Poor Pa completes 'his' hundredth century, particularly as his scores on the few occasions I have seen him play amounted to 'nil'.[61]

The text weaves in assumed knowledge about W.G. Grace's recent achieve-ment with amusement at Sloper's pretensions. The picture reinforces Sloper's incompetence: a gloved and padded Sloper is hit in the eye by the ball as he makes a wild swipe, and as he steps back one of his spiked shoes treads on the stumps. The members of the women's team are mostly alert, concentrated and active, although they are dressed in flowered hats, dresses and skirts rather than cricket whites.

Conclusion

Sports historians take sport seriously, as do its fans. Yet the humour that surrounds sport is a field ripe for further exploration. The combination of visual material and humorous text in sporting cartoons provides a potent way to help to tease out the meaning of the discursive sporting practices that constitute our understanding of sporting reality. Comic cartoons open up new ways of exploring the attitudes, values and social relationships within sporting participation and spectatorship, and of unpacking the contested meanings of 'respectability' and 'unrespectability'. The cartoons published in *Punch* and *ASHH* demonstrate different class-based and cultural ways of seeing different sporting activities, different approaches to topics such as field sports, national sporting events, women's roles in sport, or the cult of athleticism, but the full potentialities of comics and sporting cartoons remain to be explored. This chapter simply marks out the beginnings of a new and exciting field of exploration for the cultural history of sport.

The increased focus on the visual in modern societies and the burgeoning literature on visual culture have yet to be fully reflected within sports history, although, as part of the 'postmodernist' shifting of interest towards looking at images and the messages they carry, television has become a favoured focus in recent studies of sport.[62] Like some forms of television, cartoons dramatise experience in an immediate, compact way, and provide a code that can help in deconstructing popular interest in sport, and in charting the constantly changing terrain over which battles for sporting respectability have been fought.

The huge amount of other Victorian visual material that has high coverage of sport, such as the *Illustrated London News*, the *Illustrated Times* or the *Day's Doings*, with its unrespectable account of 'romantic events, reports, sporting and theatrical news at home and abroad', has yet to be interrogated. This chapter should be seen as a foray into the field. The satirical attacks on sports such as hunting, the attacks on women's participation or on athleticism in the public schools all stress that the meanings of sport were deeply contested. In the two periodicals surveyed the same activities could be seen as either respectable or unrespectable, depending on audience, artist, context and class. We need to do more to explore what sport actually meant to different sections of Victorian society.[63]

In conclusion, one might point out that until recently sports historians have almost entirely neglected the evidence of the auditory – the history of sporting noise, the language of the terraces, the changes in the technical language of particular sports and the songs sung – although Jeff Hill's recent exploration of the role of 'Abide with Me' in rituals of collective remembrance and social unity between the two world wars provides an excellent example of the potentialities of the field.[64] There has also been a brief analysis of the important rituals, roles and functions of football chants in soccer culture, but we still lack any substantive historical perspective on these.[65] But then noise too is unrespectable.[66]

Part 3:
Vice, violence and virility across Victorian Britain

A heart of darkness? Leisure, respectability and the aesthetics of vice in Victorian Wales

ANDY CROLL AND MARTIN JOHNES

The chapel that Abel attended...was full to capacity. It was a special occasion. The chapel was being visited by a preacher famous for his mane of white hair and the howling vigour of his rhapsodies that had been known to drive the peccant so fast into the arms of conversion they bounced back and returned to their normal quota of dirt all on the same night. (Gwyn Thomas)[1]

And then, suddenly, out of the West, came the Welsh John the Baptist...and like wildfire the great revival spread through Wales. A pale-faced young collier armed with power from God started on his task of saving Wales from the wrath to come. Baptisms in brooks; prayers in pits, sermons in streets...Then, just as suddenly as they had flared and spread, the cleansing fires died down, though not quite out. The young collier–revivalist broke down under the strain, and many of his converts returned to their vomits. But not Harry. (Jack Jones)[2]

Conversion was an important concept in Victorian Wales. Perhaps we should expect little else from a country in which Nonconformity had become woven into the very fabric of 'Welshness' itself.[3] If imaginative literature is any guide, some sinners managed to turn their backs forever on the most dissolute of pasts. For others, the fall from grace was as speedy as it was inevitable. Yet no matter how short-lived the effects of the periodic religious revivals that swept through the land, no matter how quickly the inspiring words of generations of white-haired preachers were forgotten, the notion that the virtuous were engaged in an ongoing struggle against the vicious was a powerful one that surfaced repeatedly in public discourse. The battle was given added significance after the nineteenth century's mid-point. In the late 1840s Welsh respectables were sent reeling by the findings of a royal commission that had been set up to inquire into the state of education in the Principality. The resulting document became known less for its pronouncements on the schooling system than for its slurs on the morality of the Welsh people. It alleged that Welsh women were lascivious, that the Welsh language was a brake on the progress of civilisation and that the chapels had singularly failed in their role as moral guardians. The 'Treason of the Blue Books', as the episode became known, was a seismic event whose shock waves reverberated throughout the remaining decades of the century.[4] Nonconformity was galvanised as a political force and scores of opinion-shapers, commentators and public figures did all they could to repair the damage that they believed had been done to the country's reputation.[5] Increasingly, the public image projected to the wider world and, indeed, to the Welsh themselves was of a Wales that was fervently religious, intensely moralistic and decidedly pure.

Such a mindset produced a peculiarly Manichaean world-view. One was either on the side of the respectables or against them; in the *Cymru bur* ('pure Wales') of the imagination there was no place for moral ambiguity. Moreover, there was a firmly held belief, shared by Victorians on the other side of Offa's Dyke, in models of behavioural consistency.[6] It was generally assumed that the roughs were always rough, the respectables always respectable. That this technique of thinking had its reassuring qualities is clear. Moving through a world populated by knowable and stable groups was infinitely preferable to facing an undifferentiated mass of morally unpredictable strangers. Thanks to the idea of conversion, there was always the possibility of rescuing those lost souls who wanted to substitute one way of life for another.

However, notwithstanding the deepest-held hopes of many contemporaries, historians have become increasingly aware that the boundary between the respectable and its ever present 'Other', the disreputable, was far from stable and fixed. Lived experiences were too complex to be boxed; deviations from the paths of righteousness could, and did, occur. Thus, Peter Bailey has noted how a fictional working-class character, Bill Banks, is more or less respectable depending upon the social context within which he operates. When mixing with his social betters, Banks is capable of conforming to their expectations; conversely, when out of their gaze he is just as capable of getting drunk and behaving in an altogether 'rough' fashion.[7] Others have drawn attention to the way in which many reputable, well-heeled males saw prostitution as 'both necessary and inevitable'.[8]

Yet if historians fully recognise that the precise meanings of 'respectability' depended upon the contexts within which they were being articulated, the sheer multiplicity and fluidity of those contexts has often gone unnoticed.[9] Rapid industrialisation and urbanisation, both processes that were particularly pronounced in Wales during the second half of the century, served only to problematise respectability even more. Far from leading to a relaxation of standards, such uncertainties merely heightened the concerns of 'civilised' society. If the roughs were to be kept outside the gates, respectability had constantly to be defined, policed and redefined. It is argued here that, because of these anxieties, 'virtuous Wales' was necessarily obsessed with the very things that it claimed so vigorously to detest: the salacious, the scandalous and the disreputable. A preoccupation with viciousness lay at the heart of *Cymru bur*.[10] This obsession is examined through the lens of leisure, a vital field within which many of these concerns about respectability were registered. Further, it is contended that the fascination with the disreputable was so deep-seated that contemplation of the vicious became something of a leisure pursuit in its own right.

The moving frontiers of respectability

That notions of respectability were contested and malleable is not surprising, given that Victorian Wales was itself in flux. The nation was becoming increasingly urbanised, with the southern ports and coalfield emerging as the most significant nodes of growth. Thousands traded in the poverty and dreariness of Welsh rural life for the excitement and regular wages of the burgeoning industrial towns and valleys. Because respectability was an inherently spatial concept, such sweeping changes helped to disrupt further already contested notions of what constituted acceptable behaviour. This truth frequently revealed itself to contemporaries in the realm of popular leisure.

Take, for instance, the bewildering situation facing inhabitants of the iron settlements located on the northern rim of the coalfield. The townships clustered around Merthyr Tydfil were pre-eminent among these, both in size and in their importance in the iron trade.[11] In the first half of the nineteenth century decades of rapid urban growth required individuals to familiarise themselves with an ever-changing landscape. Within a single lifetime the relationships that obtained between urban dwellers and the spaces through which they moved every day could be redrawn a number of times. An indication of just how often that relationship could be renegotiated was provided in 1861, during a dispute between Merthyr Local Board of Health and one

William Evans, a property-owner in Dowlais. The board was keen to determine who owned Union Street, in order to decide who should pay for any
improvements. In the ensuing court case Lewis Lewis, an agent of the
Dowlais Iron Company since 1826, was called as an expert witness. He was
asked to share his remembrances of old Dowlais, and to trace the constantly
shifting boundary between public and private space. Lewis recalled the
street in question before houses had been built, when it was the property of
the company 'and nobody was allowed to pass along it; I was ordered to
oppose people passing that way'. At that stage it was primarily used by
horses moving from their stables to the lower works. However, following
the construction of the nearby Market House the horses had to share the
street with a tram-road, which was laid down to bring stone for the building.
Lewis then described nearby Chapel Street: 'neither the horses of the
company nor the public were allowed to pass through it; it was considered
private property, and the company's men were fined if they passed up that
way'. He was responsible for instructing the local population in the correct
use of the street: 'I have turned them back many times; I turned the
Company's hauliers off, and told them they must not pass up that way, and
believe they abstained from doing so after this caution.' Union Street
appears to have been a rather more tempting thoroughfare, however, and the
company was forced to leave wagons in the road all night and on Saturdays
to make it impossible for people to pass.[12] Thus, as Lewis charted the ebb
and flow of human beings, horses and building materials through certain
urban spaces at certain times, the magistrates were presented with a micro-
history of two or three streets in Dowlais. As the built form of the town
developed, so individuals had to learn the new geographical patterns that
marked out private from public.

It is clear that such spatial niceties mattered in the mushrooming iron
towns. If their inhabitants forgot to update their mental maps of their town,
or had not made the effort to construct such maps in the first place, the local
magistrates were always on hand to educate them. When, in 1896, a boy was
summoned for playing with a bat and ball in a Merthyr street, his mother
explained to the bench that 'she had herself played in the street 40 years ago,
and games had always been played there, as the children had nowhere else
to play'.[13] The magistrate sympathised with her argument, but fined the boy
two shillings anyway. Similar lessons were dispensed to those 'greenhorns'
who had just arrived in the town. When another William Evans was caught
playing quoits in a field owned by the Dowlais Iron Company, he was
charged with causing 'wilful damage' to the company's land, to the extent
of one penny. In his defence Evans explained that 'he came from
Cardiganshire, where they were allowed to play where they liked, and

having only been in Dowlais for a week, he did not know that he was doing any harm'. His ignorance cost him five shillings.[14] Conversely, those with the necessary geographical knowledge could skilfully evade the clutches of the law. In 1861 two men were charged with being drunk and riotous, after having both been found stripped to the waist in readiness for a prize-fight. Despite compelling evidence against them and the fact that the police sergeant urged the magistrates to make an example of them, the men walked free from the court simply because they chose to hold their pugilistic encounter in a privately owned field rather than on a public thoroughfare.[15] The 'where' of popular leisure was often crucial.

This was as true in rural Wales as it was in the new urban centres. Different attitudes to poaching, for instance, largely depended upon notions of ownership and expectations regarding popular rights.[16] There was a wide-spread feeling among many members of the rural working class that, notwithstanding the pronouncements of the law, poaching was a perfectly legitimate activity. Thus, it was common for poachers to appeal to the 'immemorial rights' of locals to take game and fish from particular loca-tions, or even from the entire countryside. The local prevalence of such attitudes may have been the reason why many landowners in Carmarthenshire had to employ English gamekeepers. Class tensions undoubtedly played a role in determining attitudes towards poaching. As the *Cambrian News* noted, 'The workmen of this county do not recognise the divine rights of a game-preserving class.'[17] That may have been the case, but those workmen still found themselves at the mercy of local landowners. When, in 1881, a young man was hauled before Merthyr magistrates for trespass after fishing on Lord Aberdare's land, he protested that Aberdare himself had met him there on previous occasions and had not complained.[18] His protestations fell on deaf ears and a former respectable found himself turned into a rough because of changing spatial sensibilities on the part of his social superiors.

If notions of respectability were in part determined by spatial considera-tions, they were also influenced by temporal concerns. Nostalgia was the key here. For many observers in England looking back to a golden age became an important way of making sense of a turbulent present and an uncertain future. In the process towns came to embody spiritual and physical decay, while rusticity was seen as an integral component of a wholesome 'Englishness'.[19] Such sentiments also came to the fore in Wales, where some held urbanisa-tion and industrialisation responsible for the decline of the Welsh language and its associated 'folk' culture. There was a proliferation of romanticised images of the *gwerin*, the 'thoughtful and intelligent peasantry' that was deemed to be the only true carrier of 'Welshness'.[20] At the same time there developed a yearning for information about 'traditional' rural pastimes. *Cnappan*, a form of folk football made famous by George Owen's vivid description of the game in early seventeenth-century Pembrokeshire, was the subject of particular interest. Contrasts were drawn between the failings of contemporary football and the glories of a nobler past:

> If only as a slight protest against the barbarous game as it played at present, I should be glad to see the matter [*cnappan*] discussed in your columns...Hundreds *then* played, *now* hundreds, nay, thousands, look on at others playing. There were many thousands present at Shrewsbury on Easter Monday, and the concomitants of betting, drinking and bad language were fearful to contemplate, while the shouting and horse-play on the highway were a terror to peaceful residents passing homewards.[21]

Yet such an understanding relied upon forgetting an inconvenient history that had seen a generation of respectables working to quell a decidedly unruly tradition of folk football, replete with violent behaviour and boisterous nights of drinking.[22] It seems that *cnappan*'s status as a respectable sport could be secured only after it was safely dead.

The same could be said about *gwylmabsantau*, the Welsh equivalent of the English wakes. Richard Suggett has argued that by the mid-Victorian period 'the festival had entered middle-class mythology as a symbol of the values of a departed village community whose harmonious relationships had been destroyed by social changes'.[23] Late-Victorian commentators might praise the festivals as 'healthy, spontaneous, and full of [a] heartfelt sense of enjoyment',[24] but they were far less forgiving when their pleasure-seeking contemporaries indulged in the sort of violence and drinking bouts that had made the wakes so enjoyable. Such misremembrances abounded in late nineteenth-century Wales. Thus, in 1882 one observer could even set about romanticising the public drunk. Thinking of 'the pugnacious character of Merthyr people' in the 1830s and 1840s, he recalled a row of inns and public houses opposite a local churchyard, 'and bad indeed would be the luck if no colliers or miners quarrelled over their cups in some one of them, and streamed out in to the road to "have it out" in a pitched battle'. The immense confusion, flowing blood, shouting spectators and production of black eyes would 'generally' end with 'each fighting man shaking hands with his antagonist, and swearing eternal friendship, both declaring they had always thought each other the best of fellows alive and, now being sure of it, they must return to the public to wash away the little misunderstanding in deep potations'.[25]

This nostalgic evocation of drunken violence was penned at a moment of intense concern about the problem of public drunkenness in urban South Wales. The Welsh Sunday Closing Act had just been introduced, and newspapers were full of reports pondering the scale of the problem and gloomily speculating about the parlous state of modern 'civilisation'. As such, articles celebrating the drunks of a bygone era suited the mood perfectly. Current angst about public drunkenness was justified because today's male and (even worse) female drunkards 'prowled' around the streets, terrorised neighbourhoods, insulted women and molested children, and were clearly devoid of any noble sentiments.[26] How different from the good old days when drink-inspired (and always male) pugilists were at heart honourable colliers who kept their fights to themselves, and resolved their differences amicably. As was the case with the rehabilitation of events such as the *gwylmabsantau*, in the face of a recalcitrant present in which the vicious was apparently all around, at least an unruly past could be *made* respectable.[27]

The impulse to romanticise and 'respectabilise' a past that was just within the grasp of living memory was given added urgency by the 'revolution in leisure' that was unfolding throughout the British Isles. While recent years have seen a move away from arguments predicated upon notions of sharp disjunctures in leisure history, there is still widespread agreement that the second half of the nineteenth century was a period marked by innovation and invention.[28] The explosion of new pursuits and pastimes during these years posed fresh challenges to those intent upon categorising recreations into the rational and the irrational. Faced with the prospect of having to contend with such novel characters as the woman cyclist or the woman footballer,[29] many a moraliser cast a longing eye, perhaps not surprisingly, back to an earlier age, in which things seemed somehow more straightforward.

Nostalgia could offer only a temporary hiding place, however. In the real world of mid-Victorian and, especially, late-Victorian Wales the proliferation of entertainments and diversions resulted in a continually moving frontier of respectability, as the forces of commercialisation and popular demand led to the promotion of formerly disreputable pursuits into the pantheon of the respectable. Take cycling, for instance. An activity that generated all manner of fears, including worries about 'bicycle face', a condition said to be produced as a consequence of moving against the wind at great speeds,[30] it was particularly well-placed to provoke concerns about the involvement of women. When female cyclists first appeared on the streets of urban South Wales during the bicycle craze of the 1890s, notions of what constituted the 'feminine respectable' were well and truly disrupted. In addition to worrying about the range of medical problems that were thought to accompany the pursuit, a number of observers were disturbed by the overtly sexual aura of the 'bloomer'-wearing women sat astride their cycles.[31] Given such attitudes, the early pioneers were frequently subjected to 'gross abuse by the boorish curs and loafers that loiter by the roadsides'.[32] One woman felt so threatened riding around the centre of Merthyr in her 'rational dress' that she wore a skirt during her travels through the public streets and then changed into her bloomers only when she had left the town. Yet notwithstanding the initial widespread hostility to female cyclists, within only a few years there were signs that they were being assimilated into the respectable mainstream. As the *Merthyr Express* put it in 1897, 'why shouldn't lady cyclists wear bloomers? The old argument that it is unwomanly is played out. Nothing is unwomanly that is natural, and "bloomers" form the most natural riding habit for the lady cyclist.'[33] When a new cycle club was established in Merthyr in the following year, enough progress had been made for another commentator, writing in the same newspaper, to note that the 'traveller on wheels' was no longer regarded as a 'savage invader'.[34] Familiarity, in this case at least, bred a grudging acceptance.

Cycling was just one among many crazes and innovations that swept the urban areas in particular during the second half of the nineteenth century. Entrepreneurs of leisure kept a careful eye on changes in popular taste as they attempted to cash in on the latest fads. Skating rinks, billiard halls, bicycle race-tracks, running tracks, coffee houses, gymnasiums, and fish-and-chip stalls were among the new leisure institutions that appeared during these years. Promoters of events as varied as pedestrianism and 'ping-pong' worked hard to capture the imagination, and the pennies, of the pleasure-seeking public. Against such a kaleidoscopic and ever-changing background respectability necessarily had to be flexible enough to accommodate all suitable newcomers and reformed old-stagers. Ultimately it is the concept's malleability that emerges as one of the most striking features of the landscape of late-Victorian leisure. Of course, the members of what has since come to be known as the 'moral majority' were always going to find some pastimes wanting, yet there was still room for manoeuvre, even in the case of activities that had previously appeared to be unproblematically 'rough'. In pugilism, for example, the introduction of gloves at least softened the more brutalising aspects of the old bare-knuckle days. Moreover, the increased regulation of many of the venues in which the sport was carried out also added at least a fig-leaf of respectability.[35] The same came to be true of the drink trade, that erstwhile bastion of the disreputable and the sinful. The latter years of the century witnessed members of the trade effecting large-scale improvements in commercial drinking places, partly as a consequence of more stringent surveillance on the part of the licensing authorities, but also because it made good business sense to refashion the old, cramped beerhouses. The future lay with bigger, brighter and more open public houses, which could accommodate more drinkers, *and* satisfy the ever-watchful magistrates and police.[36] To be sure, old habits died hard and some chapels continued to debate whether publicans could ever be true Christians. A few went so far as to try to expel licensed victuallers from their congregations, although on at least one such occasion, in Merthyr in 1893, the majority of the congregation voted against the proposal.[37] By the latter decades of the century, even in Nonconformist Wales, members of the trade could rise through the ranks of respectable society and occupy the highest offices of local government. For example, David Williams, the owner of the Taff Vale brewery, was High Constable of Merthyr three times in succession, as well as being a member of the Board of Health and the Local Board of Guardians.[38]

Contemplating disreputable Wales

Thus far, attention has been concentrated upon the manner in which the ever-changing contexts of leisure in a rapidly urbanising society served to problematise and disrupt easy categorisations of 'respectable' and 'rough'. Such a state of flux did not result in an abandonment of the belief that meanings could and should be fixed. On the contrary, many late Victorians remained as convinced as their predecessors had been that the disreputable could be identified and surgically separated out from the reputable. As a consequence, the contemplation of the disreputable 'Other' became something of a cultural obsession, an obsession that was satisfied during leisure hours through the careful perusal of the newspapers. Not only was the vicious encountered in the realm of recreation; its study was elevated into a national pastime.

Local newspapers were well-placed to facilitate the circulation of images depicting the darker side of late nineteenth-century life. The repeal of many of the various newspaper taxes and duties, plus the presence of a sizeable and growing reading public, combined to have a massive impact upon the newspaper industry. In 1855 alone some 17 new provincial papers appeared, although it was the 20 years leading up to 1890 that saw the real transformation of the provincial press in Britain.[39] By the 1890s every self-respecting town possessed its own local paper; many could boast two, three or even more. Recent work has highlighted how many respectable contemporaries despaired of the 'low-class' nature of the national Sunday papers, such as *Lloyd's Weekly Newspaper* or the *News of the World*.[40] However, it is worth noting the extent to which even the 'better class' of local dailies and weeklies were content enough to fill their pages with the sensational and the salacious. Reports detailed the unedifying goings-on in the local courts; correspondence columns gave readers opportunities to describe their own narrow brushes with the 'hobble-de-hoys' and 'Yahoos' that could be found on every street corner;[41] and the work of the 'social explorers', those most Victorian of authors, was written precisely with the respectable readers of these newspapers in mind. The diligent study of the degraded and demoralised became a necessary activity in a world in which maintenance of character and reputation was everything. After all, only by regularly confronting the vicious in all its terrible glory could self-confessed respectables remind themselves that they were indeed located on the right side of the sometimes wafer-thin line. Only by coming face to face with the 'Other' could they attempt to effect social closure, and draw a comforting line between themselves and their uncivilised counterparts in the slums and rookeries; only by reading about the fallen could they hope to avoid the same fate themselves.

Aspirants to respectability read about such calamities voraciously and in great detail – indeed, the greater the detail the better. Newspapers sold to members of respectable society were filled with gratuitous accounts of the sordid, the disreputable and the sinful. When, in 1903, news broke that a William Lewis from Aberfan had been arrested on a charge of persistent cruelty to his wife, the papers made sure their readers were kept apprised of all the relevant facts. The case was all the more newsworthy because Lewis was a pastor of a Welsh Baptist church. When it transpired that he had been of 'drunken habits', his fall from grace was complete. Editors determined that this instance of domestic unhappiness, hypocrisy and individual frailty contained enough lessons to justify running it for two weeks. Such stories served as timely reminders of the need to keep to the paths of righteousness, or, failing that, of the need at least to keep all such misdemeanours out of the public gaze.[42]

If the everyday misery and cruelty of others was considered worthy of coverage in depth, it was made all the more alluring if it contained a sexual dimension. Russell Davies, arguing against the idea that Victorians were 'almost entirely repressive and repressed', has put a convincing case to the contrary; in fact, he writes, 'sex was an obsession', albeit one 'which [they] sought to keep quiet'.[43] In important respects they failed miserably. Of course, public discourse was not considered the place for explicit discussions of sexual matters. However, rather than maintain a discreet silence, writers used euphemisms that served as cues to be taken up by the respectable imagination. Prostitutes were accused of 'behaving indecently' or of consorting with their clients round the back of beerhouses 'for a bad purpose';[44] young couples were observed committing 'acts of familiarity' in public places; and narratives of sexual crimes were broken off at key points because the evidence 'proved the charge, but is unfit for publication'.[45] The very silences invited speculation on just what those intimate details might have been. Everything was implied; everything was left to the respectable imagination.

Any doubts as to whether that imagination was capable of overly dwelling on the sexual are dispelled by the observations of Edwin Roberts, a middle-class writer who published an account of his visit to the ironworks of Merthyr Tydfil in 1852. Throughout his narrative he indicates that he is intrigued by the sight of 'girls' working around the kilns and furnaces in the company of '[s]trong brawny men'.[46] More than once he pauses to contemplate the 'tall well-grown girls', who seem to him to be 'as fine-grown and elegantly limbed young creatures' as he has ever seen. Hard work, in itself, has not hurt these young women, for in his estimation, 'handsomer arms and finer busts could not be met with'. He also declares himself impressed by their 'rounded forms'.[47] However, he believes that he has reason to fear for their virtue, as he demonstrates by devoting a considerable amount of space to imagining the countless ways in which it might be lost. While passing an opening near one of the kilns, Roberts observes a 'huge giant of a fellow' playfully wrestling with a woman on the ground: 'while she was half-laughing, half-screaming, and ineffectually struggling in his great grasp, he was stifling her with kisses'. None of their fellow workers pays the slightest attention to the gambolling pair, but Roberts is spellbound. As he watches the man's 'large limbs' sprawl about, the eminently virtuous author finds himself thinking salacious thoughts: 'the whole suggested a grossness', he confesses. Then he has to correct himself, for actually such grossness 'did not exist, for it was only a "lark" – a piece of play – though coarse enough in all conscience.' Or, to be more precise, 'coarse enough' in his 'respectable' conscience. A few moments later, he feels compelled to return to the subject of the 'girls', noting that he has 'never seen anything so soft and charming in its retiring femininity'. They are all the more striking given the sexually charged landscape in which they labour: 'the noise of hammers,... the sounding of the pistons, the hissing of the steam'.[48] It is hardly a wonder then that Roberts is told, presumably after making enquiries, that there have been 'seductions' in such a place and that the 'young masters' play 'the parts of so many sultans among these dingy sultanas... it is not hard to imagine with what success'. He gravely announces that, while not all the women fall victim to such abuses of power, more often than not they do.[49]

Was Roberts the only bourgeois respectable to spend time pondering the various ways in which working-class 'girls' could become 'fallen women'? Such an imagination was certainly well-placed to read the euphemistic Victorian newspapers, turning the implicit into the explicit in the process.

In matters of violence and cruelty, often precious little was left to the imagination. The extent to which this was a world in which the 'aesthetics of vice' were well-appreciated is evidenced by an account of the 'savage brutality' involving a butcher and a live ram published in the *Merthyr Telegraph* in 1855. Notwithstanding the fact that there was no local dimension to the story – the incident occurred in Lutterworth in Leicestershire – the editor clearly thought that it was interesting enough to merit inclusion in the paper. After being introduced to the butcher, Thomas White, readers were invited to consider the full horror of his actions:

[H]aving purchased the animal in question, [White] brought it home in a cart, and deposited it in a hovel adjoining his slaughter-house. He then fetched a large butcher's knife used in the ordinary process of killing, and, having first firmly secured the ram's head, he inserted the knife beneath each of the animal's eyes as far as the bone would allow. The blood spirted [*sic*] out from both wounds, and [the] defendant then stabbed the knife into the creature's nostrils in three distinct places, producing jagged wounds of a frightful character, from which the blood also flowed freely. Some bystanders having remonstrated with the defendant, he burst out into a loud laugh, and adding some coarse observation left the animal in the state described. Shortly afterwards the ram was observed...with its head against a wall, in an almost torbid [*sic*] state, licking into its mouth the blood which poured down its cheeks and nostrils.

The beast was finally put out of its misery 'after suffering extreme agony for more than three hours'.[50] Readers doubtless expressed their revulsion at White's behaviour; indeed, it was assumed by the newspaper that they would be horrified by the account. This, after all, was the 'civilised' mid-nineteenth century, a period in which the campaign against blood sports and cruelty to animals was being vigorously prosecuted.[51] However, apparently no complaints were made against the paper for printing such a graphic depiction of the cruelty inflicted upon the poor animal. This may have been a society that was refining its sensibilities in all sorts of ways, but it was far from being squeamish when it came to contemplation of the visceral.

Squeamishness was also absent when it came to dwelling on viciousness somewhat closer to home. Again, through local newspapers this examination of the unsavoury was elevated into something of an art form. Reports of the proceedings in the police courts were a staple of every local paper throughout the Victorian period and were popular features with many readers. Evidence that the details of the court proceedings were favourites with many ostensibly respectable readers is provided by an incident that occurred in a newsagent's in Dowlais in 1893. A man 'who disported a stand-up collar of snowy whiteness, with cuffs to match, and appeared to be altogether faultlessly dressed', walked into the shop and asked for a copy of the *Merthyr Express*. When he was informed that it was sold out, he inquired: '"Do the *Times* give an account of the trials at Merthyr?"... "Yes" was the reply, "all the trials are reported except the dirty ones." "Have it got anything about the gel swearing the child on Wednesday?" "No." "Then 'tis no good for me; 'twas only for that did I want the *Express*."' The editor of the *Merthyr Times* attempted to cast the man into the ranks of the disreputable: 'We have nothing but the strongest loathing for a thing, calling itself a man, who openly declares that he buys a paper only to read the revolting details of filthy crimes – that he expends his penny only to gloat over woman's shame and man's abuse of trusting confidence.'[52]

Yet such protestations overlooked a number of uncomfortable facts. First, the man's respectable appearance made it difficult to condemn him as a typical 'rough'. Second, despite assurances that details of the 'dirty' trials were left out, there were usually more than enough salacious details included in most weeks' reports to titillate, scandalise and amuse: the endless lists of those convicted for drunk and disorderly offences; the numerous accounts of prostitutes 'behaving indecently' in public; the harrowing details of scores of affiliation orders and bastardy cases; even the most superfluous contextual information in rape cases, including the names of the victims; in short, the airing in public of all manner of private anguishes.[53] The editor may have had only 'the strongest loathing' for those who openly admitted reading about such crimes for amusement, but a nagging doubt must have remained, for if this 'faultlessly dressed' individual admitted to enjoying such material, who could say that other professedly respectable readers did not feel the same?

A final example of the newspapers' willingness to dramatise the disreputable is to be found in their publication of the work of the 'social explorers'. Alan Mayne has drawn attention to the manner in which 'slumland representations were cultural performances'. These performances in part 'explored and sought to resolve bourgeois concerns about the indeterminacies of urban scale', but, as Mayne notes, the popularity of such writings lay in 'the entertaining zestfulness of slumland sensationalism'.[54]

That sensationalism could be found in the pages of the most earnest of news-papers and Wales was no different in this respect from the rest of Victorian Britain. Indeed, with more than enough areas of urban decay of its own, industrial South Wales became a favoured destination for all manner of commentators keen to seek out the degenerate 'Other' and report their find-ings back to civilisation. Once again, much was made of the idea that the world was divided neatly – and immutably – into the virtuous and the vicious. The crossing of that fixed boundary generated much of the excite-ment that lay at the heart of the entire genre of social exploration.

Take, for example, an account of a visit to the 'China' district of Merthyr on a Saturday night in 1866. It was undertaken by one 'Saunterer' on behalf of the readers of the *Merthyr Telegraph*. Only a few hundred yards from the High Street, 'China' comprised a tangle of courts and alleys situated on the banks of the River Taff. During the first half of the nineteenth century it had earned itself a fearsome reputation as a centre of vice and crime, and, despite the achievements of the new police force in tackling some of these prob-lems, in the 1860s the 'Celestial City', as it was popularly referred to by non-residents, still possessed the ability to strike fear into the hearts of civilised citizens.[55] 'Saunterer' depicts the moments leading up to his entrance into 'China' with a high degree of dramatic tension, employing the imagery, the language and the plot structure of adventure stories in an effort to convey the excitement experienced during this foray into the unknown. After reminding his readers of the 'real nature' of the place and the impos-sibility of giving an exact description through the medium of a newspaper, 'Saunterer' recounts his preparations for the journey into the slums. He and his two companions meet in a local inn, where they 'discoursed hot brandy and water, mingled with a quantity of cigar smoke'. While imbibing, they 'freely canvassed the probabilities and improbabilities of our getting safely through our dangerous journey, or the greater likelihood of getting our three adventurous skulls knocked together by some of the "Chinese" bullies'. Because they have heard that 'no ordinarily dressed human being would be safe' in the district, they disguise themselves as policemen, using artificial whiskers to cover their faces. Thus dressed, they begin their 'secret expedi-tion' as the clock strikes one, armed with another bottle of brandy that is to serve as a '"disinfectant" while we passed through the slums of the "Celestial City"'. The tension mounts as these representatives of respectable society pick their way through the streets towards the threshold of 'China'. As they step across the borderline between safety and danger 'Saunterer' pauses to declare dramatically, 'Here, our adventures begin.'

Throughout the report (and others like it[56]), the present tense is invariably used to convey the breathless nature of the intrepid explorers' enterprise.

Meanwhile, numerous asides to the 'gentle reader' are included as means of ensuring the 'correct' response to each new scene. Thus, when the three explorers come across a brothel, 'Saunterer' reminds his readers of the precise nature of his situation: 'here is a real danger. Here I am about to enter an unknown house in a false character, and near an unsafe locality.' Moreover, the vicarious qualities of the project surface frequently as the readers are written into the narrative: 'let us just imagine...'; 'let us, therefore, proceed onwards through this narrow passage before us'; 'Then, here goes!' This is a shared adventure, a shared exploration, that takes crime, viciousness and sin as its subjects. In the tradition of all the best adventure stories, it is episodic. After the excitement of entering the 'Celestial City', meeting prostitutes and their drunken clients, and experiencing the filthy alleyways of 'China', 'Saunterer' brings his tale to a temporary close: 'But, we will rest! Yes, we *must* rest to take one draught from the brandy bottle and nerve ourselves. With this rest, too, I shall close the present letter, as space does not permit me to embody in it my full narrative of "China". Adieu, then, for another week.'[57] His respectable, 'gentle' readers are safely returned to their familiar – and, perhaps, all the more civilised-seeming – surroundings until the next journey into the slums.

So close was the connection between the work of the 'social explorers' and that of imaginative writers that, on more than one occasion, the name of Charles Dickens was invoked by commentators trying to convey the dreadfulness of the urban landscape in South Wales.[58] While the explorers' ostensible aim was to educate, in fact entertainment lay at the heart of the enterprise. Significantly, when the slum-dwellers themselves managed to make their voices heard above the din created by bourgeois respectables they complained about the heightened imagery deployed by such 'cultural outsiders'. The contrast between the two styles highlights the extent to which slumland literature was intended to titillate and thrill. For example, when, in September 1884, 'Polonius', the gossip-columnist for the *Merthyr Express*, commented upon the manner in which 'China' was still 'a disgrace to the town and the respectable inhabitants who reside therein', he reached for the stock phrases that had become shorthand for the awfulness of the slums. He informs his armchair travellers that 'China' and Pedwranfach, another area of poor housing in the town, are 'dens of iniquity', 'colonies of vice and fevers, and filth and degradation', sources of 'disease and corruption'. Those who have not seen such places cannot realise 'the abject state of dilapidation and wretchedness which the appearance of both buildings and inhabitants conveys to the mind'.[59] However, the following week 'Polonius' was chastised for his lazy deployment of the old stereotypes by a resident of the district, one 'I.B.', who argued that:

> All the persons who live at the back of the Black Bull are hard
> working industrious people, who get their living by their
> labour... I am very glad to be able to say that there are not any of
> the persons of the character he refers to living in the neighbour-
> hood of China... I have known... the neighbourhood for
> upwards of eighteen years, as I have lived in Pontstorehouse
> during that time, so that I should know, I think, more of the neigh-
> bourhood than 'Polonius', or any one else that may merely take a
> chance walk to inspect the place... Again, 'Polonius' writes in a
> rather sensational tone about the dilapidated state of both build-
> ings and the inhabitants, but again I can assure him that is not true
> of the cottages at the back of the Black Bull and Ivy Bush, as they
> are kept quite weather proof, and are very comfortable little
> cottages of the class.[60]

Stripped of the 'sensational tone' that characterised the literature that
members of respectable society pored over during their leisure hours, the
discourse of this cultural insider is much more matter-of-fact and sober.
Gone are the gratuitous references to 'vice', 'sin', 'demoralisation' and
'corruption', which gave the social explorers' work such charges of excitement. Gone, too, are the references to the repulsive drunken wretches, to the
'slums', to the exotic-sounding 'Celestial City' and even to 'China' itself,
for 'I.B.' uses that term only when discussing the characterisation of the
neighbourhood by 'Polonius', preferring the more workaday name of
'Pontstorehouse' to describe the district that he says he knows so well.
Instead, readers are presented with a picture of people who are hard-
working and industrious, and live in comfortable little cottages. This may
have been a more accurate representation of a lived reality, but it was much
less histrionic and much less entertaining. As such it was ill-suited to satisfy
the appetites of self-confessed 'respectables', who, in learning about their
binary opposites, could confirm their own civility and vicariously enjoy the
vicious in the process.

Cymru bur's heart of darkness

The highpoint in the history of *Cymru bur* appears to have been reached in
the early years of the twentieth century. In the winter of 1904–5 Wales was
gripped by 'revival' fever as a small group of evangelists toured around the
fleshpots of the South in an effort to save lost souls. They were well

rewarded for their troubles. The idea of conversion was pressed into service, enabling thousands of former sinners to bridge the yawning chasm that – under ordinary circumstances – was supposed to keep the fallen at a safe distance from the saved. The local and regional newspapers detailed the spectacular successes enjoyed by the revivalists and located Wales at the epicentre of a revival that was spreading throughout Christendom. Waves of prostitutes, drunkards, rugby-players and even choral singers renounced their worldly ways and embraced a more spiritual way of life. Publicans were hit as increasing numbers of formerly loyal customers rejected drinking places in favour of prayer meetings. Sports clubs folded and theatres saw audience numbers fall dramatically.[61] The chapels appeared to be the direct beneficiaries of these changes in public taste and their membership figures rose throughout the winter months. At last it seemed that the slurs made during the episode of the 'Treason of the Blue Books' had been shown to be unjust: Wales was indeed the home of pure morals.

Yet at the very moment when the virtuous ethos had apparently triumphed, it proved impossible to eradicate viciousness completely. As befitted a culture that promoted a fascination with the scandalous, the darker side of the revival began to attract public attention. The activities of the evangelists themselves came under suspicion in certain quarters. Unease was registered when it transpired that a photograph of the leading male revivalist, Evan Roberts, 'comforting a female penitent' had in fact been posed for publicity purposes.[62] This revelation merely fuelled speculation regarding the genuineness of the revival. Leading religious figures began to talk about a 'sham Revival, a mockery, a blasphemous travesty of the real thing' and charged Roberts himself with leading this 'mock Revival'.[63] Matters deteriorated further when rumours circulated casting doubt on the propriety of Roberts's relationship with his female evangelists. The 'Welsh John the Baptist', as Roberts had become known, is reported to have been a shy and retiring figure, but he found himself having to issue public statements denying that he had secretly married Annie Davies.[64] Nevertheless, the whiff of scandal remained in the nostrils of many, and this at a time when *Cymru bur* was supposedly at its purest.

Within months the revival had blown itself out and the majority of converts gradually slipped back to their old ways. Ten years later 'pure Wales' was dealt a blow as profound as any dispensed by the education commissioners in 1847. This time it was an 'insider' who caused offence. The stories in Caradoc Evans's pointedly entitled *My People*, a collection first published in 1915, are set in rural West Wales, one of the spiritual homelands of the *gwerin*.[65] Evans's stories paint a picture of a society dominated by the chapel and obsessed with outward displays of piety, yet rotten to the very core. According to Evans, hypocrisy, fear and ignorance were then the predominant values at work in Nonconformist West Wales. He shows the lot of women, commonly idealised as domestic angels, to be utterly miserable, with madness awaiting those who could stand the cruelty of their menfolk no longer. The poor and the uneducated are exploited by their social superiors in every conceivable way. Over them all rule the ministers and their henchmen.

Given that the demons of 1847 had once again been liberated, the reaction of respectable Welsh opinion to Evans's collection of short stories was predictable enough. According to the *Western Mail* it was 'a farrago of filth...the literature of the sewer'.[66] Others agreed: David Lloyd George condemned the author as 'a renegade' and concerted attempts were made to ban the book under the Obscene Publications Act of 1857.[67] News that it had received highly favourable reviews in England served only to heighten the outrage. Such was the extent to which Evans and his work were excoriated that it seems clear that he had touched a raw nerve: if his vignettes had really borne no relation to any reality, they would have been easy to ignore. Few felt that they could ignore *My People*. However, its compelling qualities do not spring not from any depiction of actual happenings. As Evans pointed out to his critics, none of the stories is true; they are merely pieces of fiction. Nevertheless, Evans believed that, taken together, they capture something of the essence of Welsh rural life, something of the hypocrisy that was then a vital lubricant in a culture obsessed with the maintenance of respectable appearances. In writing about such an essence he had exposed *Cymru bur*'s heart of darkness.

As we have seen, in fact, Caradoc Evans was far from being alone in concentrating upon the disreputable. Contemplation of the vicious was something of a national pastime in Wales during the nineteenth and early twentieth centuries. In the realm of leisure there was a constant policing of the boundaries between rough and respectable, as the multiple contexts within which old and new popular cultural practices took place changed and developed. Respectability was a spatial concept: rapid urbanisation problematised behaviour that had hitherto been tolerated. In the countryside, too, the acceptability of 'traditional' customs frequently depended upon the whim of landowners. Temporal concerns also came into play. Those convinced that they were living in a decaying present looked to the past for confirmation of the fact. They rediscovered yesterday's 'rough' pursuits, lamented their passing and bestowed respectability upon them posthumously. They were then used as sticks to beat today's immoral generation. The guardians of virtue and civilisation thus found themselves endlessly on the look-out for viciousness and barbarism, wherever they might lurk. In the process they became veritable connoisseurs of the disreputable. It was this highly cultivated sense of the aesthetics of vice that helped to ensure that their efforts to keep the rough 'Other' outside the boundaries of 'pure Wales' were destined to fail: as Caradoc Evans had reminded them, it had been an ever-present feature of *Cymru bur* all along.

Violence, gamesmanship and the amateur ideal in Victorian middle-class rugby

TONY COLLINS

How much of a 'gentleman' was the Victorian sporting gentleman? The question is not simply one of historical curiosity. The moral tenor of modern sport is still largely derived from, and shaped by, the tenets of Victorian middle-class sporting ethics. Discussions about the use of drugs in sport are framed in terms of a debate about what constitutes 'fair play'. Concerns are regularly voiced about the levels of violence in football and rugby. Players' disputes with match officials, whether tennis umpires at Wimbledon or football referees at Old Trafford, are used by the press to demonstrate the allegedly sad decline in sportsmanship. In addition, the tendency to hark back to a golden age, when sports were apparently played for pure enjoyment, without concern for financial considerations, is a feature of almost all popular discourse on sport.

However, the reality of Victorian middle-class sport was rather different from both its self-image and its image as viewed through the somewhat rosy spectacles of later generations. Not only was violence widespread, but it was privately held to be one of sport's most appealing features. The art of twisting the rules to one's advantage – 'gamesmanship' – was commonplace and outright cheating was often ignored if it was done in the right context. Monetary rewards were regularly paid. Far from playing for pure enjoyment, winning was critical to those who played; and if they could not win many simply stopped playing.

Rugby presents possibly the most illuminating example of this contradiction between the Victorian gentleman's words and his deeds. Until 1995 the Rugby Football Union (RFU) steadfastly upheld the Victorian principles of amateurism, insisting that rugby had a moral quality that set it above all other sports. The RFU's determination to keep its amateur ideals pure in the 1890s led to the cleavage in the game that resulted in the vast majority of its clubs in the north of England leaving the RFU in 1895 to create the semi-professional Northern Union, which later became the Rugby League. The official centenary history of rugby union, published in 1970, claimed, in language possibly more suited to 1870, that it was the sport's amateur ethic that made it unique as 'a chivalrous and character-building game'.

For its devotees rugby union was, to quote the motto of the Barbarians club, a 'game for gentlemen of all classes but never for a bad sportsman in any class'.[1] However, precisely what constituted gentlemanly behaviour was, like 'respectability' itself, a fluid and dynamic category, which involved both the invention and 'uninvention' of traditions in response to the changing circumstances in which rugby football found itself in the second half of the Victorian era.

Gentlemen and players

Who was the Victorian sporting gentleman? In his *Sport and the British* Richard Holt gives a precise definition:

> Fair play was the watchword of the gentleman amateur. The term 'amateur' has come to mean anyone who does not play for pay, but the original meaning was more subtle. Amateurs were gentlemen of the middle and upper classes who played sports that were often enjoyed by the common people – athletics, rowing or cricket, for example – but who played these and other games in a special way. Fair play meant not only respecting the written rules of the game, but abiding by what was generally understood to be the spirit of the game.

Holt develops this theme further: 'The middle-class amateur…had greater pretensions to be "civilised"…The middle-class sportsman saw himself as someone who could hold his passions in check and for whom the enjoyment of the game was more important than the result.'[2]

That many apparent paragons of Victorian sporting virtue failed to live up to such standards is perhaps not surprising. Over the past 20 years a number of historians have uncovered the extent of 'shamateurism' among gentlemen cricketers who were ostensibly amateurs. The highly profitable amateurism of W.G. Grace in particular has come under scrutiny, and the work of historians such as Keith Sandiford, Wray Vamplew and Derek Birley has highlighted the extensive financial arrangements that county cricket clubs entered into in order to support the cricketing ambitions and expenses of their gentlemen amateurs. Indeed, many amateur cricketers received more money from their county clubs than the professionals in the same team did. Possibly the most egregious example of this state of affairs was highlighted by the strike declared by some of the professionals in the England side to play Australia in August 1896. While the captain, W.G. Grace, picked up £40 for each match, double the normal expenses he was paid by his county, Gloucestershire, the professionals in the side received £10 wages for each match and the amateurs received £25 'expenses'.[3]

However, cricket had always had a place for professionalism, albeit a strictly subordinate one until recently. The fact that money made its way across the divide to many of the gentleman amateurs of the sport was generally viewed with equanimity by the cricketing world. Rugby, however, believed itself to be different. In 1886 the RFU introduced a strict code of amateurism, which forbade not only direct payments to players but every other form of remuneration too, including gifts, jobs or payments in kind. Violation of these laws was punished by banishment from the game. Nevertheless, 'understandings' about expenses, similar to those in cricket, were not unknown in the oval ball game. For example, Andrew Stoddart, captain of England at both rugby and cricket, took over as captain for the rugby tour of Australia and New Zealand in 1888 for a payment of at least £200. His fellow tourist, the Welsh international and Cambridge rugby blue W.H. Thomas, was paid £90 for the 30-week tour and demanded a further £3 a week when the tour was extended to cash in on its success. Closer to home, William Bromet, an Oxford blue who played for Tadcaster, claimed expenses of £6 and 13 shillings for turning out for the Yorkshire county side in 1895. The biggest outrage for many of Yorkshire's leading clubs, such as Bradford, Halifax, Huddersfield or Leeds, was the fact that the leading southern sides charged for travelling north to play them. In 1887 Bradford paid Blackheath players £57 and 15 shillings and those of Richmond £42 and 10 shillings in match expenses.[4] The antagonism caused by such financial demands was exacerbated by the fact that the southern teams refused to reciprocate and pay expenses to northern teams that travelled south to play. When Bradford declined to pay Blackheath's expenses in 1893 'The Club', as Blackheath proclaimed itself, immediately cancelled the fixture. Nor was this was a practice confined to devotees of the rugby code of football: the Corinthians, a name even today synonymous with amateurism, charged their soccer opponents £150 a match and were well-known for their liberal dispensation of expenses.[5]

Hacking and violence in rugby

These examples of breaches in the gentleman's code could be thought to be aberrations, untypical of the game as a whole. Such a defence, which was occasionally advanced by supporters of the RFU, would be tenable if it could be demonstrated that such behaviour was indeed anomalous when compared to the conduct of the game as a whole. To what extent therefore did the way that gentlemen played rugby otherwise conform to the ideals of 'fair play'?

As could be expected of a sport that was so closely associated with young men who had been educated at public schools, the pattern for its playing styles and ethics was set in those schools where it was the sport of choice. At its heart was a belief that the violence of the sport would help to foster 'manliness', the ability to give and receive violence without flinching, either physically or metaphorically.[6] Even a cursory glance at Thomas Hughes's novel *Tom Brown's Schooldays*, based on his childhood experiences at Rugby School, demonstrates how central this belief was to the sporting activities of the boys at the school and at those other schools that shared its form of football. East, the character who befriends the new boy Tom Brown, and provides the book's commentary on the culture and norms of the school, proudly describes Rugby's version of football to his new friend: 'it's no joke playing-up in a match, I can tell you. Quite another thing from your private school games. Why, there's been two collar-bones broken this half, and a dozen fellows lamed. And last year a fellow had his leg broken.' The violence of the game is seen as an opportunity for boys to demonstrate their imperviousness to pain and injury; indeed, as East makes clear in the same conversation, many boys took special measures to flaunt their disregard of the dangers inherent in the sport: 'Our house plays the whole school at football. And we all wear white trousers, to show 'em we don't care for hacks.'[7] Hacking, the deliberate kicking of an opponents' shin bones regardless of whether he had the ball, was, after running with the ball in the hands, the most distinctive feature of the school's code of football. Two years after the spectacularly successful publication of Hughes's book a senior pupil writing in the school's magazine, the *New Rugbeian*, pithily described his, and presumably many other pupils', philosophy when playing the game: 'My maxim is hack the ball on when you see it near you, and when you don't, why then hack the fellow next to you.'[8] Even as late as 1923 Old Rugbeians who had been at the school in the 1850s and 1860s could still be found to defend the moral qualities instilled into young boys by the long-abandoned tradition of hacking.[9]

Hacking and the Rugby game's attendant violence was no less prized by those schools that took their lead from Rugby and its sport. Thus Harry Garnett, President of the RFU in 1889, had been introduced to hacking as a boy at Blackheath Proprietary School: 'Boots were made specially with an extra sole piece at the toe, pointed like a ship's ram, and hardened against the bars of the fire, or with a hot poker.' Hacking was inflicted on opponents 'with the utmost violence'. None of this was surprising to those involved in rugby at the time, not least because Garnett's old school was notorious for its unswerving devotion to hacking. Despite being asked by the school's headmaster to stop the practice in the 1860s, they continued to hack their way through opponents and at one point forced the adult Richmond club to abandon a match with them in protest against their tactics. Further north, E.H. Dykes, who founded the Leeds Parish Church rugby team in 1874, had learned the importance of hacking and tripping as a pupil at Durham School: '"Hack him over" was the cry when anyone was running with the ball, and it was the commonest thing to see fellows hacked off their feet. A scrummage was mainly an opportunity for hard hacking.' Such was the seriousness with which hacking was taken that Durham boys would prepare for rugby matches by hammering their shins with pokers in order to harden the skin.[10]

Although Rugby School's version of football was unique in conferring legitimacy on hacking, it would be a mistake to assume that other codes of public school football were free of hacking or violence in general. A debate on the desirability of a common code of football rules to enable the playing of inter-school matches, which took place in *Bell's Life* in the late 1850s, quickly degenerated into a dispute over the 'manliness' of different schools and their codes of football. Perhaps inevitably, a partisan of Rugby's game sought to assert its superiority by expressing the hope that 'no school is so far degenerated as to fear to expose their shins to the chance of a little rough treatment'. However, it was a partisan of Eton's 'dribbling' code of football, which had more in common with modern soccer, who pointed out the dangers of contests between schools: 'shinning [kicking at an opponent's shins] is carried to such an extent at our public schools that it would be greatly increased where jealousy exists (which it is sure to do) on either side'. Harrow, another school that played a dribbling form of football, was also noted for the ferocity with which players' shins could be attacked during matches. Indeed, a motion to allow hacking, presented to a meeting to codify the rules of the newly formed Football Association (FA) in November 1863, was defeated by only ten votes to nine.[11]

Despite the FA's rejection of hacking the practice continued among those clubs that followed Rugby School's tradition and eventually formed their own union, early in 1871. Given the rivalry between the different codes of play and the growing interest in football being taken by the middle class, it was perhaps inevitable that such extreme displays of violence by those ostensibly being educated to become society's leaders would come to public attention. The immediate catalyst for the formation of the RFU was a challenge issued by Scottish rugby players in December 1870 for an England-versus-Scotland match under Rugby School's rules, intended in large part to combat the growth of the Association code of football, which had arranged its own England-versus-Scotland fixture in November. However, the underlying context was a public outcry over violent play and serious injuries in games of football played according to Rugby School's code. A letter from 'A Surgeon' had appeared in the *Times*, complaining about the number of injuries he had dealt with that had occurred during games of football at Rugby School and ascribing them all to hacking. The seriousness of his complaint may be gauged by the fact that his letter called into question the competence of the school's headmaster, for allowing the practice to continue. In recognition of the hostility that his opposition to the game's ethos would engender, the writer also withheld his name, preferring anonymity in order to protect his son, who was a pupil at the school.[12] The letter was reprinted in the medical journal the *Lancet* and brought the question of violence in football to widespread public attention for the first time.

Defenders of Rugby School's version of the game, including current pupils and old boys, leapt to its defence, either by disputing the facts of the surgeon's claims or by defending hacking as 'entirely legitimate', in the words of an old boy who had gone on to Trinity College, Oxford.[13] Mounting a defence that was later to be used by rugby union players to justify the raking of feet against opponents who sought to protect the ball after a tackle, the writer went on to say that hacking had been dying out but that 'a new evil has arisen, and to prevent this evil, known as that of "mauling" [whereby the ball was shielded from the defending side through the use of bodies and hands] a certain amount of hacking is absolutely necessary'. The controversy grew to such heights that the school's medical officer, Dr Robert Farquharson, felt it necessary to write to the *Times* early in December 1870, admitting that a boy had been killed while playing the game but that his death had been due to an abdominal injury caused by a collision, rather than to hacking, which, Farquharson claimed, was not responsible for any major injuries. In a gesture apparently intended both to assuage the critics of the sport and to deflect attention away from the school, he called on the other public schools to gather data on the number of accidents that had occurred due to the playing of football under their respective rules.

The controversy caused consternation among the adult players of Rugby School's code of football, and led to a call from the Richmond and Blackheath clubs, late in December 1870, for the formation of a union of Rugby rules football clubs, with the stated intention of countering the adverse publicity that the sport was attracting. Richmond had opposed 'unnecessary' hacking since 1866, although even it was not opposed to hacking at players who were running with the ball or those who were contesting for the ball in a scrum. The aim of the new union, which was founded on 26 January 1871, was to draw up a common code of rules that would enable matches between adult clubs to be played without their having to negotiate compromises over the idiosyncrasies of each others' rules. Hacking was explicitly forbidden under rule 57 of the new union, although it was generally understood that clubs playing each other could make their own arrangements about its enforcement during matches. It is also safe to assume that the RFU's rule 58, outlawing the use of 'projecting nails, iron plates or gutta percha' on boots, was a direct response to the activities of those players who were most devoted to hacking.[14]

Despite the formation of the RFU and its public banning of hacking, it was clear that the practice was not merely a predilection of overly aggressive schoolboys, for it continued across the adult game throughout the 1860s and 1870s. Although many of the newly founded clubs played their own varia-tions of Rugby School's rules of football, violence was an integral – not to say very appealing – part of the game. Blackheath, despite being one of the founding teams in the FA, continued to play under Rugby School's rules, with full hacking. Nor were there any appreciable differences between the attitudes adopted by clubs in the north of England and those adopted by clubs in the south. W.H.H. Hutchinson remembered that Hull's original rules forbade hacking but allowed tripping, a feature that was also explicitly outlawed in the RFU's first set of rules. The nature of the games that were played at that time can be gauged by Hutchinson's memory of a match against Harrogate, when an opposing player 'got me by the hair of the head and stuck to it for all he was worth'. J.G. Hudson, one of the founders of the Leeds club, also looked back fondly at a Leeds-versus-Manchester match of 1865, which consisted predominantly of 'a good set-to at each other's shins in mid-field'. Herbert Gregg, a founder of the Manchester club, also looked back fondly at the 'many bloody battles I have taken part in against Liverpool, also Preston, Rochdale and many other clubs', during the 1860s and 1870s. The first Yorkshire-versus-Lancashire match in 1870 was marked by the Lancashire players' keenness to indulge in hacking their opponents.[15]

Harry Garnett continued to be as enthusiastic about hacking when he was an adult player as he had been in his school days. Throughout his career he disdained to wear shinguards, believing them to be 'unmanly', and forbade his team-mates to wear them too, telling a fellow Otley player in the 1870s: 'If you don't take that off, I will see if I cannot hack it off.' Nor was he unique in taking such an uncompromising stance. When York played a game against York Training College, in the mid-1870s, the players were aghast to see that their opponents turned out wearing shinguards. York's captain,

Robert Christison, protested but, perhaps forewarned against what was about to transpire, the Training College players refused to abandon their protection. Undeterred, York proceeded to hack away at the covered shins of their adversaries. Christison proudly recalled 30 years later that, despite the College players' precautions, they still looked 'a good deal worse for wear' when they removed their shinguards after the match. As late as 1879 Manchester played Manchester Free Wanderers in a game in which both sides agreed to allow hacking.[16]

Even after hacking disappeared from the adult game, the 1880s still saw examples of violent play on the part of teams composed of 'gentlemen'. When Bradford toured Scotland in 1885 its game against Edinburgh Academicals was marred by 'some of the foulest play ever perpetrated' by the Scotsmen, who left four Bradford players seeking hospital treatment following the match. The fact that some of this rough play was, on occasion, due to middle-class players seeking to assert their dominance over the more working-class northern clubs can be seen by the comments of C.B. Grundy of Blackheath about a game against a Yorkshire team in 1881: 'Their idea evidently was, "There's a team of southern amateurs, let's frighten them by playing rough." And they did play rough! But they never made a greater mistake in their lives. At half-time Blackheath had thirteen men left and the others eleven. The rest had been taken in cabs to the nearest hospital.' Given the evidence, it appears to be a fair assumption that such behaviour during matches was not uncommon in the 1880s. It is also worth pointing out that the soccer amateurs of Corinthians FC were also widely noted for their 'robust' style of play, in which individual dribbling of the ball and the shoulder-charging of opponents played a prominent part, a style that was viewed by many as being more violent than the style of play based on passing the ball, used by the professional sides in the north and the Midlands.[17]

'It's not the winning but who is taking part'

It was not just the violence of playing styles that suggests that the ideal of 'it is not the winning, but the taking part that it is important' was honoured more in the breach than in practice. Until 1885 neutral referees were not obligatory at rugby matches and the common practice was for disputes over the rules to be decided through discussion between the captains of the two teams. Although in theory this appeared to be the perfect application of gentlemanly ethics, in practice it was far from it. Looking back on the 1870s Harry Beardsall of the Huddersfield club remarked that, in his playing days, 'the captains were the referees and if any disputes occurred they squabbled until one or the other gave way'.[18] Indeed, it became an unwritten rule that the time spent arguing over disputed points during the course of a match had to be added on, in much the same way that injury time was added to the length of a match. As Robert Christison of York admitted, such arrangements meant that team captains tended to be drawn from among the more argumentative members of a club.

Gamesmanship, perhaps best defined as using the letter of the law to undermine the spirit of the law, was also rife. A Leeds player, Ben Cariss, allegedly became the first person to deliberately kick the ball out of play deep into his opponents' half of the field in order to give his side a territorial advantage. Although this tactic subsequently became a feature of rugby union and has continued for the past 120 years, at the time Cariss was frowned upon by many because the traditional aim of the game had been to avoid putting the ball into touch. In 1878 controversy ensued after A.N. Hornby, a member of one of Lancashire's major textile-manufacturing families with an outstanding reputation as a player of soccer, rugby and cricket, sought to protect a slender Lancashire lead in a Roses match by instructing his team to kick the ball out of play as soon they received it, in order to waste time. Perhaps the most notorious example of a departure from the 'spirit of the game' occurred in 1889 during England's game against a touring New Zealand Maori team at Blackheath. Andrew Stoddart had his shorts ripped in a tackle and players of both sides formed a circle around him so that he could protect his decency while changing. However, as the circle was being formed Frank Evershed picked up the ball and scored a try for England. Despite vigorous protests by the Maori side, claiming that this was ungentlemanly conduct, the referee Rowland Hill, who, as Secretary of the RFU, was one of the strongest advocates of the amateur ethos, allowed the try to stand.[19]

As can be seen from these examples, winning was vitally important to those gentlemen of the Victorian middle class who played rugby. Arguably, this was not least because their victories in sporting contests confirmed their own belief in their superiority over those they saw as members of lower social orders or lesser races. Indeed, for many members of the middle class any sport without a victory lost its meaning; defeat undermined both their sense of the natural hierarchy of society and their self-confidence. If they consistently lost, many simply withdrew from the sport. For those who espoused the Corinthian belief that it was 'the playing of the game for its own sake' that was important, rather than the result, defeat should not have detracted from their enjoyment of, or participation in, rugby, yet it did. In 1881, for example, the original Hull club, founded in 1865 by local ship-owners' sons who had been to Rugby

School, passed a resolution 'that this club cease to exist' after suffering a series of crushing defeats by clubs that they viewed as being composed of their social inferiors. The following year York, one of the oldest rugby clubs in England, decided to fold and merged with the local York Melbourne club following a similar string of heavy defeats by clubs with members from lower down the social scale. In 1883 Yorkshire Wanderers, which claimed to be the oldest and most socially exclusive rugby club in Leeds, voted not to continue playing after losing every single match of the previous season.[20]

While some withdrew from the sport, the reaction of other middle-class players and administrators was to seek to restrict the involvement of working-class players in the game in order to reduce the perceived threat to their control. The introduction in 1886 of strict regulations outlawing any form of payment or reward for play was an attempt to curb the growing dominance of working-class players on the field. The great fear was that the introduction of professionalism would result in the complete eclipse of gentleman players by working-class professionals, as had happened in soccer following the acceptance of professionalism in 1885. Until 1886 (and contrary to the myths of its official historians) the RFU had no formal rules either promoting amateurism or banning professionalism, although at the local level the Yorkshire Rugby Union, for example, had stopped some forms of payment in 1879. It was only the increasing prominence of working-class players from the late 1870s that caused the question of amateurism to be raised. The intention of the amateur code of 1886 was explicitly to apply ever-more stringent regulations to rugby players and any material benefits they may have derived from playing the sport, in order to keep the balance of power within the game firmly on the side of the young businessmen and professionals who had always led it.

These growing fears about working-class participation in rugby were also related to the gradual extinction of hacking. In part, hacking's decline was due to new attitudes to violence in sport. As the RFU's keenness to officially oppose hacking demonstrated, significant sections of middle-class public opinion were not favourably disposed to the violence engendered by the hacking game. Rugby could not be expected to increase its popularity as a vehicle for the education of young men while its players insisted on engaging in such bloody practices, especially when these were viewed alongside the seemingly less violent code of football played by teams in the FA. Growing middle-class intolerance of cruel and bloody sports involving animals, which had culminated in the outlawing of sports such as cock-fighting in the middle of the century, was mirrored by concerns about human recreations, most prominently voiced by supporters of the 'rational recreation' movement of the mid-nineteenth century. Although the rational recreationists directed their attention at the working class's leisure pursuits, the idea that the middle class should set an example for others to follow became increasingly important to the administrators of newly popular sports in the 1870s. Such leadership was especially important to the enthusiasts of 'muscular Christianity', which became the moral thread running through the philosophy and attitudes of many of those leading rugby, and helped to give the game an evangelical tenor that was not to be found in most other sports.

It was no coincidence that the decline of hacking coincided with the entry of working-class players into the game. While rugby's rulers generally welcomed the new adherents of the game, their participation was accepted only as long as it did not call into question or threaten the leadership of the sport, either on or off the field. Hacking and other associated forms of violence in the game were to be confined to those social strata that shared a common moral culture. They were not to be indulged in between or across classes, only within classes. Thus by the mid-1880s there was a new outcry against the growth of violence in the game, this time initiated by the RFU itself, which, it alleged, was caused by working-class players who did not understand the rules, or, more ominously, by working-class 'veiled professionals', who were prepared to use violence in order to win at all costs in pursuit of monetary gain. The irony of such complaints when viewed in the context of rugby's history was unintentionally highlighted by a supporter of the RFU, writing to the *Yorkshire Post* in 1886:

> A great many of the Horbury team were artisans and colliers. Now, I don't object to any working man – collier or whatever he may be – as long as he understands the game he is playing, but when in ignorance he puts on his working boots...I am not surprised at smashed legs...It is a disgrace to the prestige of 'Dear Old England' for time-honoured fair play.[21]

A mere ten or 15 years earlier many players would have viewed 'smashed legs' as an predictable and possibly not undesirable outcome at the end of a match. Such a shift in opinion illustrates just how much the ideals of fair play and gentlemanly conduct had changed. Rather than being a fixed set of norms and values, as imagined by the supporters of amateurism, these concepts had evolved in direct response to the internal and external pressures on rugby in the latter half of the nineteenth century.

Conclusion

Such comments also revealed the underlying tension in the construction of rugby's gentlemanly ethos. No matter how strongly rugby's rulers emphasised its chivalrous characteristics, they could not (nor, indeed, did they want to) escape the fact that the game's violence was central to its appeal. As C.B. Fry, often seen as an embodiment of the 'Corinthian gentleman', put it in 1899, when arguing that all codes of football had become 'too civilised': 'clothe it as you will in law and order, it nonetheless fascinates and appeals to us by reason of that in us which desires the stress and excitement of fighting'.[22] Such beliefs were held not because rugby's participants were inherently more aggressive than players of other sports, but because the sport saw its role in society as being the third aspect of a trinity that joined together masculinity and national identity. This tended to be more implied than expressed towards the end of the Victorian period, although it was to resurface very strongly during and after the First World War. Yet the link had been made very explicit in the earlier decades of the sport. In 1863 F.W. Campbell of Blackheath, a supporter of Rugby School's code, had argued on behalf of his club at the foundation meeting of the FA that abolishing hacking would 'do away with all the courage and pluck of the game, and I will be bound to bring over a lot of Frenchmen who could beat you with a week's practice'. In 1872, at the founding of the Wakefield Trinity club, one of the curates had pointed to the physical virtues of the game, 'which were supposed to make one Englishman equal to five Frenchmen'. In 1876 a writer in the Manchester-based periodical *Athletic News* had responded to those who felt that the game was too violent and dangerous by arguing that 'English youths inherit the traditional pluck and energy of their race' by taking part in it.[23]

The point is not that Victorian middle-class rugby players were any more violent, or more inclined to bend the rules of the game, than working-class players were; rather that there was no appreciable difference in the type of behaviour displayed by members of either class on the playing field (although crowd behaviour, which lies beyond the scope of this chapter, was a different matter altogether). As A.A. Sutherland, the rugby correspondent of Robert Blatchford's *Clarion*, pointed out, there were great similarities between hacking and 'purring', a working-class activity common in the Northwest of England in the early and mid-nineteenth century, which had involved two men kicking each other's shins until one could no longer continue.[24] The only difference was that such behaviour was perfectly acceptable when employed within the shared social circles inhabited by the former public school boys who led the game, but was unacceptable to the game's rulers when used against them by those of a less exalted social background.

The growth of the ethos of the 'gentleman amateur' in rugby was there-fore not the result of a codification of ideals, but a changing and fluid response both to suspicious sections of middle-class public opinion and to the influx of working-class players into rugby in the 1880s. The earlier, more overtly violent traditions of public-school and middle-class rugby were in effect 'uninvented', and replaced by an ethical system of 'fair play' that was used to justify the continued control of the game by its public-school-educated rulers. The gentleman rugby player may or may not have existed, but middle-class sporting bodies such as the RFU felt that it was necessary to invent him.

Ludism, laughter and liquor: homosocial behaviour in late-Victorian Scottish harriers clubs

HAMISH TELFER

Within sport there has always been a tension between the importance of serious sporting competition and the wish to take part for straightforward pleasure. In late-Victorian Scotland the pursuit of sporting pleasure provoked powerful polarities and cross-currents. On the one hand, sporting rhetoric provided elevated, serious and purposeful reasons for participation. Sport was presented as respectable and as a constructive force, and, wherever possible, arguments for its rational and improving nature were marshalled to support it. On the other hand, as Richard Holt has indicated, 'conviviality lies at the heart of sport'.[1] In part this was a broader sense of camaraderie and companionship, but in the case of many sports clubs, including the harriers' clubs that form the subject of this chapter, elite male conviviality, social activities and general clubbability were certainly as great attractions for many members as the manly and virile images of the sport itself. The complex relationships between sociability and the social pleasures of ludism, laughter and liquor on the one hand, and the more 'rational', 'respectable' or religious reasons for sporting participation, on the other, can be illustrated by a study of the Scottish harriers clubs over the period 1885–1900.

Harriers clubs were athletic clubs that enjoyed a form of winter cross-country running in which one or two runners, known as the 'hares', were given a short start and the rest of the runners, known as the 'hounds', set out to overtake them within a specified distance. Its origins lay in the English public schools, so it could be portrayed as clearly respectable, but in its late-nineteenth-century Scottish manifestations such respectability had to be re-established. Many aspects of the sport, including its patterns of organisation and participation, and its sociability, could be represented as either respectable or unrespectable, depending on circumstances and audiences. Indeed, images of the sport could sometimes be used to depict social, political and economic tensions in society in satirical ways.

The chapter begins by providing some contextual information about the origins and the spread of harriers clubs in Scotland. It then examines some of the factors that could be exploited to give the sport a more respectable image. These included the socially exclusive nature of much of the membership; links with other 'respectable' sporting institutions, the police, the military or churches; and examples of good works. Yet not all views were positive. There were concerns over a number of issues, including trespassing, littering, cheating and betting. The social functions that supported and sustained the majority of Victorian sports clubs, and those less respectable activities – the humour, the noise and the sheer fun that they often generated in the evenings, well after the sporting competition itself – were also ambiguous, open to different interpretations. The final section explores the important and often under-emphasised role of alcohol, smoking and similar activities in harriers' sociability. The extensive calendar of homosocial 'smokers' and 'socials', with their drinking, smoking, entertainment and revelry, was probably far more of an attraction than the relative sobriety and propriety of the Grand Annual Dance, where women were permitted.

Origins and spread

The harriers clubs were among a number of new sporting organisations spawned in the late nineteenth century as part of the tide of new leisure. As with almost all other sporting organisations in Victorian Britain, the formation of harriers clubs in Scotland stemmed from a variety of key opportunistic factors. Public schools and universities were often key catalysts in the formation of athletic clubs, while the general growth in 'sports days' in villages and towns, coupled with the organisation and development of sport generally in the mid- to late-nineteenth century combined well with the new Victorian liberalism. The first Scottish harriers club, Clydesdale Harriers, was formed on 4 May 1885, predating Edinburgh Harriers by some five months and the West of Scotland Harriers by just over one year. There is evidence of some sporadic organised cross-country activity pre-dating these first three clubs, such as the Red Hose Race of Carnwath in the early nineteenth century or the activities of Edinburgh medics in Holyrood Park in the mid-nineteenth century, as well as reports of a Towerhill Athletic Club based in Springburn, Glasgow around 1885.[2] However, these three clubs are recognised as the first harriers clubs in Scotland.

Although the main geographical axis of interest in harrier running was the Edinburgh–Glasgow corridor, further clubs developed in Perth, Dundee, Forfar, Arbroath and Aberdeen within the next few years. Members of these clubs were often drawn from the ranks of the professions, moving around the country in jobs that carried expectations of public service and community leadership, and they spread the sport throughout Scotland. The burgeoning industrial economies of the major cities meant that respectable forms of recreation were in demand by ever-growing numbers of middle-class men. The city of Dundee, for example, supported some 17 harriers clubs between 1887 and 1890, with a further seven clubs in the surrounding area. The new-found enthusiasm for the harrier 'tradition' appealed to young men who found this sporting activity a mark of distinction. Young Scots even took the sport to the rest of Britain and overseas. Clydesdale Harriers had a London branch, the London Clydesdale Harriers.[3] Early reports of cross-country running in New South Wales, Australia, gave the winner of the championship of 1897 as R.M. Gibson, a native of Largs, Scotland.[4]

A peculiarity of the growth of the sport was the way in which Clydesdale Harriers developed a patriarchal control over its development. As interest developed Clydesdale Harriers developed a missionary zeal, encouraging the formation of associate clubs, which, rather than becoming separate organisations in their own right, became 'sections' of Clydesdale Harriers. Thus its membership swelled rapidly. By 1888/89 membership of the club stood at 200 and by 1890 the opening run of the season involved 120 members. Membership had risen to 1,000 by 1900, even after some of the 'sections' had declared themselves fit to run their own affairs and had broken entirely from the parent club.

For many members 'hare and hounds' was only one of their interests. Some harriers were footballers, taking part in running for reasons of fitness and camaraderie.[5] In addition to running, harriers clubs of this period opened 'sections' for members interested in skating, boxing, cycling, swimming and gymnastics. The West of Scotland Harriers developed out of groups with strong interests in cycling, rowing and football, while Edinburgh Harriers had strong gymnastics and skating teams. Harrier clubs often took on more established sporting opposition. By the 1890s Clydesdale Harriers had beaten Preston North End, the 3rd Lanark Rifle Volunteers and Celtic FC at soccer. It seemed that wherever a harrier went there was a connection to be made with either another sport or gentlemen of 'clubbable values'.

Select image

Clydesdale Harriers may have been the first club, but it soon found itself opposed by a powerful and even more select club when the premier Scottish football club of the day, Queen's Park FC, aided the formation of the West of Scotland Harriers. This provoked an attack from the sporting press, which accused Queen's Park FC of creating an unwelcome rival to Clydesdale Harriers that was more socially exclusive. Queen's Park FC was itself seen as a socially exclusive group compared to many of the other football clubs of the day, an image that its amateur status still partially supports to this day. Its overt patronage of 'the West' lent the club the slightly effete air associated with gentleman amateurs. The 'omnium gatherum institution', as the *Scottish Athletic Journal* called the West of Scotland Harriers, was said to have a committee comprising 'the most influential athletic men in the West of Scotland'.[6]

This select image was also enhanced by the inclusion of patrons from among the 'great and good' of society. The Clydesdale Harriers and the West of Scotland Harriers vied with each other to create the most impressive list of patrons for the club's yearly handbook. By 1889/90 Clydesdale Harriers could boast five members of Parliament, the Lord Provost of Glasgow and two knights. By 1903/04 the West of Scotland Harriers had caught up, with seven members of Parliament (including Andrew Bonar Law), two knights and the then Lord Provost of Glasgow, Sir John Ure Primrose, who was to further his sporting connections as Chairman and director of Glasgow Rangers FC.[7] Other clubs attempted to replicate the pattern of the leading Glasgow and Edinburgh clubs. In the case of Forfar Harriers, for example, the honorary president and the president were drawn from the Union Bank and the British Linen Bank respectively.

The press of the day depicted the actual membership of the Scottish harriers clubs as being rather mixed, but largely drawn from socially superior middle-class groups. Most were in professional occupations or were small businessmen. Many aspired to rise in status, and there were also some skilled working men among them. Like the high-status patrons, the membership appeared to be highly respectable. Club rules assumed that members would know how to behave and therefore there was not the same need to control club activities. In the new harriers clubs 'belonging' was taken to mean identification with values associated with aspiration, class and social standing. Enjoying life without fear of criticism was the construct that was ascribed to the social activities of the clubs. In this sense the harriers clubs were different from some of the football clubs, where religion and local community were more important.

Other connections could also confer respectability on the sport. The hares and hounds tradition had strong roots in English public schools, and many of the leading harriers had themselves gone to English public schools or universities. In addition, masters at Scottish public schools were often recruited from their English counterparts, and the process and diffusion of athleticism was affecting the Scottish public schools. Thus the sport was supported in its early days by a calling and justification that other forms of organised sport could not claim, and the impact of these schoolboys and students on the sport was important in transforming and, indeed, inventing a sporting form. The practice of hares and hounds in the Scottish public schools was supported both by the Kingsleyan tradition of the 'tireless stride for Christ' and more general elements of the amateur ideal. It offered a way to realise Montague Shearman's definition of a sportsman as 'a man who kept his engagement, never mind under what difficulties, and accepted defeat without a murmur, and success with becoming modesty'.[8] Even so, private schools in Scotland varied in the emphasis they placed on harrier activity. A good example of a school that organised hares and hounds clubs in open competition was George Watson's College, Edinburgh (Watsonians). In the 1890s Fettes had numerous packs that ran in the fields around Barnton and Cramond in Edinburgh. By contrast, as *Scottish Sport* noted, Dr Almond of Loretto had relatively little success in instilling some sort of enthusiasm for the sport among the boys of his school, although he was a keen advocate of cross-country running and Loretto had donated a cup for competition as early as 1888.[9]

The harriers clubs also tried to justify the service they provided by associating it with ideals of authority, discipline, militarism and public service. They did this in a variety of ways. One was to use relevant facilities, such as the military barracks at Maryhill or the gymnasium facilities of the Govan Police, both in Glasgow.[10] Another was to forge links with the recently established Boys' Brigade, which attached great importance to the role and function of physical education for boys, as well as other forms of physical activity. General Chapman's exhortation to have more physical activity based on the Merchant Schools policy of recruiting former NCOs from the Army inspired attempts to link schooling, the Boys' Brigade, the military, and physical activity and drill.[11] In linking the role and place of forms of physical activity to militarism, the Boys' Brigade provided the strong muscular (and Scottish) Protestant *raison d'être* for the use of physical activity for the betterment of self, country and empire. By 1890 the Boys' Brigade at Airdrie just outside Glasgow was using cross-country running as one of a number of regular activities for its members.[12]

Football, rugby and other team sports often organised charity cups, as a way of establishing their respectable credentials and giving something back to the communities that supported them. It is therefore, perhaps, not surprising that another example of harriers' respectable sociability was activity in connection with charity and 'good works'. For example, in an attempt to emphasise the social status of the club, and to reinforce the inherent 'good' of the club and its activities to the citizens of Dundee, Dundee Thistle Harriers provided more than 500 poor children of the city with a treat of 'a substantial tea, a bag of fruit and a couple of half pennies'.[13]

Less respectable aspects

Despite its emphasis on 'muscular Christianity', the role of the Church as an arbiter of manliness and virtue was something of a mixed blessing in Scottish sport generally, and for running in particular, as not all clergymen saw harriers as entirely respectable. Some clubs did enjoy the patronage of ministers of the Church of Scotland. Paisley Harriers, for example, recruited the Rev. W.E. Lee of Greenlaw Church, who clearly saw the activity as a wholesome distraction.[14] However, the tireless tirades against the frivolous activities of the harriers from other churchmen, such as the Rev. Beveridge of Port Glasgow, were reported with enthusiasm by the press and were a constant thorn in the side of the sport. More generally, the temperance leagues, the evangelical associations, the Reccabites and the various Sabbatarian movements were always dubious of the value of sport, despite the strong advocacy of physical activity by the armed forces and schools in relation to disciplining and moulding youth for manly service. Baillie Chisholm of the United Evangelical Association of Glasgow, for example, denounced football as 'a temptation to youth leading many into habits of foul profanity, to intemperance and gambling'.[15]

There was certainly a less respectable side to harriers' sporting behaviour. There is, for example, evidence to suggest that their activity over the countryside was sometimes seen as a public nuisance. Littering was occasionally reported and must have been a constant problem. Packs of runners descending on estates every Saturday afternoon raised issues of privacy and challenged the status of landowners. In some cases there were reports of harriers being beaten by estate managers intent on keeping them off the lands of their masters. Reports of runs are peppered with occasional glimpses of the hazards of running over private land, and confronting gamekeepers, barbed wire and dogs. The following extract is typical:

> Greenhead Harriers' run on Saturday was abruptly terminated on Aitkenhead estate grounds by the appearance of a brutal gamekeeper armed with a formidable stick, and accompanied by a ferocious-looking dog. After using very threatening and abusive language, he brutally assaulted one of the members who had

become detached from the pack, by knocking him down, kicking him, and causing blood to flow freely from his mouth. As this is not profitable for defenceless harriers, clubs intending to cover this district should take note.[16]

Usually the club would attempt to use the simple expedient of making the landowner a club patron, thus removing the obstacle.[17]

On occasions the 'Corinthian' values of the clubs were compromised from within their own ranks, rather than by perception of public nuisance, with reports of more clearly unrespectable, if not dishonest, behaviour. After one incident *Scottish Sport* carried a somewhat indignant report of a run on the outskirts of Glasgow: 'a runner, who knew the country, cut the trail by a couple of miles, ferried himself across the canal and thus easily won the handicap. When the result was made known, a pal, who had been in the same boat, but was unplaced, split, with the result that he too was disqualified, and rightly too.'[18]

Some groups were intent on making the sport into an opportunity for profit based on self-interest. Cross-country running fought off an early attempt by betting syndicates to use the sport for betting purposes. Brian McAusland[19] details the activities of a syndicate known as the 'Co-Partnery Ring', which appears to have been involved in rigging handicap races and saw the formation of the new harriers clubs, and Clydesdale in particular, as a threat to its business. At this time athletics in the broadest sense suffered from a degree of corruption, with betting syndicates essentially defining the outcomes of races where they existed at football clubs and as more local events. The advent of organised clubs posed a threat to this lucrative business as the new clubs set about controlling and defining the conditions under which they would train and race, thus effectively wresting the racing calendar away from the syndicates.

Sociability and respectability

For most Scotsmen sporting sociability had long provided a potentially cathartic outlet, an escape from the seriousness of work, from household and family affairs, and from the potential prison of 'respectable behaviour'. Pure pleasure, enjoyment and sociability have always played key roles in promoting participation in sport. In his study of the evolution of the many and varied club and sporting organisations in England, Neil Wigglesworth shows that in the first half of the nineteenth century many clubs styled themselves 'societies' to reflect this emphasis. His research into these early 'societies' shows that many were formed by small groups of friends seeking diversions and that there was a host of 'societies' whose purpose was essentially social.[20] A similar early Scottish example was the Edinburgh-based 'Six Foot High Club', founded in 1826. The object of this club was to 'practise the national games of Scotland and gymnastics'. Membership was, as the name suggests, limited to those who were at least six feet tall, but honorary membership was also bestowed on leading literary figures of the day, such as Sir Walter Scott, James Hogg (the 'Ettrick Shepherd'), Lockhart (Scott's biographer) and Christopher North. The club provided a guard of honour for the hereditary Lord High Constable of Scotland in 1828. The club met at Hunter's Tryst, five miles from Edinburgh city centre, at an inn that was reputedly well-patronised and was run by two 'respectable old ladies'. The club's town rooms were in East Thistle Street and later at Malta Terrace. Practising field and throwing events, as well as running, shooting, golf and curling, the club enjoyed the attendance of ladies at its sporting days. Scott himself wrote in his journal on 5 March 1829: 'What a tail of the Alphabet I should draw after me, were I to sign with the indications of the different societies I belong to, beginning with the Presidency of the Royal Society of Edinburgh and ending with Umpire of the Six Foot High Club.'[21]

A similar emphasis on Scottish sociability could be found throughout the nineteenth century. Neil Tranter's work on the sporting organisations of Stirling shows that a number of sports clubs, such as the Borestone Bowling Club, founded in 1858, and events, such as the Callendar Highland Games of 1888, were inaugurated 'solely to provide amusement'.[22] Sociability was central to the sport of hare and hounds too. Social standing, and the role and place of masculine ideals, were lived out in the runs and in the exclusivity associated with the structured nature of the sport. There was clear demarcation in the allocation of roles as 'hares' or 'hounds', with fast and slow packs, as well as 'whips'. In addition, each 'pack' had a pace runner and the run was regarded as a pack affair rather than as a matter of racing between individuals. It was usual for the packs to be assembled only within the last mile and then runners were permitted their head in racing each other. The strong emphasis on packs functioning together created a bonding within groups of runners who preferred to run with certain friends, emphasising the social and manly ideal of the 'selfless man', and the co-operative nature of the club runs. This created an image of the harriers as young Victorian gentlemen capable of co-operating with each other, and of accepting the values and aspirations of the 'right' club, while still allowing runners to see themselves as heroic individuals striving to make their way over natural countryside. The 'heroic' is captured superbly in an account of the hares of

Clydesdale Harriers, a club run from Ibrox Park (the home of Glasgow Rangers FC), laying a trail for the hounds:

> Valour and discretion were exemplified by the hares on Saturday. Two of them, when the paper went down, plunged into the River Cart, which was then in high flood, and swam to the other side, thus saving fully two miles, whilst the third hare, when the water reached his neck, scrambled back and walked home. Good old 'discretion'! Good old 'valour'! The pack preferred taking the longer route, and crossing by the bridge.[23]

The nature of competition generally emphasised the club rather than individual endeavour in these early days. There were pack runs of differing abilities and squadron runs, as well as the inter-club competitions and national championships. Few spectators attended. Collaboration and sociability were far more important than competition. Yet at the same time members wanted to improve their levels of fitness and endurance. This could mean some compromise with strict amateur ideals. There were occasional examples of clubs that enlisted the services of professional trainers to supervise training: the select Edinburgh Harriers club replaced Geordie Wood with a younger trainer in 1897[24] and Dennistoun Harriers employed a trainer in January 1898.[25]

Sociability was reinforced by the recruitment of members from similar social backgrounds. In the case of the Scottish harriers, social activities and cross-country sport both formed part of the fabric of club identity. Wholesome fresh-air activity with friends of similar social standing, coupled with convivial social activity, lay at the heart of the sport. In 1886 the *Scottish Athletic Journal* reported on the arrangements to form the 'West of Scotland Harriers'. It commented upon the arrangements to consider every application for admission and added: 'Their aim will always be to have in the West of Scotland Harriers a club in which gentlemen will find companions with whom they can associate both in the close and at the social board.'[26]

The accommodation used by the clubs could be more ambiguous in its message. Football, cricket, rugby and rowing clubs each had their own club rooms at their sporting venues, which served both sporting and social functions. Inevitably these club houses were at the fairly basic level associated with the rough and ready early provision of sporting facilities. In contrast, many gymnastic clubs and private swimming clubs had the luxury of providing both members' lounges and refreshments, as well as the sports facilities themselves, all under one roof. The harriers clubs, lacking any such permanent base for either social or sporting provision, set about hiring rooms in 'reputable' hotels, with lounges and facilities for members, such as food and newspapers, as well as, in some cases, provision for overnight accommodation to satisfy their social aspirations. They also set about establishing their sporting bases at notional 'headquarters' by using inns, public swimming baths and the new football grounds. Initially, therefore, the new harriers sought accommodation at both sporting and social levels. In the case of Edinburgh Harriers this was achieved through a relationship with the Royal Gymnasium in Edinburgh, which provided both types of facility for some time.

While no harriers club initially had its own grounds, pavilion or social rooms, the clubs nevertheless came to be associated with not only the premier sporting venues but also the premier meeting places. Even in the earliest days of the clubs the provision of convivial meeting and recreational facilities was seen as a key requirement. Hotels, relying on the publicity that attended the associated social events, vied to offer the best rates and facilities, and to be regarded as the focal point for harriers' functions, often putting aside rooms for their exclusive use. The Langholm Hotel in Glasgow was known for its 'handsome' rooms, and for providing newspapers, comic weeklies and sporting papers such as the *Graphic*, the *Illustrated London News*, *Punch* or *Bell's Life*. Most other harriers clubs tried to secure a base with good meeting rooms, such as public baths or a good inn. The summit of ambition was to acquire separate 'rooms' in a city where 'gentlemen' members could live out the ideal of their acquired status.

All clubs had notional 'headquarters', and clubs' meeting rooms and hotel venues in city centres soon came to represent the epitome of the Victorian middle-class ideal, and assumed key importance. Their aim was to take on the aspect and appearance of 'gentlemen', so the more select the venue the better. Clydesdale Harriers acquired club rooms in the centre of Glasgow for the benefit of members.[27] The more peripatetic West of Scotland Harriers favoured the Langholm Hotel, although rooms at the Conservative, Liberal and St Andrew's Clubs were also used, while Ingram Harriers secured the Parkhead Masonic Halls as 'headquarters'. The Langholm and Lauder Hotels in Glasgow, both used by harriers, were also used by other sports clubs.

The perceived need to emulate the respectability of gentlemen's or political clubs was highlighted by a correspondent who wrote to the *Scottish Athletic Journal* in 1886 to argue for a meeting place that athletes could use 'without having to resort to bars and public houses'. The Langholm Hotel was 'adequate', but in his view it was 'not ideally suited to men of active dispositions':

How much more satisfactory would it be if they could resort to a comfortable club – practically a home for the time being – where there would be a certainty of meeting friends; where a game at billiard, a hand at whist, a little music, together with the concomitant drink and smoke, could be comfortably and temperately indulged in; where, for those who require it, a comfortable tea or supper could be had, and where for country members comfortable and reasonable sleeping accommodation could be secured?[28]

When Edinburgh Harriers began offering the complete gentleman's service of 'rooms', in October 1899,[29] it completed the creation of an elite grouping of pre-eminent harriers clubs, comprising Clydesdale, West of Scotland and Edinburgh Harriers.

This sometimes grated on contemporary commentators, who saw aspiring gentleman 'toffs' continuously pleading poverty in other contexts. In 1897 an article in the *Scottish Sport* commented on harriers' 'impecuniosity' by pointing out that:

In the main, the expenses of harriers are comparatively small. Their outfit is not difficult to maintain; yet it is a humiliating fact that many of the clubs are continuously pleading poverty and appealing for subscriptions to gentlemen who are known to look with kindly eyes on every sort of legitimate effort in the direction of physical education and recreation. Were this a case of mere boys or apprentice lads appealing for aid, no one could grudge them a little support, but when we find clubs, many of whose members are tradesmen, in fairly prosperous circumstances, appealing for aid, then, we say it is time to call a halt.[30]

The article went on to accuse the clubs and their members of attempted blackmail, and rebuked them, exhorting them to 'apply their hands to their own pockets'. Clubs were clearly reluctant to dig too deep. Even the Clydesdale Harriers were unwilling to purchase rooms outright, taking the view that the financial risks were too high, and decided to rent rooms instead. If there were no rooms available, meetings for the purpose of organising club activities were generally held at hotels of good social standing. As we have seen, this became the norm for the sport.

Much of the harriers' sporting life revolved around the winter calendar of runs at set venues. The locations of these winter Saturday runs changed regularly and there was no regular sporting base, although more favoured venues were sometimes used for the weekly post-run social activities. Identity and social class seem to have been emphasised in the hiring of complete train carriages and 'brakes' to take the harriers to their Saturday venues, as well as in the quality of the hotels booked for changing and socialising after the event. The social exclusiveness of these sportsmen may well have helped to reinforce their sense of order within a rapidly changing and industrialising Scotland, emphasising that the boundaries in sport were perhaps not as clear as they were elsewhere in society. With venues for Glasgow runs as far-flung as Bothwell, Helensburgh, Chryston, Kirkintilloch, Beith, Renton, Kilmarnock, Hamilton and Paisley, up to 40 miles from the city centre, it required some considerable organisation to assemble up to 60–80 men for a run, a meal and a social. Advertising train times, hiring railway carriages dedicated to club members only and hiring special 'brakes', in addition to making arrangements at suitable venues, ensured that the activities of the harriers clubs were welcome elements in the new leisure economy. Many venues became popular with the clubs and runs became integral features of the economy of certain hotels and inns. Fixture calendars bore names that soon became familiar to harriers, including the Queen's Hotel, Helensburgh (the West of Scotland Harriers); the Bull, Milngavie (Clydesdale Harriers); Mather's Hotel, Broughty Ferry (Airlie and Broughty Harriers); and Gemmell's Restaurant, Govan (Bluevale Harriers). For Edinburgh Harriers the inns and hotels surrounding their city became favourite venues, replicating the form of the sport in the west of the country. The Harp Hotel at Corstorphine, the Volunteer Arms at Morningside, the Sheep Head at Duddingston, the Old Inn at Roslin and Mr Clark's Inn at Coltbridge were a few of the venues that catered for the new harriers.

Gentlemanly standing was enhanced not only by the selection of venues for runs but also by the nature and quality of the social functions by which each club was judged. The small but elite grouping of sporting polymaths that led the harriers clubs used their connections and backgrounds to great effect in publicising their events. The harriers clubs tried to represent late-nineteenth-century sportsmen as healthy, well-connected and leisured through events such as gatherings for card games (Dundee Harriers), socials in the rooms of the Co-operative Society (Bellahouston Harriers), *conversaziones* in the Town Hall (Motherwell Harriers) or grand dances (West of Scotland Harriers).

Smokers and socials: less respectable pleasures

The harriers' social structure essentially revolved around the socials after their cross-country runs and the smokers held during the week. The subtle complexities in the ways in which behaviour was defined, regulated and controlled within the social fabric of sports clubs are exemplified in these events, which were enthusiastically engaged in, often reported on and understood to be the main attractions offered by the clubs. Additional events – such as the dinner held to mark the International Exhibition in Glasgow in 1888 – provided further excuses for collective enjoyment. There were also occasional inter-club socials, including dinner dances, which ladies were permitted to attend.

Smoking and the drinking of alcohol were problematic, especially when they were carried out by members of the working class. Within Scottish sport more generally there was a variety of attitudes to both these activities. The alehouse where the Six Foot High Club met typified the importance of alcohol in almost all sports in the early nineteenth century. By the later nineteenth century a tiny minority of sportsmen, many of them Methodists, Nonconformists or secular political reformers, opposed the convivial, pleasure-seeking pub-based culture, which they saw as harmful. Gerry Finn's work on John Hope's Edinburgh-based movement in sport in general and football in particular, which was committed to evangelicalism, radical Protestantism, temperance and 'no Popery', illuminates the issues that such critics raised.[31] The strong temperance movement in sport was mainly associated with ensuring the respectability of working-class participants. Hope's devotion to the cause of providing respectable leisure to the citizens of Edinburgh was based on maximising the appeal of the temperance cause through the game of football, as this was 'the game of the masses'.[32] For a short while he was successful in his attempts to provide a wholesome activity whose practitioners did not succumb to the sinful pleasures of drink. Through his position as a city councillor, by the donation of a sizeable area of land for a public park and through the volunteer movement, Hope moved the agenda of sport and drink firmly into the minds of the citizens of Edinburgh. Using the volunteer movement, Hope founded the 3rd Edinburgh Rifle Volunteer Football Club, which was to enjoy early success in winning the Edinburgh Cup; the club also embodied Hope's abstemious anti-Catholic crusade through sport.[33] The early association of football with the temperance movement was exemplified further in the activities of both Hibernian in Edinburgh and Celtic in Glasgow, both of which had strong associations with the Catholic Young Men's Society and the League of the Cross, a Catholic temperance movement.[34]

However, trying to present an image of respectability by disassociation from the world of drink was extremely difficult when changing rooms were in inns, pubs and hotels. The temperance leagues were quick to point to the evils of drink in relation to wholesome athletic activity. In 1898, for example, the *League Journal* carried an article powerfully condemning strong drink in relation to sport. It cited as supporters of this view W.G. Grace and Prince Ranjitsinhji in cricket, George Orton, the US mile champion, Hanlon the sculler, J.G. Clegg of Sheffield and others, perhaps surprisingly including the Newport Rugby team of 1891 and 1892. The article specifically stressed the bad effects of alcohol:

> We know what medical men say about the effect of alcohol upon parts of the body – how its action overworks the heart, and therefore decreases the staying power; how it renders the muscles flabby, thus taking from them their snap and spring; how it upsets the stomach, lowers the temperature, muddles the brain, and generates nervousness when coolness is essential... alcohol not only decreases the staying power, but it also weakens the nerve or will power.[35]

The article exhorted readers to remember that the function of athletic exercises is to develop the athletic man, whom it characterised as a better citizen, with higher mental attainment and strength of character, and as the epitome of 'physical, mental and moral manhood'. Intelligent athleticism was therefore predicated on total abstinence, whatever the sport. However, the appeal of certain sports was rooted in cultural values of clubbability and camaraderie within the developing sporting culture.

To take another example from the wider world of sport in Scotland, in 1889 a sketch in the *Scottish Umpire*, exploiting the ever-increasing public interest in the background to football matches, gave an account of the Scottish Cup Final between Celtic and Third Lanark Rifle Volunteers. It included a vignette of the pavilion dressing room, where beef tea, sherry 'fzip', nettle beer and brandy were all in evidence.[36] After-match celebrations were sometimes periods of heavy drinking and club officials were not immune. At the dinner that followed the Scottish Football Association's match with England in 1890 the bill included a conspicuous £33 for champagne alone.[37] Once professional football clubs became incorporated it was even more difficult to preach temperance, as the drinks trade was soon heavily involved. In the case of Celtic FC, for example, its committee was dominated by publicans and publicans numbered some 23.3 per cent of the club's shareholders.[38]

There was a similar ambiguity in relation to smoking. In a brief but pointed commentary *Scottish Sport* remarked in 1897 that:

> A question that is a thorn in the flesh of all the masters of our
> schools is smoking ... All the methods adopted by schoolmasters
> seem to be of no avail to stop the evil, and we think that the best
> and only way is to appeal to the good sense of the boys them-
> selves. We do not speak as anti-tobacco leaguers. We smoke
> ourselves; but what we earnestly ask boys is to smoke only when
> they have become men. It stops growth and spoils training. A boy
> smoker will never play football so well as he otherwise would.[39]

The article went on to depict the dangers of inhalation as a pernicious habit
and depicted the dangers of the craving once acquired. It encouraged the use
of pipes as an alternative, a sure sign that the assumed audience was public
school boys and pupils at the 'senior secondaries'. At the same time,
however, the extent to which the smoking rooms of hotels and inns were
frequently advertised in the athletic and sporting press, with an emphasis on
the provision of facilities for sporting clubs, suggests that little notice was
taken of such strictures.

In some circumstances the harriers positively exuded the mores and fashions underpinned by middle-class respectable values. Yet many harriers
appear to have felt that exhortations to abstinence were meant for others less
capable of controlling their alcoholic intake, implicitly because of their
lower social standing. Convinced of their relatively high social station,
harriers copied the customs, values and rituals associated with the other
sporting clubs to which they belonged.

Some individual harriers occasionally took a stand on issues such as
smoking and drinking. Andrew Hannah of Clydesdale Harriers, arguably the
pre-eminent harrier of the day, having won the national championship five
times between 1890 and 1896, was an outspoken advocate of total abstinence and was noted for advising up-and-coming harriers on the virtues of
a good diet, plenty of sleep, and avoidance of cigarettes and alcohol.[40] Yet
such opposition rarely prevented abstainers from attending the social occasions that characterised the harriers clubs. Harriers' smokers were hugely
popular occasions, and tickets for these and the *conversaziones* were in great
demand both among club members and among the members of other clubs,
who saw these occasions as providing opportunities to develop links with
other harriers. Thus the relaxed conviviality of a smoker in a good location
embodied all the pleasures of Victorian clubbability.

Smokers were not the exclusive preserve of harriers, but were associated
with most sports clubs. The breakaway Scottish Amateur Athletic Union
held a successful smoking concert at Ancell's Restaurant in Glasgow in

1895, with guests from the Scottish Cyclists Union, on the occasion of the Union's medal presentations. The local press reported such occasions with enthusiasm. However, the harriers' smokers appear to have been more frequent and, perhaps, more important.

As the harriers clubs grew so too did the pressure on the venues they used to receive larger numbers for Saturday runs and the social events that followed them. This meant that the socials acquired even greater significance, becoming planned events catering for upwards of 100 participants. It was the smokers and the 'socials' that gave the clubs their distinctiveness. Often the social was the event that gave the edge to the occasion, rather than the quality of the run, and clubs vied with each other to hold the most enjoyable and distinctive gatherings. Information about the 'socials' was emphasised in the information that the clubs gave to the press.

The first inter-club run, between Edinburgh Harriers and the West of Scotland Harriers in 1886, mustered some 53 runners. The social after the event was held not at the venue of the run (the Sheep Head Inn, Duddingston) but at the Prince of Wales Hotel in Edinburgh. In addition to speeches and toasts, the piano was featured as singing and recitations carried on until 9.45 in the evening. In the case of one 'at home' held by the Clydesdale Harriers, the evening finished at 2 a.m. The Royal Hotel on George Square, Glasgow, was a favoured post-race venue for the West of Scotland Harriers when they were entertaining other clubs at inter-club competitions. On the return match with Edinburgh Harriers in December 1886, for example, the club ran from the Victoria Baths on the south side of Glasgow, retiring to the Royal Hotel at 5.30 p.m. for tea and ending the evening at 9 p.m. It was not uncommon to invite officials from other clubs as guests on such occasions. Usually there was a ham and eggs tea followed by toasts and cigars, as well as singing and recitations.

According to one particularly enthusiastic piece of reporting in the *Scottish Athletic Journal* on 1 February 1887, the West of Scotland Harriers club run at Erskine Ferry the previous week seems to have contained all the elements of carnival. The late arrival of the harriers, due to the horses overheating, meant a two-hour journey, with the run commencing at 4.30 p.m., when it was getting dark. The proprietor of the hotel had not been forewarned that some 30 runners would arrive, but given one hour his staff had managed to prepare a meal. The social after the run, with recitations, singing and toasts, was well-received, and the club dog indulged in a fight with another dog under one of the tables, which caused the members to get up onto their chairs. Departing at 8 p.m. did nothing, it seems, to ensure the safety of the journey home for the driver of the coach left the road and landed the coach in a ditch more than once. Glasgow was reached at 10p.m.[41]

At a Bellahouston Harriers club smoker in October 1895 the revelry included conjuring acts by a 'Professor' Lawrie, 'who fairly brought down the house'; a performance by the Maxwell quartet; and a reading by T. Robb Lawson. Gifts awarded for long service included silver-topped umbrellas, gold badges and a gold Albert watch. In most harriers clubs impending marriages were celebrated with a gift to the groom and, though much more rarely, to the bride. Such awards and exchanges of gifts became potent symbols of the exclusiveness of the clubs, enhancing the desire to 'belong' and marking recipients as individuals who had served with distinction, service being the valued commodity of Victorian club gentlemen.

A sense of burlesque was not always confined to smokers. The harriers were noted for the often innovative and enthusiastic ways in which they engaged in their sport. Activities on New Year's Day had long been a feature of Scottish cultural life and inter-club races were organised to celebrate the occasion. On New Year's Day 1897 the harriers of Dundee took part in traditional 'bun racing', 'cookie shines' and 'dumplin' fechts'. On New Year's Day 1898 Elderslie Wallace Harriers met Cambuslang Harriers for a day trip to Ayr: it was reported that local men joined in their celebrations, which included the playing of bagpipes. Edinburgh Northern Harriers frequently held 'Benedicts versus Batchelors' races. In all these cases the social after the event was an eagerly anticipated gathering.

Whether the 'socials' were grand affairs or involved relatively small numbers gathered in the snuggery of hotel kitchens, it was these occasions that gave the harriers' sport its character and its emerging form as a liminal activity. The homosocial nature of the occasions was evident from the start, with the virtual exclusion of women as participants and even as spectators. Women, or rather 'ladies', were allowed to attend the clubs' grand annual dances, but these were occasions of relative sobriety and propriety compared to the all-male smokers.

It was the smokers that gave the harriers the edge over other sporting forms because of their sheer sociability. While Queen's Park FC could boast that its annual dance was the 'dance of the year in football circles',[42] the harriers transformed convivial gatherings from planned and formal annual occasions into weekly and monthly events, encompassing the spectrum of entertainment from grand balls to post-run revelries.

At one of the first smokers held by the West of Scotland Harriers in Glasgow there were 'gold medal' singers, comics and general recitations, while at the Edinburgh Harriers' 'smoking concert' on Boxing Day 1885 the Richmond Hotel saw some 60 members attend, with prizes being presented to race winners as well as general entertainment, singing and toasts. Edinburgh Harriers also held a popular annual billiard tournament. To be included on the guest list of a smoker as an invited member representing another club became a much sought-after honour. In addition to the smokers, clubs held 'at homes' to which members of other clubs were invited. Essentially less boisterous but no less convivial, these 'at homes' came to be the hallmark by which clubs expressed their status as purveyors of good taste.

The services of proven entertainers became a feature of smokers. Professional entertainers invited to perform for harriers clubs included the infamous 'Herr Iff', but there were also turns from members noted for their skills in singing, recitation, comedy, conjuring and music. Dundee Harriers were noted for the quality of the cigars provided at their smokers, which were usually lit at 7.30 p.m. prompt. Word got around as to the relative merits of the performers and professional entertainers doing the circuits of the sports clubs. For one particular smoking concert held by the West of Scotland Harriers on 28 December 1886 the services of a musical association were engaged as well as a comic vocalist who had 'served his time' at the socials of Rangers Football Club.[43] By the turn of the century films were beginning to be a feature of clubs' social activities. In October 1898, for example, the Edinburgh Harriers used 'cinematograph photo.' at a club run and showed the result at an 'at home' a few weeks later. These smokers and gatherings were popular with other clubs and served as key entertainment for young sporting men, who did the rounds of club smokers, hoping to be seen, and to have chances to talk and influence the direction of the sport. The clubs themselves relied upon the income generated by these events. Edinburgh Northern Harriers declared a profit of two hundred pounds from smokers and dances in 1897, and announced a diversification into picnics as a new venture to augment its ever-popular annual fish supper at the Peacock Hotel, Newhaven.

The patterns of sociability and the distinct character of each of the clubs were evidenced through the structure of their social events, which provided rites of passage and a gradual process of socialisation into the world of Victorian sporting manhood. Modelling the harriers clubs on gentlemen's clubs provided a respectable veneer for what might otherwise have been condemned as frivolous and sinful pleasure. Enjoying life without being criticised was apparently one of the greatest challenges facing young middle-class males. Respectable club activity centred on the way in which runs were organised rather than on the quality of the run itself, although great pride was taken in the quality of trail-laying by the 'hares'. By focusing on the process of the sport and inventing its 'ethos', the clubs were able, by and large, to navigate through the difficult waters of respectability by virtue of the social background of their members, the attachment to respectable rituals and also their association with other forms of social activity. The quest for acceptable leisure activity was exemplified more through the structure and organisation of the clubs, and their constructed sense of respectability, than through their sporting activities. Indeed, sport served as an instrument for change, with the image of the sportsman and the image of the club interacting dialectically.

The sport therefore claimed a moral foundation, despite being based on somewhat hedonistic pursuits that combined the simultaneously individual and collective nature of the run with the camaraderie of the socials. These occasions emphasised both the sensual and the masculine, celebrating the ostentatious virility of the all-male club. The sport offered a healthy image of youthfulness and the open air, while the socials and the smokers kept up traditions of indoor socialising (in both senses of that word).

Epilogue: The dogs bark but the caravan moves on

MIKE HUGGINS AND J.A. MANGAN

In *Mid-Victorian Britain, 1851–1870* Geoffrey Best claimed that during the period he surveyed, in contrast to the earlier, more pleasure-loving Georgian era, 'the great Victorian shibboleth and criterion, respectability...was the sharpest of all lines of social division, between those who were and those who were not respectable: a sharper line by far than that between rich and poor'. He argued further that certain criteria of respectability were absolute and that respectable people did not get drunk or behave riotously.[1] He described those who did not maintain a respectable front as social deviants and claimed that there were few departures from the 'gold standard' of respectability, apart from a colourful segment of aristocratic and county society, which positively flaunted its 'disreputable' pleasures in a sporting milieu, and a 'bohemian' circle of artists and writers in mid-Victorian London who 'deliciously' defied convention.

More recently historians have questioned Best's model, suggesting that the reality was rather more subtle, with a line that wavered, was broken and certainly did not constitute an absolute divide.[2] Assuredly there were moralists, vociferous, well-organised, highly visible, severe, pledged to self-restraint; and there were hedonists, discreet, equally well-organised, sensibly 'invisible', sensual, given to self-indulgence. However, as *Disreputable Pleasures* has revealed, there were moralists who could also be hedonists, were capable of crossing and recrossing the changing lines of respectability, and were sometimes 'pure' and sometimes 'impure'. *Disreputable Pleasures* has also suggested that hedonism was widespread, if more discreet than in earlier times. Indeed, more than a few Victorians enjoyed multi-layered disreputable pleasures.[3] Best himself recognised that respectability came in a variety of styles, some lighter and some heavier. He certainly appreciated that the requirements of respectability appeared to vary from place to place and from group to group, and suggested that further research might well indicate that places such as Liverpool, Manchester or Glasgow contained interestingly immoral but as yet largely unrevealed communities.

Disreputable Pleasures has taken up Best's request for further inquiry, exploring variations in the definitions and varieties of respectability across Britain and across social classes, and attempting to locate various social contexts in which absolute constraints of respectability were loosened or even abandoned.

Initially the apparent simplicity of a rigid, dichotomous model of Victorian society, as composed of a majority of 'respectables' and a minority of 'unrespectables', had a strong appeal to historians, in much the same way that an uncomplicated triadic approach to class structures long maintained its appeal. More recent surveys of Victorian social history warn against such simplifications. For example, Patrick Joyce, a leading figure in recent 'postmodernist' approaches to history, has pointed out that we need to guard against simplified notions of culture, and that the tendencies of social historians to ascribe quite precise cultural identities to both general social categories and specific occupations should be resisted. Such 'precision' needs qualification. Joyce has further reminded his readers that in both the mid- and late-Victorian periods, despite the impact of demographic change, urbanisation and industrialisation, there were lots of pressures making for continuity.[4] Past practices were not wholly replaced. His caveats have clear relevance to the view that a new Victorian 'respectability' is unlikely to have been unshakably maintained.

In recent years, while our understanding of social class has shifted significantly, many historians of sport, leisure and recreation still find conventional models acceptable, if only as shorthand. Although Britain has been for centuries, as David Cannadine has remarked, an 'unusually classbound society', historians need to be wary of the dangerously naïve certainties associated with a too narrowly class-based analysis.[5] Joyce has provided a particularly useful warning about the use of over-simplistic models of social class in relation to work and leisure. For one thing, among the working class there were huge differences in values, attitudes and behaviour between the desideratum, who had very little money to spend on leisure and whose pleasures had mainly to be free, and the members of the 'labour aristocracy', who were less constrained.[6] E.P. Thompson explained the 'making' of the English working class through reference to its common experiences, but in reality, work, leisure and life chances were by no means as unified as Thompson claimed they were.[7]

The Victorian middle class was much more fractured and fragmented than it has all too often been presented as being, with significant cultural, economic and geographic divisions. The structure of the middle class, it is now clear, was very different as between towns, ethnicities, generations and neighbourhoods. A whole range of collective identities had their effects on

attitudes to leisure. Peter Bailey's recent thoughtful identification of 'significant second-order collectivities – fractions, taste-publics, strata, subcultures
– and the privileging of the individual subject' has further challenged the
limitations of earlier class analysis.[8] Such insights are highly suggestive,
implying as they do that notions of reputable and disreputable identity are
likely to have been highly contingent constructions, and that simplistic
dichotomies need to be abandoned if the dangers of over-simplification are
to be avoided. One thing must never be overlooked: that individuals, to a
lesser or greater degree, always had the capacity for independence of action
and thought, and were capable of moving in and out of 'respectable' social
roles in different social settings. Bailey has further sensible observations to
make regarding the need for more extensive work of recovery and interpretation, the need for greater alertness to 'internal' realities as much as to
'external' forms, and the consequent pressing need for more profound
studies of pleasure and performance, as well as contest and control.[9]

While the essays in *Disreputable Victorians* challenge the still too widely
embraced conventional view that the leisure of most middle-class and artisan Victorian men had mostly a respectable and serious purpose, there is still
much to be done before an adequately sophisticated and sensitive understanding of the exact extent of reputability and disreputability in Victorian
society is achieved. We still need a more refined comprehension of the
complex ways in which the Victorians themselves defined respectability. To
a large extent historians' interpretations of the term have been based on the
more vocal, visible and literate outpourings of those opposed to 'unacceptable' pleasure, who exaggerated the evils of its votaries' actions. A modern
equivalent might be to base our understanding of modern foreign holidays
wholly or mainly on the television programme *Wish You Were Here*: what of
Tourists from Hell? In reality, respectability and 'unrespectability' were
continually negotiated and renegotiated. They shifted in meaning in
response to fashion. Respectability was always a subjective concept, without question always a power in society, but with shades and nuances that
become fully apparent only through a detailed scrutiny of beliefs and behaviours. The variations in period use have meant that perceptive historians,
including the contributors to this volume, sensibly employ the term in different ways. There has, perhaps, been too much consistency of approach.
Multiple meanings, if sensitively located, add depth to any analysis.[10]

There is also still a need to draw out more fully the chronology of the
Victorians' changing definitions of respectability. The heyday of middle-
class attempts to impose 'rational recreation' seems to have been the 1830s
and the 1840s. In 1852 there appeared the apparently confident assertion
that 'no person above the rank of a labouring man or artisan would

venture...into a public house',[11] yet even then, as a recent overview of urban leisure indicates, the assertion did not apply to those who could afford to ignore or risk their reputations, including, in London alone, sporting aristocrats, professional 'men about town', the 'bohemian' set, Freemasons in pub-based lodges, many journalists, and a large number of businessmen and provincials enjoying the anonymity bestowed by the capital's size.[12] The assertion certainly also excluded, as *Disreputable Pleasures* reveals, an assortment of public schoolboys in the rural West of England. Historians should be ever-conscious of the need to avoid any tendency to over-polarise period attitudes. Even if many in Britain remained wary of the moral temptations of the beckoning new anonymous urban leisure world, it is clear that by the end of the Victorian period those with sufficient income and time were enjoying greater opportunities for self-indulgence. There was a liberal, assured and pleasure-seeking tone to *fin de siècle* middle-class life.[13] If the late 1860s, the 1870s and the 1880s were periods of transition, and thus pivotal, there remains the requirement to locate with greater care the trajectories through which the nature, constraints and power of 'respectability' changed direction and emphasis over this period. This came at a time when leisure had secured a place in the public's mind as 'a necessary amenity, a basic overhead in the maintenance of an industrial society', although for some the notion still persisted that it was 'a dangerously open-ended world'.[14] How many trajectories, decorous and debauched, did it have?

The term 'respectability' ultimately derives from the Latin verb *respicere*, 'to look at' or 'to regard'. Nineteenth-century semantics often treated respectability as a social or moral quality worthy of note or observation. Respectability thus had a link with outward show, formal propriety and the observance of overt codes of behaviour, and was therefore at its most influential in homes, immediate neighbourhoods and workplaces, where individuals were known, and respectability was often both expected and demanded. However, as *Disreputable Pleasures* has shown, there were many places, such as schools, universities, racecourses, inns, sporting clubs and sports grounds, where the constraints were far looser. Nor is this an exhaustive list. London's advantages in this regard have already been touched on. Geoffrey Best himself pointed out that the anonymity of London provided cover for licentious behaviour, a point also made by Lynda Nead in her *Victorian Babylon: People, Streets and Images in Nineteenth-Century London*. Nead offers an innovative account of modernity and metropolitan life, and argues that the new social configurations of the Victorian city caused confusion concerning expectations of public morality, and offered the chance of alluring immoral adventures. The large cities of Victorian Britain – notably, but not only, London, Liverpool, Glasgow and

Manchester – were huge, dark, dangerous, alienating and brutal, but they also offered better and bigger excitements, enticements and enjoyments. They were new topographical landscapes of seductive licentiousness.

What were the ways in which the new uses of urban space, the increasingly diverse urban recreations and their leisure opportunities challenged respectability? Inquiry is far from exhausted. Pubs, of course, have been ever-present and easily accessible centres for association, conviviality and amusement, both legitimate and illegitimate. Thus the entrepreneurial activities of Victorian urban landlords such as Jack Warner, who organised boxing, cycling, fishing, hunting, pedestrian, skating, swimming and wrestling events for clients of all classes at the Old Welsh Harp Inn at Hendon, on the northern edge of London, were fundamental to broadening sporting opportunities in the 1860s and 1870s. There must have been many such places the length and breadth of the new urban Britain. Pub landlords, like bookmakers, were to be found on elected town councils, local boards of health or parish vestries, and as directors of football, racing or other sporting organisations, and were suspected by some of being disreputable simply because of their calling, no matter how they actually behaved or how they used their wealth. Perhaps there was substance behind the suspicion.

Conventional wisdom has it that churches, chapels and other religious agencies, anti-gambling and temperance groups, trade unions and radical politicians were among the main proponents of consciously reformist models of rational, respectable and edifying recreations. Thus attitudes to recreation were closely linked to religion, work and politics. It is surprising, therefore, that historians of rational recreation have until recently paid too little attention to these influences. Leisure's relationships to religion, work and politics were highly significant, but could also be very complicated.[15] Leisure, like work, involved social struggles that made it highly politicised.[16] In this regard, community responses, regional differences and individual actions could be confusing. In the case of horse-racing, for example, actions at times transcended political party lines. While Tories were generally supporters of racing, the Liberals in general were hostile both to horse-racing itself, and to the betting and intemperance associated with it. Thus in some Liberal heartlands, such as Wales, horse-racing never became a major sport. However, in those parts of England where horse-racing had firm, long-standing foundations even local Liberal MPs were forced to endorse and sometimes attend the races, and some local Liberal voters enjoyed the sport. Thus political affiliation was not always an absolute guide to attitudes to leisure.

Those with strong religious convictions were presumably less likely to be attracted to the more sinful pleasures and more likely to be concerned about conscience, which was central in shaping attitudes to respectability. The role of the churches in the generation and sponsorship of respectable and rational recreations has yet to be adequately explored. This is especially the case with regard to nineteenth-century sport. Much has been made, for example, of church links with football clubs, although many teams may have simply represented friendships formed at Sunday School or Bible class, rather than the moral enthusiasm of sporting clerics. A great deal of scope for closer inquiry is available here. Attitudes to respectability were partly driven by the potent power of Protestantism, but the latter was beginning a slow retreat even in 1851, according to the religious census, especially north of the line from the Severn to the Wash, although higher-status districts within cities generally retained relatively high levels of church involvement. It is possible, therefore, that the importance of religious sponsorship has been overestimated. On the other hand, religion's continued success in helping to determine the habits of the late-Victorian Sunday should serve as a warning against underestimating its impact. In Leicester, for example, three symbolic attempts by the Leicester Secular Society in June 1885 to play cricket on corporation land, to show that 'the first day of the week might profitably be devoted to amusement', met escalating resistance. On the first occasion this was from the police, who took names and addresses, on the second from interruptions by a Sabbatarian 'mob', and on the third by 'over a thousand who turned up to obstruct play'.[17] The role of organised Sabbatarianism in delaying the development of Sunday sport, especially those sports with strong proletarian followings, has yet to be adequately investigated. Most local authorities banned Sunday football in their parks until the 1920s or 1930s, or even later. Nor has there yet been any satisfactory attempt to explore the disparate attitudes to sport within the churches. What were the different approaches, attitudes and beliefs of the Nonconformist, Anglican and Catholic churches, and were there differences within these communities? In nineteenth-century Britain, as, for example, in nineteenth-century Australia, Catholics were frequently punters, jockeys and bookmakers, and were far less inhibited than members of some of the non-Catholic churches with regard to gambling and temperance.[18] Horse-racing also offered opportunities for other religious minorities: Jews were increasingly prominent as owners and bookmakers towards the century's end.

Contributors to *Disreputable Pleasures* have had some observations to make about gender and disreputability in Victorian sport. Masculinity and sport went hand in hand. However, class made its impact too. In the men-only harriers clubs social background was of crucial importance. This was also true of the prestigious clubs and meetings that dominated horse-racing, among which the Jockey Club at Newmarket, the Dublin Turf Club and the

Royal Caledonian Hunt Club were the most 'respectable', and of the Marylebone Cricket Club and 'gentlemen's clubs' in the larger cities. Nevertheless, there were also less respectable equivalents to be found, often with wider clienteles, ranging from the Junior Tattersall's Club, a short-lived betting club in London, to the Post Office Inn in Manchester, a centre for betting in northwest England. All-male informal 'fraternities' in pubs, sports clubs and elsewhere were a feature of late-nineteenth-century Britain, and the complex interpenetration of sport and masculinity is certainly worth much more exploration than space in *Disreputable Pleasures* has allowed.

Women's relationship to 'less respectable pleasures' has only been hinted at here and also needs far greater consideration. Women made up a significant proportion of the audiences at music halls,[19] attended race meetings and placed bets in significant numbers.[20] Respectable middle-class women could be found in the grandstands of many sports grounds, representing a new type of femininity, a new diversity of manners and a new configuration of gender relations.[21]

Finally, in order to understand Victorian disreputable pleasures more completely, there is a need for a wider consideration of the varied representations of 'respectability' and 'unrespectability'. Textual analyses are all very well, but the visual should be inspected more fully – not only the cartoons and 'penny dreadfuls' but paintings, advertisements, posters and book illustrations.

Disreputable Pleasures is a beginning. Future studies will reveal yet more about the subtleties and shadings of leisure in Victorian Britain, and plug some of the gaps between ideological rhetoric and actual reality, between words and deeds, and between pure and impure actions. Leisure lay right across the main fault lines of Victorian society. The divisions found in the Victorian leisure cultures, recently described, for example, by Hugh Cunningham, are now rightly the subject of some debate and are certainly not the same as class divisions.[22] In time, this will become even clearer.

Finally, a prediction: the passage of time will also ensure that sophisticated pluralistic approaches are applied, involving an extensive and extended examination of sequential differences and similarities, and the extent of accommodation to respectability, adaptation to it, compliance with it, resistance to it and rejection of it. Past tendencies to overemphasise the extent of reputability and underemphasise the extent of disreputability may well become only too apparent.

Notes

Prologue

1. John Gardiner, *The Victorians: An Age in Retrospect* (London: Hambledon Press, 2002).
2. Raymond Williams, *Marxism and Literature* (Oxford: Oxford University Press, 1977), p. 110.
3. Two books by Raymond Williams, *Culture and Society, 1780–1950* (London: Hogarth Press, 1958) and *The Long Revolution* (London: Chatto and Windus, 1961), were particularly influential.
4. Peter Bailey, *Leisure and Class in Victorian England: Rational Recreation and the Contest for Control, 1830–1885*, 2nd ed. (London: Methuen, 1987); Hugh Cunningham, 'Leisure and Culture', in F.M.L. Thompson (ed.), *The Cambridge Social History of Britain, 1750–1940*, Vol. 2: *People and Their Environment* (Cambridge: Cambridge University Press, 1990); John Walton, *The English Seaside Resort: A Social History, 1750–1914* (Leicester: Leicester University Press, 1983).
5. See, for example, Asa Briggs, *Victorian Cities* (Harmondsworth: Penguin, 1968), p. 46.
6. Helen Meller, *Leisure and the Changing City, 1870–1914* (London: Routledge, 1976); M.R. Booth, *Theatre in the Victorian Age* (Cambridge: Cambridge University Press, 1991); T. Bennett, *The Birth of the Museum: History, Theory and Politics* (London: Routledge, 1995).
7. R.J. Morris, *Class, Sect and Party: The Making of the British Middle Class: Leeds, 1820–1850* (Manchester: Manchester University Press, 1990).
8. See Pierre Bourdieu, *Distinction: A Social Critique of the Judgement of Taste* (London: Routledge, 1992) and *The Field of Cultural Production* (Cambridge: Polity Press, 1993).
9. See, for example, Geoffrey Best, *Mid-Victorian Britain, 1851–1875* (London: Collins, 1971); F.M.L. Thompson, *The Rise of Respectable Society: A Social History of Victorian Britain 1830–1900* (London: Fontana, 1988); see also E. Ross, 'Not the Sort that Would Sit on the Doorstep: Respectability in Pre-World War I London Neighbourhoods', *International Journal of Labour and Working Class History* 27 (1985), 39–59.
10. See Cunningham, 'Leisure and Culture'.
11. Peter Bailey, 'Will the Real Bill Banks Stand Up? A Role Analysis of Mid-Victorian Working-Class Respectability', *Journal of Social History* 12 (1979).
12. Mike Huggins, 'More Sinful Pleasures? Leisure, Respectability and the Male Middle Classes in Victorian England', *Journal of Social History* 3:3 (2000), 585–600; Mike Huggins, *Flat Racing and British Society, c. 1790–1914: A Social and Economic History* (London and Portland, OR: Frank Cass, 2000).
13. Neil Tranter, *Sport, Economy and Society in Britain, 1750–1914* (Cambridge: Cambridge University Press, 1998), p. 2.
14. John Lowerson, *Sport and the English Middle Classes, 1870–1914* (Manchester: Manchester University Press, 1993), pp. 2, 268.
15. Richard Holt, *Sport and the British: A Modern History* (Oxford: Clarendon Press, 1989), p. 350.
16. Dennis Brailsford, *British Sport: A Social History* (Cambridge: Lutterworth Press, 1997), p. 88.
17. Neil Wigglesworth, *The Evolution of British Sport* (London and Portland, OR: Frank Cass, 1996), p. 11.
18. Bailey, 'Will the Real Bill Banks Stand Up?', 336–53. See, more generally, Peter Bailey, *Popular Culture and Performance in the Victorian City* (Cambridge: Cambridge University Press, 1998).

19. See Huggins, 'More Sinful Pleasures?'.
20. John Burnett, *Liquid Pleasures: A Social History of Drinks in Modern Britain* (London: Routledge 1999). See also David Gutzke, *Cultures of Drinking in Britain since 1750* (Manchester: Manchester University Press, forthcoming).
21. See Robert Stebbins, 'The Costs and Benefits of Hedonism: Some Consequences of Taking Casual Leisure Seriously', *Leisure Studies* 20:4 (Oct. 2001), 305–10.
22. David Cannadine, *The Language of Class* (New Haven, CT: Yale University Press, 1998).
23. Cunningham, 'Leisure and Culture', pp. 289–320.
24. Patrick Joyce, *Visions of the People: Industrial England and the Question of Class, 1848–1914* (Cambridge: Cambridge University Press, 1991).
25. Peter Bailey, 'The Politics and Poetics of Modern British Leisure', *Rethinking History* 3:2 (1999), 158.
26. J.A. Mangan, 'Regression and Progression: Introduction to the New Edition', *Athleticism in the Victorian and Edwardian Public School* (London and Portland, OR: Frank Cass, 2000), p. xxviii.
27. Peter Bailey, *Leisure and Class in Victorian England*, p. 71.
28. Simon Gunn, *The Public Culture of the Victorian Middle Class: Ritual and Authority and the English Industrial City, 1840–1914* (Manchester: Manchester University Press, 2000), p. 7.
29. John Springhall, *Youth, Popular Culture and Moral Panics: Penny Gaffs to Gangsta-Rap, 1830–1996* (Basingstoke: Macmillan, 1998), especially pp. 38–70.
30. This arcane expression could arguably be more usefully replaced by the term 'language usage'.
31. See, for example, Joan Chandler, *Television and National Sport: The United States and Britain* (Urbana, IL, and Chicago: University of Illinois Press, 1988); Gary Whannel, *Fields in Vision: Television Sport and Cultural Transformation* (London: Routledge, 1992).
32. Tony Collins, *Rugby's Great Split: Class, Culture and the Origins of Rugby League Football* (London and Portland, OR: Frank Cass, 1998).
33. For an earlier pragmatic use of the concept of 'fair play' – as a means of reducing the brutal anarchy of public school football and to ensure the schools' survival – see J.A. Mangan, 'From Hooligans to Heroes: Some English Historical Origins of Modern World Sport', unpublished paper delivered by invitation at various universities between 1990 and 2000.
34. Wigglesworth, *The Evolution of British Sport*, Ch. 5.
35. *Fortnightly Review* LV (1894), 679, quoted in Lowerson, *Sport and the English Middle Classes*, p. 117.
36. Richard Holt, *Sport and the British*, p. 347.
37. L. Davidoff, M. Doolittle, J. Fink and K. Holden, *The Family Story: Blood, Contract and Intimacy, 1830–1960* (Harlow: Addison Wesley Longman, 1999), p. 27.
38. Dahn Shaulis, 'Pedestriennes: Newsworthy but Controversial Women in Sports Entertainment', *Journal of Sport History* 26:1 (1999), 29–50.
39. J. Hargreaves, 'The Victorian Cult of the Family and the Early Years of Female Sport', in E.G. Dunning, J.A. Maguire and R.E. Pearton (eds), *The Sports Process: A Comparative and Developmental Approach* (Champaign, IL: Human Kinetics, 1993) pp. 71–84.
40. J. Sterngass, 'Cheating, Gender Roles and the 19th-century Croquet Craze', *Journal of Sport History*, 25:3 (1998), 398–418.
41. Lewis Carroll, 'Sylvie and Bruno Concluded', in *Complete Works* (New York: Modern Library, 1936), p. 597.

Chapter 1

1. Boris Johnson, 'The Only Reason for Envying the French', in *Daily Telegraph* (7 Sept. 2000), 8.
2. Andrew Gimson, 'Let Children Leave School at 14 if They Want To', in *Daily Telegraph* (20 Aug. 2000), 8.
3. The Schools Inquiries Commission Report (the Taunton Report), 1868, p. 47.
4. A.G. Bradley, A.C. Champneys and J.W. Baines, revised and continued by J.R. Taylor, H.C. Brentnall and G.C. Turner, *A History of Marlborough College* (London: John Murray, 1923), p. 200; henceforward *A History of Marlborough College* (1923). Another history, *Marlborough College 1843–1943: A Brief Survey to Commemorate the Centenary* (Cambridge: printed privately by W. Lewis, MA, at the University Press, 1943), states that 'within 20 years of its

precarious infancy Marlborough College had taken its place among the half-dozen schools which had hitherto stood head and shoulders above the rest' (p. 19).

5. Sir Lionel Earle, *Turn Over the Page* (London: Hutchinson, 1935), p. 17.
6. Edward Lockwood, *The Early Days of Marlborough College*, (London, Simpkin, Marshall, Hamilton and Kent, 1893)
7. Quoted in J.A. Mangan, 'Social Darwinism and Upper-class Education in Late Victorian and Edwardian England', in J.A. Mangan and James Walvin (eds), *Manliness and Morality: Middle-Class Masculinity in Britain and America, 1840–1940* (Manchester: Manchester University Press, 1987), p. 143.
8. 'Marlburiania', also known as the Kemble Notes, comprises two pages of typed comments based on marginal notes made by W. Kemble, a pupil contemporary of J.S. Thomas at Marlborough, on Rev. J.S. Thomas, 'Reminiscences', the end chapter of Newton Mant (ed.), *The New Chapel at Marlborough College* (London: W.H. Allen Lane, 1889). The copy owned and annotated by Kemble is in the Marlborough College Archives.
9. Earle, *Turn over the Page*, pp. 16–17.
10. *A History of Marlborough College* (1923), p. 124.
11. Earle, *Turn Over the Page*, p. 16.
12. John Betjeman, *Summoned by Bells* (London: John Murray, 1960), p. 155.
13. *A History of Marlborough College* (1923), p. 145.
14. Ibid., p. 144.
15. See the brief biography of James Franck Bright by 'AHJ', *Dictionary of National Biography, 1912–1921*, pp. 66–67.
16. Ibid.
17. Anonymous, 'Marlborough College Thirty Years Ago', in *All the Year Round* (10 April 1870), p. 421.
18. Thomas, 'Reminiscences', pp. 142–3.
19. Ibid., p. 142.
20. F.A.Y. Brown, *Family Notes* (Genoa: Instituto Sordomum, 1917), p. 188.
21. Ibid.
22. See 'Marlburiania', Marlborough College Archives.
23. See AHJ on James Franck Bright, *Dictionary of National Biography, 1912–1921*, p. 66.
24. Disreputable sexual pleasures are not fully discussed here. There is simply no space. I deal only, and briefly, with flagellation, seemingly the pre-eminent sexual indulgence of Victorian public schoolboys. I do not discuss other sexual practices such as homosexuality. There is no reason to believe that it was not widespread, however. John Addington Symonds has left a frank description of its prevalence at Harrow – see Phyllis Grosskirth, *John Addington Symonds: A Biography* (London: Longman, 1964) but see more especially 'Memoirs of John Addington Symonds', Vol. 1, manuscript copy in the London Library. Since Harrow was typical of the public schools of the period in most things Symonds's description of behaviour could, in my view, be reasonably taken to have wider applicability in the public schools of the time. The veil of silence, of course, was heavy and hid a great deal.
25. *Marlborough College 1843–1943*, p. 11.
26. Ibid., p. 13. However, another pupil who arrived on the first day wrote: 'The ride was very beautiful. When we arrived, the house, and as far as I have seen the rooms, arrangements, fare, etc., far exceed my expectations': L. Warwick James, 'Marlborough College 3. The Opening', in *Kennet* (Summer 1951), p. 14.
27. Ibid., p. 13.
28. Ibid., p. 14.
29. *Marlburian* (1880). I am grateful to Dr T.E. Rogers, archivist of Marlborough College, for this reference.
30. Ibid.
31. Ibid.
32. There is a mould for 'squalers' in the Natural History Museum in London. 'Both word and weapon were of Wiltshire origin', according to *A History of Marlborough College* (1923), p. 18.
33. *A History of Marlborough College* (1923), p. 126.
34. Ibid., p. 180.
35. Ibid., p. 144.
36. Ibid., pp. 77–8.
37. *Marlburian* (1880).

38. Thomas, 'Reminiscences', p. 154.
39. Thomas was an early assistant master, then a senior housemaster and, finally, a long-serving bursar, who played a major part in the financial resuscitation of the College in the second half of the nineteenth century. Thus, he was a loyal servant of Marlborough but also an honest recorder of early realities. He is indirectly accused of exaggeration by another contemporary at Marlborough in the 1840s, William Gildea (1848–51). Gildea, writing many years later in reaction to the Centenary History of Marlborough published in 1893, energetically denied the existence of poaching and painted an impossibly noble picture of the school in the 1840s, which runs contrary to the ethos of the times, the reports of other contemporaries and the official history. Gildea was also dismissive of the coverage of the Rebellion in the History of 1893.

    In my view, Gildea does not merit much attention. The present archivist of Marlborough College, Dr T.E. Rogers, has observed that 'Gildea with the passage of time had forgotten much of the excesses of the Rebellion and was indignant that the reputation of the Prefects (and by extension himself) was impugned by "The [1893] History" version': letter to the author dated 22 Nov. 2001.

    Rogers also remarks in the same letter that the College Archives contain a letter written in 1926 by A.G. Bradley, the author of the History of 1893, stating that 'he had interviewed many old boys who had been at the college in 1851 and whose memories of the event were substantially unanimous except in matters of detail and consistent with what he had written in The History'. Rogers adds that Bradley 'further goes on to say that Gildea was not one of those he had canvassed and wonders whether he had taken umbrage at not being asked'. Perhaps Bradley is rather over-defensive in making this remark, but there can be little doubt that Gildea was ridiculously over-defensive in his own reminiscences.
40. Thomas, 'Reminiscences', p. 154.
41. Ibid., pp. 187–8.
42. *Marlburian* (1880).
43. Ibid. The nickname was derived, it appears, from the mocking apocryphal tale of a group of Wiltshire rustics who once tried to rake the reflection of the moon out of a pond, thinking that it was a large cheese. It was a taunt that the 'primitives' could not bear. See Anonymous, 'Marlborough College Thirty Years Ago', p. 419.
44. Ibid.
45. *A History of Marlborough College* (1923).
46. R.G. Van Yelyr, *The Whip and the Rod* (London: Gerald G. Swan, 1941), p. 194.
47. Ian Gibson, *The English Vice: Beating, Sex and Shame in Victorian England and After* (London: Duckworth, 1978), p. 66.
48. Lockwood, *Early Days of Marlborough College*.
49. Ibid.
50. Brown, *Family Notes*, p. 96.
51. G.E. Hodgson (1847–54), who later became Superintendent of Gymnastics at Cheltenham College. The master was named as Clayton. See 'Marlburiana'.
52. Brown, *Family Notes*, p. 96.
53. Thomas, 'Reminiscences', pp. 144–6.
54. Lockwood, *Early Days of Marlborough College*, pp. 12–13.
55. See Mangan, 'Social Darwinism and Upper-class Education', p. 150.
56. Ibid.
57. *A History of Marlborough College* (1923), p. 148.
58. Quoted in Van Yelyr, *The Whip and the Rod*, p. 193.
59. Ibid., p. 189.
60. Ibid., p. 190.
61. Lockwood, *Early Days of Marlborough College*, p. 90.
62. Ibid., p. 13.
63. Ibid.
64. Ibid.
65. *A History of Marlborough College* (1923), pp. 148–9.
66. Thomas, 'Reminiscences', pp. 147–8.
67. See Gibson, *The English Vice*.
68. For further inspection of this 'flesh' than is possible in this chapter, see James Brinsley-Richards, *Seven Years at Eton* (London: Richard Bentley and Son, 1883); Rev. C. Allix Wilkinson, *Reminiscences of Eton (Keate's Time)* (London: Hurst and Blackett, 1888); *Eton under Hornby*

(London: A.C. Fifield, 1910); R.H. Hadden, *Reminiscences of William Rogers* (London: Kegan Paul, Trench, 1888). Edward Anthony, *Thy Rod and Staff* (New York: Little, Brown, 1995), remarks that Eton as the 'last school in English to abolish the use of the birch rod...has always had a tradition of stern and frequent corporal punishment', and points out that Tim Card, in *Eton Renewed: A History from 1860 to the Present Day* (London: John Murray, 1994), 'revealed that the last but two of the Eton headmasters, the late Anthony Chevenix-Trench, had been well up in the tradition of doctors Keate and Hawtrey, [being] like them a flagellator of passionate energy and questionable motives' (p. 31).

Incidentally, Anthony takes issue with Gibson over his insistence that flagellation was an 'English vice'. Anthony comments: 'In sole pursuit of the thesis embodied in his title, he ignores or overlooks the enormous books of flagellant tradition and erotica produced by other cultures and national groups' (p. 88).

69. John Lewis Deleware, 'Eton Thirty Years Since', in *Macmillan's Magazine*, 32:187 (May 1875), 46.
70. Ibid., p. 47.
71. *Marlborough College 1843–1943*, p. 2.
72. 'Marlburiana', Marlborough College Archives, p. 1.
73. Letter to Rev. W.A. Bradford (dated 31 Jan. 1857), in Marlborough College Archives.
74. Deleware, 'Eton Thirty Years Since', 47.
75. Christopher Tyerman, *A History of Harrow School, 1324–1991* (London: Oxford University Press, 2000), p. 257.
76. See J.A. Mangan 'Regression and Progression: Introduction to the New Edition', in *Athleticism in the Victorian and Edwardian Public School* (London and Portland, OR: Frank Cass, 2000), pp. xxviii–xxix.
77. Van Yelyn, *The Whip and the Rod*, p. 196. Tim Card, *Eton Established: A History from 1440 to 1860* (London: John Murray, 2001) is interestingly casual about flogging at Eton in the first half of the nineteenth century: 'it is...arguable that the Eton system of punishment was ineffective, indeed wrong...too much reliance by far...was placed on flogging. It was wrong not because most boys minded, but because they did not and because it was less alarming to be flogged for the tenth time than the first' (p. 179). Earlier Card writes, equally casually: 'some psychiatrists would argue that certain boys became habituated to flogging, and that they developed an addiction to flagellation. This behaviour pattern was known at the time, but was not a matter of such fascination as it would be today' (p. 138). Perhaps 'concern' would be a more appropriate term than 'fascination'.
78. Donald Pearsall, *Night's Black Angels – The Forms and Faces of Victorian Cruelty* (London: Hodder and Stoughton, 1975), p. 257.
79. Van Yelyr, *The Whip and the Rod*, p. 196.
80. Gibson, *The English Vice*, p. x.
81. Ibid., p. 262.
82. Steven Marcus, *The Other Victorians: A Study of Sexuality and Pornography in Mid-Nineteenth-Century England* (New York and London: W.W. Norton, 1985), p. 253.
83. Lockwood, *Early Days of Marlborough College*, p. 2.
84. *Marlborough College 1843–1943*, p. 2.
85. Ibid., p. 15.
86. *A History of Marlborough College* (1923), p. 123.
87. Ibid.
88. Robert Few, a member of the promotion committee that was instrumental in establishing the school: see *Marlborough College 1843–1943*, p. 9.
89. See *Marlborough College 1843–1943*, p. 130.
90. Thomas, 'Reminiscences', pp. 71–2.
91. Lockwood commented on absconding as follows:
My Master eyed me when I went up to class with a look of love, and soon proceeded to apply his cane to my back, which had hardly healed from the bruises it had received before. I would have run away had there been any hope of keeping away, but several boys had made the attempt, and after wandering about the country for some time, were caught, brought back and flogged (Lockwood, *Early Day of Marlborough College*, p. 66).
92. George Orwell 'Such, Such were the Joys', *Partisan Review*, Vol. 19 (1952), 521.
93. Ibid., 521.
94. See J.A. Mangan, 'Muscular, Militaristic and Manly: The British Middle-Class Hero and Moral

Messenger', in Richard Holt, J.A. Mangan and Pierre Lanfranchi (eds), *European Heroes: Myth, Identity, Sport* (London and Portland, OR: Frank Cass, 1996), p. 29.

95. Ibid., p. 32.
96. Ibid.
97. John Chandos, *Boys Together: English Public Schools, 1800–1864* (London: Hutchinson, 1984), p. 138.
98. Tim Card, *Eton Established*, p. 109. John Chandos has provided fuller details of the fatal fight: In a distraught letter to his mother, Milnes Gaskell wrote home, 'A most awful and horrible warning not to fight in the playing fields happened last night.' Two boys, Charles Woodman and Francis Ashley, the youngest son of the Earl of Shaftesbury, having quarrelled, their respective friends entered into an engagement for the principals to settle their differences in a fight in the afternoon of 2 March. Reports of what happened vary in many particulars, but what is known for certain is that the two boys – Ashley, aged 13, and Wood, aged 14 but considerably bigger – fought for about two and a half hours and at the end of that time they both collapsed. Wood was assisted from the field; Ashley in a state of coma was carried back to his house by two friends and placed on his bed. He never regained consciousness and died that night (*Boys Together*, p. 142).
99. Card, *Eton Established*, p. ??.
100. *A History of Marlborough College* (1923), p. 130.
101. Ibid., pp. 129–30.
102. Thomas, 'Reminiscences', called it 'notorious' and stated that it was named after the school's drawing master.
103. Thomas, 'Reminiscences', p. 139.
104. Ibid.
105. Ibid.
106. *A History of Marlborough College* (1923), p. 150.
107. Thomas, 'Reminiscences', p. 140.
108. Ibid., p. 141.
109. Brown, *Family Notes*, p. 88.
110. *A History of Marlborough College* (1923), p. 163.
111. Thomas, 'Reminiscences', p. 169.
112. Orwell, 'Such, Such were the Joys', p. 519.
113. *A History of Marlborough College* (1923), p. 72.
114. Thomas, 'Reminiscences', p. 176.
115. *A History of Marlborough College* (1923), p. 142.
116. Ibid., pp. 143–4.
117. *Marlborough College 1843–1943*, p. 2.
118. *A History of Marlborough College* (1923), p. 156.
119. Ibid.
120. 'Marlborough College Thirty Years Ago', *Marlburian*, p. 153.
121. I follow the spelling in L. Warwick James, *Marlborough College Register 1843–1952*, 9th ed. (1952). Elsewhere Warwick James (see *Kennet* [1951]), like Wilkinson in his letters, uses the spelling 'Pevier'. Whatever the correct spelling of his surname, his role in the Rebellion has ensured him a kind of immortality.
122. Thomas, 'Reminiscences', p. 174.
123. *A History of Marlborough College* (1923), p. 157.
124. 'Marlborough College Thirty Years Ago', p. 153.
125. L. Warwick James, 'Marlborough College: The Rebellion', *Kennet* (Winter 1951), 13.
126. Brown, *Family Notes*, p. 92.
127. Ibid., p. 93.
128. *A History of Marlborough College* (1923), p. 158.
129. Ibid.
130. Ibid.
131. 'Marlborough College Thirty Years Ago', 151.
132. *A History of Marlborough College* (1923), pp. 158–9.
133. Ibid.
134. Ibid., p. 160.
135. Ibid., p. 161.
136. According to Gerald Murray, in discussion with the author in the 1970s, the thrashing of Peviar and the throwing of fireworks into fires were exaggerations written for effect in the earliest

school history (1896). However, the main author of this history did interview witnesses of the Rebellion, who were all long dead by the time Murray offered his opinion.

137. 'Marlborough College Thirty Years Ago', pp. 153–4.
138. Brown, *Family Notes*, p. 94.
139. Thomas, 'Reminiscences', p. 182. Edward Lockwood recounted that some time later Wilkinson asked him 'to come into his private room, and there I found him in a state of considerable distress... when I entered the room I saw one whom hitherto I regarded almost as a god, but now when I came out he had henceforth in my estimation to take his place with other mortal men' (*Early Days of Marlborough College*, p. 138).
140. *A History of Marlborough College* (1923), p. 161.
141. See Warwick James, 'Marlborough College: The Rebellion', 15. Earlier in this article (on page 12) Warwick James warned his readers that, while there was obviously some foundation for the stories of the Rebellion, it was equally clear that none of the events had lost in the telling.
142. Quoted by Warwick James, 'Marlborough College: The Rebellion', 13.
143. L. Warwick James, 'Marlborough College 3. The Opening', *Kennet* (Winter 1951), 16.
144. See Canon W. Gildea, *Recollections of School Days at Marlborough College, 1848–1851* (London: privately printed by Arthur L. Humphreys, 1918).
145. Copy of letter in the Marlborough College Office. Thanks are extended once again to the school's archivist, Dr T.E. Rogers, for drawing it to my attention.
146. Matthew Wilkinson, Letter 257, to Mrs Twyford (dated 6 Nov. 1851). This letter and others cited below are included in 'Letters of Matthew Wilkinson 1849 Onwards, Transcribed from his Original Carbon Copies by L. Warwick James', photocopied and supplied to the author by Gerald Murray (then Marlborough College's archivist) in October 1975.
147. Wilkinson, Letter 266, to Rev. F. Webber (dated 10 Nov. 1851).
148. Wilkinson, Letter 279, to Rev. W.F. Cobb (dated 14 Nov. 1851).
149. Wilkinson, Letter 281, to F.A. McGeachy (undated).
150. Wilkinson, Letter 258, to W.H. Turner (dated 6 Nov. 1851).
151. Wilkinson, Letter 262, to Rev. L.B. Luther (dated 7 Nov. 1851).
152. Wilkinson, Letter 246, to Rev. G.F. Piggot (dated 31 Oct. 1851) .
153. Wilkinson, Letter 250, to Rev. H. Lee (dated 1 Nov. 1851).
154. Quoted in Warwick James, 'Marlborough College: The Rebellion', 14.
155. Quoted in L. Warwick James, 'Marlborough College 1. The Idea', *Kennet* (Winter 1950), 14.
156. See J.A. Mangan, *Athleticism in the Victorian and Edwardian Public School*, Ch. 2.
157. Letter in the Marlborough College Archives. Copy supplied to the author by Gerald Murray. G.T.L. Carwithen was the son of a West Country clergyman, Rev. G.W.T. Carwithen of Frithelstock, Torrington, Devon, and was at Marlborough from October 1850 to Easter 1856. Subsequently he had a distinguished military career, eventually commanding the King's Own Scottish Borderers. The author is indebted to Dr T.E. Rogers for this information.
158. Richard Reynolds, 'Tom Brown Would Not Recognise School Now', *Daily Telegraph* (1 Oct. 2002), 25; written in response to Bella Bathurst, 'Live-in Hell', *Daily Telegraph Magazine* (28 Sept. 2002), 56–8.
159. Ibid.
160. Ibid.

Chapter 2

1. *Daily Telegraph* (1 Nov. 2001), 3.
2. Ibid.
3. Ibid.
4. The *Daily Telegraph* (10 Nov. 2001), 11, reported on the Sirens, the women-only drinking club at St John's College, Cambridge; the all-female Magdalene Wyverns and the St John's all-male drinking society the Muff Divers; and 'excessive revelry', which included male and female students who 'urinated on the floor and walls of the lobby to A1, First Court'.
5. Edward Paice, *Lost Line of Empire: The Life of 'Cape to Cairo' Grogan* (London: HarperCollins, 2001), p. 16.
6. Ibid., p. 17.

7.   Ibid., p. 17.
8.   Ibid., p. 21.
9.   Ibid., p. 22.
10. Summary of Contents, St John's College Senior Dean's and Junior Dean's Disciplinary Books, St John's College, Cambridge, Archives.
11. Ibid.
12. Junior Dean's Disciplinary Book (1853).
13. Ibid.
14. Ibid.
15. Ibid.
16. Such men were numerous. They included, in particular, missionaries and educationalists who proved to be exceptionally enthusiastic promoters of the then largely English-inspired 'modern games' and their allegedly associated moral virtues. For an overview see, for example, J.A. Mangan, *The Games Ethic and Imperialism: Aspects of the Diffusion of an Ideal* (London and Portland, OR: Frank Cass, 1998).
17. Quoted in J.A. Mangan, 'Oars and the Man: Pleasure and Purpose in Victorian and Edwardian Cambridge', *History of Higher Education Annual*, Vol. 4 (1984), p. 52.
18. The term in its late Victorian and Edwardian meaning is defined and discussed in J.A. Mangan, *Athleticism in the Victorian and Edwardian Public School: The Emergence and Consolidation of a Victorian Ideology* (London and Portland, OR: Frank Cass, 2000).
19. See Mangan, *Athleticism*.
20. Especially in Mangan, *Athleticism* and *The Games Ethic*.
21. Hugh Kearney, *Scholars and Gentlemen: University and Society in Pre-Industrial Britain, 1500–1700* (London: Faber and Faber, 1970).
22. Ibid., p. 1.
23. J.A. Mangan, 'Lamentable Barbarians and Pitiful Sheep: Rhetoric of Protest and Pleasure in Late Victorian and Edwardian Oxbridge', in Tom Winifrith and Cyril Barret (eds), *Leisure in Art and Literature* (London: Macmillan, 1992), p. 130.
24. Ibid., p. 131.
25. T.E.B. Howarth, *Cambridge Between Two Wars* (London: Collins, 1978), pp. 16–17. See also Mangan, 'Lamentable Barbarians', p. 131, for a fuller quotation.
26. Noel Annan, *Leslie Stephen* (London: Weidenfeld and Nicolson, 1951), p. 30.
27. Rowland Prothero, *Whippingham to Westminster: The Reminiscences of Lord Ernle* (London: John Murray, 1938), p. 43.
28. Mangan, 'Lamentable Barbarians', p. 135.
29. William P. Baker, 'Sport and University Life in England 1879–1914', unpublished paper presented at the Clemson University Conference on Sport and Society (April 1982), p. 1.
30. Mangan, 'Oars and the Man', p. 53.
31. Ibid.
32. Baker, 'Sport and University Life in England', p. 2.
33. Mangan, 'Lamentable Barbarians', p. 131.
34. Mangan, 'Oars and the Man', pp. 52–3.
35. Ibid., p. 55.
36. See John Honey, *Tom Brown's Universe: The Development of the Public School in the Nineteenth Century* (London: Millington, 1977).
37. Mangan, *Athleticism*, p. 122.
38. Ibid., p. 123.
39. Ibid.
40. Mangan, 'Oars and the Man', p. 56.
41. Mangan, *Athleticism*, p. 123.
42. Ibid., pp. 123–4.
43. Mangan, 'Oars and the Man', p. 53.
44. Ibid., p. 54.
45. Ibid.
46. Mangan, 'Lamentable Barbarians', pp. 134–5.
47. Mangan, *Athleticism*, p. 125.
48. Ibid., pp. 125–6.
49. Ibid., p. 126.
50. Ibid.

51. Ibid., p. 125.
52. Mangan, 'Oars and the Man', pp. 54–5.
53. Mangan, 'Lamentable Barbarians', p. 139.
54. Charles Tennyson, *Cambridge from Within*, (London: Chatto & Windus, 1913), P. 166.
55. Mangan, *Lamentable Barbarians*, p. 139.
56. Ibid.
57. Mangan, *Oars and the Man*, p. 251.
58. Ibid.
59. Ibid.
60. Ibid.
61. Ibid.
62. Ibid., p.252.
63. B. H. Stewart, *Reminiscences* (1945), p. 1.
64. Ibid., p. 253.
65. Ibid., p. 257.
66. Arthur Gray, *A History of Jesus College* (Cambridge: Heffer, 1902), p. 224.
67. Mangan, *Oars and the Man*, p. 254.
68. *Blackwoods Magazine*, Oct, 1912, pp. 576–7.
69. Mangan, *Oars and the Man*, p. 255.
70. Steve Fairbairn, *Fulham of Jesus*, (London: 1937), p. 71.
71. A. Gray and F. Brittain, *A History of Jesus College*, (London: Heinemann, 1960), p. 171.
72. Mangan, *Oars and the Man*, p. 250.
73. Ibid., p. 255.
74. *Granta*, 17 May, 1894, p. 334.
75. Gray and Brittain, *Jesus College*, p. 155.
76. *Punch*, 29 July, 1893, p. 37.
77. Mangan, *Oars and the Man*, p. 260.
78. Ibid., p. 261.
79. Ibid., p. 261.
80. Ibid., p. 262.
81. Ibid.
82. Ibid.
83. Ibid.
84. Ibid.
85. Ibid.
86. Mangan, *Lamentable Barbarians*, p. 136.
87. Ibid., p. 151.
88. Mangan, *Oars and the Man*, p. 263.
89. Ibid., pp. 263–4.
90. "'My Tutor' by a Cynical Undergraduate", *Granta*, Vol. IX, No. 144, 7 December, 1895, Series 4 and 5, p. 18.
91. *Granta*, Vol. IX, No. 121, 11 November 1893, pp. 77–8.
92. *Oxford Review*, 21 January, 1885, p. 72.
93. Ibid., p. 75.
94. Mangan, *Athleticism*, p. 124.
95. Mangan, *Oars and the Man*, p. 265.

Chapter 3

1. W. Vamplew, *The Turf* (Harmondsworth: Allen Lane, 1976), p. 133.
2. See, for example, Mike Huggins, *Flat Racing and British Society, 1790–1914* (London and Portland, OR: Frank Cass, 2000), Ch. 3.
3. B.G. Orchard, *Liverpool's Legion of Honour* (Birkenhead: the author, 1893), pp. ix, xi.
4. W.J. Conybeare, *Perversion* (London: Smith, Elder, 1856), Ch. 14.
5. G.J. Milne, *Trade and Traders in Mid-Victorian Liverpool: Mercantile Business and the Making of a World Port* (Liverpool: Liverpool University Press, 2000), p. 4.
6. *Porcupine*, 29 Dec. 1866, 457.

7. S. Smith, *My Life Work* (London: Hodder & Stoughton, 1903), p. 108.
8. *Porcupine*, 17 May 1862, 49.
9. *Liver*, 27 May 1893.
10. B.G. Orchard, *The Clerks of Liverpool* (Liverpool: J. Collinson, 1871), p. 10.
11. *Clerks' Journal*, 3:30 (1 Aug. 1890).
12. Orchard, *Clerks of Liverpool*, p. 42.
13. *Porcupine* (5 Oct. 1867), 265.
14. G.J.S. Broomhall and J.H. Hubback, *Corn Trade Memories, Recent and Remote* (Liverpool: Northern Publishing, 1930), pp. 162–4, 263.
15. T.H. Bird, *A Hundred Grand Nationals* (London: *Country Life*, 1937), pp. 120–1.
16. *Liverpool Daily Post* (20 March 1899).
17. Huggins, *Flat Racing and British Society*, p. 79; J. Hughes, *Liverpool Banks and Bankers, 1760–1837* (Liverpool: Henry Young, 1906), p. 181.
18. E. Bradyll, *The Lays of Cotton Broking* (Liverpool: Harris, 1865), p. 4. This was published anonymously, but Bradyll's authorship was revealed in Orchard, *Liverpool's Legion of Honour*, p. 196.
19. Orchard, *Liverpool's Legion of Honour*, pp. 32, 65–6.
20. Orchard, C*lerks of Liverpool*, p. 16.
21. For a general account of racing at Liverpool see J.R. Pinfold, *Gallant Sport* (Halifax: Portway Press, 1999).
22. *Liverpool Chronicle* (19 May 1838).
23. *Liverpool Daily Post* (29 March 1879).
24. See the list in C. Pitt, *A Long Time Gone* (Halifax: Portway Press, 1996). A general history of racing in the area is given in P. Thompson, *On the Turf* (Bebington: Quarry Publications, 1991).
25. *Bethell's Life in London and Liverpool Sporting Register* appears to have lasted only from 1824 to 1827. The set of the *City Racing Record* in the British Library's Newspaper Library at Colindale covers the years 1887–97.
26. A. Birrell, *Some Early Recollections of Liverpool* (Liverpool: Henry Young and Sons, 1924), p. 10.
27. *Liverpool Daily Post* (27 March 1899).
28. *Liverpool Courier* (2 March 1836).
29. *Liverpool Standard* (1 March 1839).
30. *Liverpool Daily Post* (30 March 1899). Fry was also struck by the amounts of money that he saw changing hands. This led him to give up his drapery business and become a bookmaker. He prospered in his new business to such an extent that by the end of the century he was one of the country's leading bookmakers, being owed around £1 million in bets.
31. *Porcupine* (29 March 1879), 821.
32. J.K. Walton and A. Wilcox, *Low Life and Moral Improvement in Mid-Victorian England: Liverpool Through the Journalism of Hugh Shimmin* (Leicester: Leicester University Press, 1991), p. 79.
33. *Porcupine* (15 March 1862), 283.
34. *Liverpool Daily Post* (25 April 1870).
35. *Liverpool Citizen* (24 Sept. 1887).
36. *Porcupine* (25 March 1871), 651–2.
37. *Field Quarterly Magazine and Review*, Vol. 1 (1870), 138.
38. Walton and Wilcox, *Low Life and Moral Improvement*, p. 85.
39. This remarkable case can be followed in *Porcupine* (principally 12 April, 25 July and 26 July 1879, 264, although there are also references in the issues of 19 April, 40; 26 April, 57; 3 May, 73; and 10 May, 89). It is noticeable that even the *Porcupine* never refers to the young swells in the case by name.
40. Walton and Wilcox, *Low Life and Moral Improvement*, pp. 75–6, 84–5.
41. *Porcupine* (25 March 1871), 651–2.
42. Walton and Wilcox, *Low Life and Moral Improvement*, p. 79.
43. *Times* (17 April, 19 April and 5 May 1875).
44. *Porcupine* (27 Dec. 1879), 614.
45. Ibid. (19 July 1862), 125.
46. H. Shimmin, *Liverpool Life, Second Series* (Liverpool: Egerton Smith, 1857), pp. 13–19.
47. *Liverpool Chronicle* (11 July 1829).
48. Ibid.

49. *Liverpool Courier* (2 March 1836).
50. Letter from E.W. Topham to Halifax Wyatt (dated 24 Feb. 1872), Molyneux Muniments (Croxteth Hall, Merseyside) DDM 55.
51. *Liverpool Daily Post* (25 April 1870).
52. *Bethell's Life in London and Liverpool Sporting Register* (28 July 1827).
53. Letter from E.W. Topham to Halifax Wyatt.
54. *Porcupine* (25 March 1871), 651–2.
55. Bradyll, *The Lays of Cotton Broking*, pp. 8–9.
56. *Porcupine* (29 May 1869), 79.
57. *Liverpool Citizen* (6 June 1888).
58. *Liverpool Echo* (27 March 1897).
59. *Porcupine* (7 Jan. 1865), 327.
60. *Wasp* (4 Feb. 1882).
61. H. Shimmin, *Liverpool Life*, p. 98.
62. Ibid., pp. 100, 102.
63. *Liverpool Review* (2 Nov. 1889).
64. H. Shimmin, *Town Life* (London, 1858), pp. 152–3.
65. *Times* (3 May 1860).
66. *Wasp* (26 Nov. 1881).
67. *Porcupine* (17 March 1877), 810.
68. Ibid. (10 March 1877), 790; ibid. (24 March 1877), 823.
69. One such attempt was reported in the *Times* (21 April 1870).
70. *Liverpool Daily Post* (10 Nov. 1877).
71. This figure has been arrived at by comparing the clubs mentioned in a series of articles in the *Liverpool Review* (1883–84), with the list of Liverpool clubs in *Kelly's Directory of Lancashire, Liverpool and Manchester* (London: Kelly, 1887), pp. 639–40. Most, but by no means all, of the clubs were situated in the streets surrounding Williamson Square.
72. *Liverpool Review* (8 Sept. and 13 Oct. 1883).
73. Orchard, *Liverpool's Legion of Honour*, p. 62.
74. The Waterloo appears in the annual volumes of *Gore's Directory of Liverpool* from 1879 to 1913, but does not appear in the volume for 1917. The Waterloo was the longest-lasting of the Liverpool betting clubs, the majority of the others having disappeared by the mid-1890s.
75. *Liverpool Review* (13 Oct., 24 Nov. and 8 Dec. 1883).
76. *Times* (2 and 3 Nov. 1891).
77. *Wasp* (26 Nov. 1881).
78. *Liverpool Review* (26 July 1884).
79. *Liverpool Daily Post* (30 March 1899); *Baily's Magazine of Sports and Pastimes*, 89:516 (Feb. 1903), 134; *Index of Wills* (1903).
80. *Times* (29 and 30 Oct. 1891).
81. See, for example, the report of the case against the Caxton Club, *Liverpool Review* (1 Dec. 1883); for Raffles's views see *Liverpool Review* (15 Dec. 1883 and 26 July 1884).
82. *Liver* (3 June 1893).
83. *Times* (21 June 1894).
84. Liverpool Watch Committee, *Report on the Police Establishment and the State of Crime...*, *1894* (Liverpool: Watch Committee, 1895), p. 20. By 1902, however, the number had risen to 255.
85. *Liverpool Daily Post* (26 April 1870); *Porcupine* (30 April 1870), 50.
86. There is a considerable literature on the Maybrick case: see, for example, T. Christie, *Etched in Arsenic* (London: Harrap, 1969) or B. Ryan, *The Poisoned Life of Mrs Maybrick* (Harmondsworth: Penguin, 1977). The most recent life of Mrs Maybrick is A.E. Graham and C. Emmas, *The Last Victim* (London: Headline, 1999). The 'Ripper diary' has been published in full in S. Harrison, *The Diary of Jack the Ripper* (London: Smith Gryphon, 1993). For a spirited defence of the 'diary', which also uncovers a lot of new information about the Maybricks, see P. Feldman, *Jack the Ripper: The Final Chapter* (London: Virgin, 1998).
87. Quoted in Graham and Emmas, *The Last Victim*, p. 28.
88. *Liverpool Echo* (8 Aug. 1889).
89. Quoted in Feldman, *Jack the Ripper*, p. 304.
90. Quoted in Harrison, *The Diary of Jack the Ripper*, p. 275. All the entries in the 'diary' are undated.

91. Harrison, *The Diary of Jack the Ripper*, p. 36.
92. Christie, *Etched in Arsenic*, p. 32.
93. Ibid., p. 43.
94. *Liverpool Review* (6 July 1889).
95. *Liverpool Courier* (29 May 1889); *Liverpool Echo* (29 May 1889).
96. Ibid. (1 June 1889).
97. *Liverpool Post and Mercury* (2 May 1927).
98. *Liverpool Echo* (13 Aug. 1889).
99. *Liverpool Courier* (6 June 1889).
100. *Liverpool Echo* (8 June 1889).
101. Ibid. (14 and 23 Aug. 1889).
102. Orchard, *Liverpool's Legion of Honour*, pp. 619–20.
103. *Liverpool Echo* (12 Aug. 1889).
104. *Liverpool Citizen* (4 April 1888).
105. J.H. Hay and W.D. Scott, *Liverpool* (London: A. and C. Black, 1907), pp. 14–15. Scott also gives (pp. 116–17) one of the most lyrical descriptions of the Grand National, which deserves to be better-known.

Chapter 4

1. Henry Sell, 'The World's Press and its Developments', *Sell's Dictionary of the World's Press* (1900), p. 22.
2. See Virginia Berridge, 'Popular Journalism and Working-Class Attitudes: A Study of *Reynolds's Newspaper*, *Lloyd's Weekly Newspaper* and the *Weekly Times*, 1854–1886' (PhD dissertation, University of London, 1976) and Michael W. Shirley, '"On Wings of Everlasting Power": G.W.M. Reynolds and *Reynolds's Newspaper*, 1848–1876' (PhD dissertation, University of Illinois, 1997).
3. Harold Herd, *The March of Journalism* (London: Allen and Unwin, 1952), p. 186.
4. *Pall Mall Gazette* (9 Feb. 1889), 2.
5. See, for example, the chapter 'Working-Class Culture and Working-Class Politics in London, 1870–1900: Notes on the Remaking of a Working Class' in Gareth Stedman Jones, *Languages of Class* (Cambridge: Cambridge University Press, 1983); Ross McKibbin, *Ideologies of Class* (Oxford: Clarendon Press, 1990); T.G. Ashplant, 'London Working Men's Clubs, 1870–1914', in Eileen Yeo and Stephen Yeo (eds), *Popular Culture and Class Conflict, 1590–1914* (Brighton: Harvester Press, 1981); J. Cornford, 'The Transformation of Conservatism in the Late Nineteenth Century,' *Victorian Studies*, 7 (1963), 35–66; A. Davies, *Leisure, Gender and Poverty: Working-Class Culture in Salford and Manchester, 1900–1939* (Buckingham: Open University Press, 1992); Mike Savage, *The Dynamics of Working-Class Politics: The Labour Movement in Preston, 1880–1914* (Cambridge: Cambridge University Press, 1987); and Judith Walkowitz, *City of Dreadful Delight* (London: Virago, 1992).
6. See, for example, the chapter 'Traditions of Respectability in British Labour History' in Brian Harrison, *Peaceable Kingdom* (Oxford: Clarendon Press, 1992); F.M.L. Thompson, *The Rise of Respectable Society* (Cambridge, MA: Harvard University Press, 1988); Gertrude Himmelfarb, *Victorian Minds* (New York: Alfred A. Knopf, 1968); Asa Briggs, 'Victorian Values', in Eric M. Sigsworth (ed.), *In Search of Victorian Values* (Manchester and New York: Manchester University Press, 1988); and Peter Bailey, '"Will the Real Bill Banks Please Stand Up?": Towards a Role Analysis of Mid-Victorian Working-Class Respectability,' *Journal of Social History*, 12 (Spring 1979), 336–53.
7. For example, G.A. Cranfield, *The Press and Society: From Caxton to Northcliffe* (London and New York: Longman, 1978); Alan Lee, *The Origins of the Popular Press in England, 1855–1914* (London: Croom Helm, 1976); Lucy D. Brown, *Victorian News and Newspapers* (Oxford: Clarendon Press, 1985); R.D. Altick, *The English Common Reader* (Chicago: University of Chicago Press, 1957); Stephen Koss, *The Rise and Fall of the Political Press in Britain: The Nineteenth Century* (Chapel Hill, NC: University of North Carolina Press, 1981); Aled Jones, *Powers of the Press: Newspapers, Power and the Public in Nineteenth-Century England* (London: Scolar Press, 1996, reprinted Aldershot: Ashgate, 1998); Joel Wiener (ed.), *Papers for*

the Millions: The New Journalism in Britain, 1880s to 1914 (New York: Greenwood Press, 1988); and George Boyce, James Curran and Pauline Wingate (eds), *Newspaper History: From the Seventeenth Century to the Present Day* (Beverly Hills, CA: Sage Publications, 1978).

8. *Newspaper Press Directory* (1870), 138; Thomas Catling, *My Life's Pilgrimage* (London: John Murray, 1911), p. 231.
9. *Newsagent and Advertisers' Record* (Jan. 1890), 51.
10. *Sell's Dictionary of the World's Press* (1895), p. 360.
11. J.F. Stephen, 'The Sunday Papers', *Saturday Review* (19 April 1856), 493; *Newsagent and Bookseller's Review* (3 June 1899), 642.
12. Robert Donald, 'How Seven-Day Journalism Was Killed in London', *Outlook*, 63 (1899), 262.
13. *Pall Mall Gazette* (5 Feb. 1889), 1.
14. Quoted in *Sell's Dictionary of the World's Press* (1892), 150. This was quite similar to the claim made by the *Sunday Times*, which, with the *Observer*, was one of a small number of low-circulation middle-class Sunday papers, to be a daily paper published on Sundays.
15. I have examined the second incident in '"An Evil of Untold Magnitude": The Seven-Day Journalism Controversy of 1899 and Late Victorian Attitudes towards Sunday Newspapers', paper presented at the annual conference of the Research Society for Victorian Periodicals (1997). On the protests in 1889, see R.D. Blumenfeld, *The Press in My Time* (London: Rich and Cowan, 1933), pp. 157–8. Blumenfeld was the editor of the *New York Herald*'s London edition.
16. *New York Herald*, London edition (4 Feb. 1889), 5.
17. *Newsagent and Bookseller's Review* (20 May 1899), 604.
18. *Newspaper Press Directory* (1870), p. 139.
19. Harrison, 'Traditions of Respectability', p. 161.
20. H.H. Henson, 'The British Sunday', *National Review* (July 1899), 767–8.
21. The only full-length study of Victorian Sabbatarianism is John Wigley, *The Rise and Fall of the Victorian Sunday* (Manchester: Manchester University Press, 1980), which is rather brief and uncritical. See also the chapter 'Religion and Recreation in Nineteenth-Century England' in Harrison, *Peaceable Kingdom*, pp. 123–56.
22. *Pall Mall Gazette* (15 Feb. 1889), 2.
23. *Times* (19 July 1871), 12.
24. *Parliamentary Debates*, third series, Vol. 208 (1871), 254.
25. *Pall Mall Gazette* (12 Feb. 1889), 1.
26. *Times* (1 Jan. 1884), 6.
27. Stephen, 'The Sunday Papers', 493.
28. Catling, *My Life's Pilgrimage*, p. 202.
29. 'Newspaper Cleansing', *Saturday Review* (9 July 1870), 39.
30. *Newspaper Press* (1 Sept. 1870), 209.
31. Ibid.
32. *Newsagent and Bookseller's Review* (25 Feb. 1893), 209.
33. *Sun* (28 March 1899), 1.
34. *Newsagent and Bookseller's Review* (8 July 1899), 16.
35. Catling, *My Life's Pilgrimage*, p. 118.
36. It was the *Newsagent and Advertisers' Record*, a monthly publication, from 1889 to January 1891.
37. Although the *Newsagent and Bookseller's Review* was not included in her study, Laurel Brake has a chapter on news trade periodicals in *Print in Transition, 1850–1910: Studies in Media and Book History* (New York: Palgrave, 2001), pp. 67–83.
38. *Newsagent and Advertiser's Record* (Oct. 1889), 3.
39. *Newsagent and Bookseller's Review* (25 March 1893), 300.
40. Ibid. (30 Sept. 1893), 327.
41. Ibid. (15 April 1899), 437.
42. Ibid. (28 Jan. 1893), 108.
43. Ibid. (3 June 1899), 642.
44. Ibid. (10 June 1899), 665.
45. Ibid. (8 July 1899), 16.
46. Ibid. (11 March 1893), 246.
47. Ibid. (28 Jan. 1893), 102.
48. Ibid. (13 May 1893), 482.
49. Ibid. (11 Feb. 1893), 149.

50. Ibid. (10 June 1899), 665.
51. Ibid. (28 Jan. 1893), 102.
52. Ibid. (4 Feb. 1893), 197.
53. Ibid. (28 July 1893), 104.
54. Ibid. (10 March 1894), 234.
55. Ibid. (9 Sept. 1893), 254.
56. Ibid., 248.
57. Ibid. (28 Jan. 1893), 102.
58. Ibid. (11 Feb. 1893), 150.
59. Ibid. (25 Feb. 1893), 209.
60. Ibid. (11 March 1893), 246.
61. Ibid. (22 April 1893), 402.
62. Ibid. (6 May 1893), 446.
63. Ibid. (20 May 1893), 493.
64. Ibid. (28 June 1894), 58.
65. Ibid., 59.
66. The relevant issues of the _Newsagent and Bookseller's Review_ describing the meeting have been lost. See _Times_ (21 Aug. 1894), 9.
67. _Newsagent and Bookseller's Review_ (24 June 1899), 722.
68. Ibid., 724.
69. Ibid.
70. Even the arrival of the halfpenny _Daily Mail_ in 1896 did not seriously diminish the value of the Sunday paper, as the _Mail_ was initially an eight-page paper, about half advertisements, while _Lloyd's_ had 24 pages, about one third advertisements.
71. Richard Holt, _Sport and the British: A Modern History_ (Oxford: Clarendon Press, 1989), p. 135.
72. Wray Vamplew, _Pay Up and Play the Game: Professional Sport in Britain, 1875–1914_ (Cambridge: Cambridge University Press, 1988), p. 63.
73. _Newsagent and Bookseller's Review_ (28 Jan. 1893), 101.
74. Ross McKibbin, 'Working-Class Gambling in Britain, 1880–1939', in _Ideologies of Class_, p. 123.
75. Ibid., p. 131.
76. Holt, _Sport and the British_, 136–48. See also Peter Bailey, _Leisure and Class in Victorian England_ (London: Routledge, 1978).
77. Holt, _Sport and the British_, p. 180.
78. Joan Neuberger, _Hooliganism: Crime, Culture and Power in St Petersburg, 1900–1914_ (Berkeley, CA, and Los Angeles: University of California Press, 1993).
79. Ibid., p. 21.
80. Ibid.
81. _Reynolds's Newspaper_ (12 Oct. 1890), 3.
82. _Newsagent and Bookseller's Review_ (25 Feb. 1893), 209.
83. The _People_ did run a regular cycling column, all year round, entitled 'Mr Wheeler', which ran to about 20 per cent of its total sporting coverage, but it was the only Sunday paper to pay that much attention to cycling.
84. Sunday papers usually printed several editions, starting as early as Thursday for Continental editions, although the bulk came out on Saturday afternoons (for the provinces) or early Sunday mornings (for London). In most cases the content, including sporting columns, remained largely unchanged; only Saturday news (usually sensational) was added to the Sunday morning edition. Printing extensive match results might have involved too much typesetting for a single evening.
85. _Weekly Dispatch_ (5 Oct. 1890), 9.
86. _People_ (8 June 1890), 4.
87. Ibid. (22 June 1890), 4.
88. _Reynolds's Newspaper_ (12 Oct. 1890), 3.
89. _People_ (22 June 1890), 4.
90. Ibid. (8 June 1890), 4.
91. See, for example, the _Weekly Dispatch_ (15 June 1890), 5.
92. _Reynolds's Newspaper_ (12 Oct. 1890), 3.
93. Ibid. (25 April 1897), 2.
94. _Weekly Dispatch_ (25 April 1897), 10.
95. _Weekly Times and Echo_ (8 June 1890), 1.

96. Ibid. (15 June 1890), 6.
97. Ibid. See also 'Newspaper Happenings,' *Sell's Dictionary of the World's Press* (1891), p. 97.
98. *Weekly Times and Echo* (8 June 1890), 1.
99. Ibid. (22 June 1890), 9.
100. Ibid.
101. Ibid. (15 June 1890), 6 (emphasis in the original).
102. Ibid. (8 June 1890), 1.
103. David Cannadine, *Class in Britain* (London: Penguin Books, 1998), p. 16.

Chapter 5

1. Richard Davenport-Hines, *Gothic: 400 Years of Excess, Horror, Evil and Ruin* (London: Fourth Estate, 1999), pp. 11, 248. In the late 1950s much the same kind of outraged response greeted the first of the many Dracula and Frankenstein films produced by Hammer Films: Jonathan Rigby, *English Gothic: A Century of Horror Cinema* (London: Reynolds and Hearn, 2000), pp. 36–77. Edward Lloyd put out mass-produced weekly or monthly serials ('penny bloods') from Salisbury Square, London, such as James Malcolm Rymer's *Varney the Vampire, or the Feast of Blood* (1846–47).
2. B.R. Mitchell and P. Deane, *Abstract of British Historical Statistics* (Cambridge: Cambridge University Press, 1962), p. 12; James Greenwood, 'Penny Packets of Poison' [1869], in Peter Haining (ed.), *The Penny Dreadful, or Strange, Horrid and Sensational Tales* (London: Gollancz, 1975), pp. 357–71; Elizabeth James and Helen R. Smith, *Penny Dreadfuls and Boys' Adventures: The Barry Ono Collection of Victorian Popular Literature in The British Library* (London: British Library, 1998). For a definition of the 'penny dreadful' see John Springhall, *Youth, Popular Culture and Moral Panics: Penny Gaffs to Gangsta-Rap, 1830–1996* (Basingstoke: Macmillan, 1998), pp. 39–44.
3. Anonymous, *Tales of Highwaymen or, Life on the Road* (London: NPC, 1865–66); [Francis Hitchman], 'Penny Fiction', *Quarterly Review*, 171 (1890), 152; Walter Dexter (ed.), *The Letters of Charles Dickens*, Vol. 2 (London: Nonesuch Press, 1938), p. 548. Reading genre fiction solely for amusement continues to offend high-minded critics.
4. J.P. Harrison, 'Cheap Literature – Past and Present', *Companion to the Almanac of the Society for the Diffusion of Useful Knowledge or Year Book of General Information for 1873* (London: Society for the Diffusion of Useful Knowledge, 1872), p. 70; Edwin Hodder, *The Life and Work of the Seventh Earl of Shaftesbury*, Vol. 3 (London: Cassell, 1886), p. 469.
5. Patrick Dunae, 'The Boy's Own Paper: Origins and Editorial Policies', *The Private Library*, 9 (1976), 122–58; Greenwood, 'Penny Packets of Poison', p. 367; 'The Penny Dreadful', Correspondence, *Daily News* (28 Sept. 1895), 7.
6. Potts cited by Anonymous, 'Trashy Literature', *Bookseller*, 201 (4 Aug. 1874), 632–3; Norman Vance, 'The Ideal of Manliness', *Times Educational Supplement*, 28 Sept. 1973, 24; Jeffrey Richards (ed.), *Imperialism and Juvenile Literature* (Manchester: Manchester University Press, 1989); Marjory Lang, 'Childhood's Champions: Mid-Victorian Children's Periodicals and the Critics', *Victorian Periodicals Review*, 13 (1980), 22.
7. Springhall, *Youth, Popular Culture and Moral Panics*, pp. 163–8; 'George Savage', *Charley Wag, the New Jack Sheppard* (London: William Grant, 1860–61), pp. 3, 20, 238, 577. 'Savage' may have been the essayist George Augustus Sala, who was a member of the Savage Club.
8. J.C. Reid, *Bucks and Bruisers: Pierce Egan and Regency England* (London: Routledge, 1971), pp. 52–69; Rohan McWilliam, 'The Mysteries of G.W.M. Reynolds: Radicalism and Melodrama in Victorian Britain', in Malcolm Chase and Ian Dyck (eds), *Living and Learning: Essays in Honour of J.F.C. Harrison* (Aldershot: Scolar Press, 1996), pp. 182–98; Louis James, 'The Trouble with Betsy: Periodicals and the Common Reader in Mid-Nineteenth Century England', in Joanne Shattock and Michael Wolff (eds), *The Victorian Periodical Press: Samplings and Soundings* (Leicester: Leicester University Press, 1982), p. 358.
9. Anonymous, *The Wild Boys of London, or The Children of Night. A Story of the Present Day* (London: NPC, 1864–66), p. 2; Springhall, *Youth, Popular Culture and Moral Panics*, pp. 81–4; E. S. Turner, *Boys Will Be Boys: The Story of Sweeney Todd, Deadwood Dick, Sexton Blake, Billy Bunter, Dick Barton et al.* (London: Michael Joseph, 1948), p. 66.

10. Anonymous, *The Wild Boys of London*, pp. 2–18; Paul Schlicke (ed.), *Oxford Reader's Companion to Dickens* (Oxford: Oxford University Press, 1999), pp. 437–41, 450.

11. 'Lieut. Parker', S.U.S. [pseud.], *The Young Ladies of London; or, The Mysteries of Midnight* (London: NPC, 1867–68), pp. 3, 6–7, 10; Gareth Stedman Jones, *Outcast London: A Study in the Relationship Between Classes in Victorian Society* (Harmondsworth: Penguin, 1984), pp. 67–126.

12. *Returns of Allotments, News Agents' Newspaper & Publishing Co.*, Companies House, BT31/631/2644, Public Record Office, London; Irving Lyons, *The Boy Pirate; or, Life on the Ocean* (London: NPC, 1865); 'Lieut. Parker' [pseud.], *The Boy Rover; or, The Smuggler of the South Seas* (London: Henry Lea, 1866), pp. 4–6; Patricia Anderson, *When Passion Reigned: Sex and the Victorians* (New York: Basic Books, 1995), pp. 101–2. 'Walter' was probably H.S. Ashbee, a bibliographer of erotica: see Ian Gibson, *The Erotomaniac: The Secret Life of Henry Spencer Ashbee* (London: Faber and Faber, 2001).

13. Anonymous, *Rose Mortimer; or, The Ballet-Girl's Revenge* (London: NPC, 1865?), pp. 12, 15; Anonymous, 'Mischievous Literature', *Bookseller*, 126 (1 July 1868), 446.

14. Anonymous, *The Work Girls of London: Their Trials and Temptations, A Novel* (London: NPC, 1865), p. 38; Anonymous, *The Outsiders of Society; or, The Wild Beauties of London* (London: Henry Lea, 1866), p. 6.

15. Anonymous, *Fanny White and Her Friend Jack Rawlings: A Romance of a Young Lady Thief and a Boy Burglar* (London: George Vickers, 1865?), pp. 54–5. Like *Charley Wag*, this has been attributed to 'George Savage', G. A. Sala or Frederick 'Harry' Hazleton.

16. McWilliam, 'The Mysteries of G.W.M. Reynolds', p. 192; 'The Literature of Vice', *Bookseller*, 110 (28 Feb. 1867), 122.

17. Anna Clark, 'The Politics of Seduction in English Popular Culture, 1748–1848', in Jean Radford (ed.), *The Progress of Romance: The Politics of Popular Fiction* (London: Routledge, 1986), pp. 47–70; see also Shani D'Cruze, *Crimes of Outrage: Sex, Violence and Victorian Working Women* (London: UCL Press, 1998).

18. George Emmett, *Captain Jack; or, One of the Light Brigade* (London: Hogarth House, *c.* 1885); 'Ralph Rollington' [John Allingham], *A Brief History of Boys' Journals, With Interesting Facts About the Writers of Boys' Stories* (Leicester: H. Simpson, 1913), pp. 17, 21–5; John Medcraft, 'The Rivalry of Brett and Emmett', *Collector's Miscellany*, 7 (1947), 103–5.

19. George Emmett, *Boys of Bircham School* (London: Hogarth House, *c.* 1880), pp. 3, 12. Testifying to Dickens's all-pervasive and facetious influence, Bircham was the first in a long line of headmasters whose onomatopoeic names are indelibly linked in school stories with corporal punishment. Other examples include Thrasham and Birchoften.

20. George Emmett (attrib.), *Tom Wildrake's Schooldays* (London: Hogarth House, *c.* 1885); *Young Tom's Schooldays* (London: Hogarth House, *c.* 1880), p. 214. On Burrage see John Springhall, '"Boys of Bircham School": The Penny Dreadful Origins of the Popular English School Story, 1867–1900', *History of Education*, 20 (1991), 81–5; 'A Latter-Day Pilgrim' [E.H. Burrage], *The Ruin of Fleet Street* (London: E.W. Allen, 1885), pp. 22–3; 'Death of E.H. Burrage', *Surrey Mirror and County Post* (10 March 1916), 5.

21. John Springhall, '"A Life Story for the People"? Edwin J. Brett and the London "Low-Life" Penny Dreadfuls of the 1860s', *Victorian Studies*, 33 (1990), pp. 223–46; [W. Thompson Townsend], *The Captain of the School* (London: *Boys of England* Office, 1882), pp. 1–6 (originally serialised in *Boys of England*, July to Nov. 1867); Townsend, *Unlucky Bob; or, Our Boys at School* (London: *Boys of England* Office, *c.* 1905; originally serialised in *Boys of England*, July to Oct. 1868).

22. [Townsend], *The Captain of the School*, pp. 5–6, 34; Springhall, '"Boys of Bircham School"', 85; George Emmett (attrib.), *Tom Wildrake's Schooldays*, p. 67.

23. Anonymous, 'Our New Story', *Young Englishman*, 2 (7 Feb. 1874), 264; [Kevin Carpenter], *Penny Dreadfuls and Comics: English Periodicals for Children from Victorian Times to the Present Day* (London: Victoria and Albert Museum, 1983), pp. 6, 12.

24. Bracebridge Hemyng, 'Jack Harkaway's Schooldays', *Boys of England*, Vol. 10 (9 Sept. 1871), 241–4; Graham Greene, 'Harkaway's Oxford', *Collected Essays* (Harmondsworth: Penguin, 1970), pp. 180–3.

25. 'Ralph Rollington', *A Brief History*, pp. 7–8; E.M. Sanchez-Saavedra, 'The Anglo-American Pulp Wars: Edwin Brett vs. Frank Leslie', *Primary Sources and Original Works*, 4 (1996), 103–17; Albert Johannsen, *The House of Beadle and Adams and its Dime and Nickel Novels: The Story of a Vanished Literature*, Vol. 2 (Norman, OK: University of Oklahoma Press, 1950), pp. 138–9.

26. Anonymous, *Bicycle Bob; or, Who Will Win* (London: *Boys of England* Office, *c.* 1895), pp. 6–8, 34–5. The hobby of cycling first swept through England in the 1890s.
27. Anonymous, *The Oxford and Cambridge Eights; or, The Young Coxswain's Career* (London: Harkaway House, *c.* 1890), pp. 4–5, 6, 8.
28. Anonymous, 'Tom Floremall's Schooldays', *Boys of England*, Vol. 16 (Feb. to Oct. 1876); Tom Hopperton, 'Digging Around the Roots, Pt. 3', *Story Paper Collector*, 4 (1962), 91–6; *Leeds Mercury* cited by Anonymous, 'Penny Dreadfuls', *Public Opinion*, 46 (22 Aug. 1884), 238–9.
29. Anonymous, *The Wild Boys of London*, pp. 6–7, 18; Joseph Bristow, *Empire Boys: Adventures in a Man's World* (London: Arnold, 1991), p. 25; see also David Alderson, *Mansex Fine: Religion, Manliness and Imperialism in Nineteenth-Century British Culture* (Manchester: Manchester University Press, 1998).
30. Springhall, *Youth, Popular Culture and Moral Panics*, pp. 81–92; Springhall, *Coming of Age: Adolescence in Britain, 1860–1960* (Dublin: Gill and Macmillan, 1986), pp. 105, 121, 153.
31. See Pierre Bourdieu, tr. Richard Nice, *Distinction: A Social Critique of the Judgement of Taste* (London: Routledge, 1984); Lawrence W. Levine, *Highbrow/Lowbrow: The Emergence of Cultural Hierarchy in America* (Cambridge, MA: Harvard University Press, 1988).

Chapter 6

1. See, for example, L. Tickner, *The Spectacle of Women: Images of the Suffrage Campaign, 1907–14* (London: Chatto and Windus, 1987); Catherine Hall, *Fun without Vulgarity: Victorian and Edwardian Popular Entertainment Posters* (London: HMSO, 1996); Patricia Anderson, *The Printed Image and the Transformation of Popular Culture, 1790–1860* (Oxford: Clarendon Press, 1991).
2. Lynda Nead, *Victorian Babylon: People, Streets and Images in Nineteenth-Century London* (New Haven, CT: Yale University Press, 2000); Peter Burke, *Eyewitnessing: The Use of Images as Historical Evidence* (London: Reaktion Books, 2001).
3. See T. Benson, 'Low and the Dictators', *History Today*, 51:3 (2001), 35–43. For an example from US politics see R.A. Fischer, *Them Damned Pictures: Explorations in American Political Cartoon Art* (New Haven, CT: Archon Books, 1996).
4. A relatively early example is F.E. Huggett, *Victorian England as Seen by* Punch (London: Book Club Associates, 1978). See also A. Fowler and T. Wyke, 'Cartooning King Cotton', *Historian*, 55 (Aug. 1997), 17–20; A. Fowler and T. Wyke, 'Tickling Lancashire's Funny Bone: The Gradely Cartoons of Sam Fitton', *Transactions of the Lancashire and Cheshire Antiquarian Society*, 89 (1993), 1–53; and Ronald Pearson, 'Thackeray and *Punch* at the Great Exhibition: Authority and Ambivalence in Verbal and Visual Caricature', in Louise Purbrick (ed.), *The Great Exhibition of 1851* (Manchester: Manchester University Press, 2001).
5. S.W. Pope, 'Sport History: Into the 21st Century', *Journal of Sport History*, 25:2 (1998), iv. A rare exception is C. Lansbury, 'Sporting Humour in Victorian Literature', *Mosaic* 9:4 (1976), 65–75.
6. See A. Melling, 'Ray of the Rovers: The Working-Class Heroine in Popular Football Fiction, 1915–25', *International Journal of the History of Sport*, 15:1 (1998), 97–122; Dave Russell, *Football and the English* (Preston: Carnegie Publishing 1997); R. Dickason, 'Sport in British TV Ads: Representation or Pretext?', *Revue française de civilisation britannique* (April 2000), 89–102.
7. See Richard Altick, Punch: *The Lively Youth of a British Institution, 1841–1851* (Columbus, OH: Ohio State University Press, 1997); Peter Bailey, *Popular Culture and Performance in the Victorian City* (Cambridge: Cambridge University Press, 1998), Ch. 3.
8. Standard texts on Victorian sport have generally eschewed references to cartoons. For example, John Lowerson, *Sport and the English Middle Classes, 1870–1914* (Manchester: Manchester University Press, 1993), contains only one reference to *Punch*. J.A. Mangan, *Athleticism in the Victorian and Edwardian Public School* (London and Portland, OR: Frank Cass, 2000) is exceptional in providing references in double figures.
9. Allen Guttman, *The Erotic in Sports* (New York: Columbia University Press, 1996), uses photographs, paintings and other material to show how pictures of sport can be suffused with a sense of erotic pleasure.
10. *Punch* (26 May 1849), 218.

11. Charles Dickens and W.H. Wills, 'Epsom', *Household Words* 3:63 (7 June 1851); Hippolyte Taine, *Notes on England* (London: Caliban Press, 1995; translation of *Notes sur l'Angleterre* [1860–1870]).
12. Frank Morris, '*Punch*'s First Ten Years', *Journal of Newspaper and Periodical History*, 7:2 (1991), 67.
13. *Punch* (1 June 1872), 225.
14. Almost every volume of *Punch* contains some of these: see, for example, *Punch* (Nov. and Dec. 1887), 227, 271, 289.
15. See Altick, *Punch: The Lively Youth of a British Institution*; see also A. Adrian, *Mark Lemon: First Editor of* Punch (London: Oxford University Press, 1966); Alison Adburgham, *A* Punch *History of Manners and Modes, 1841–1940* (London: Hutchinson, 1961).
16. Taine, *Notes on England*, pp. 197–8.
17. Caroline Jackson-Houston, 'The Cheek of the Young Person: Sexualised Popular Discourse as Subtext in Dickens', in Martin Hewitt (ed.), *Unrespectable Recreations* (Leeds: Leeds Centre for Victorian Studies, 2001), pp. 31–45.
18. See Steven Marcus, *The Other Victorians: A Study of Sexuality and Pornography in Mid-Nineteenth Century England* (London: Weidenfeld and Nicolson, 1966).
19. See Raymond Carr, *English Foxhunting* (London: Weidenfeld and Nicolson, 1976); David Itzkowitz, *Peculiar Privilege: A Social History of English Foxhunting, 1753–1855* (Hassocks: Harvester Press, 1977)
20. See Grant Jarvie, *Highland Games: The Making of the Myth* (Edinburgh: Edinburgh University Press, 1991); Alistaire Durie, 'Unconscious Benefactors: Grouse Shooting in Scotland, 1780–1914', *International Journal of the History of Sport*, 15:3 (1998), 57–73.
21. On the Derby see Altick, *Punch: The Lively Youth of a British Institution*, pp. 533–4.
22. *Punch* (30 March 1872), 136.
23. Ibid. (24 Feb. 1866), 78; ibid. (30 Oct. 1875), 17; ibid. (24 Sept. 1887), 129.
24. Ibid. (15 Oct. 1864), 155.
25. Ibid. (29 Sept. 1894), 147.
26. Ibid. (24 Sept. 1864), 132.
27. Ibid. (10 Nov. 1866), 198.
28. For details of current research on the place of women in Victorian sport see the succinct summary in Neil Tranter, *Sport, Economy and Society in Britain, 1750–1914* (Cambridge: Cambridge University Press, 1998), Ch. 6.
29. See, for example, Patricia Marks, *Bicycles, Bangs and Bloomers: The New Woman in the Popular Press* (Lexington, KY: University Press of Kentucky, 1990); Marilyn Constanzo, '"One Can't Shake Off the Women": Images of Sport and Gender in *Punch*, 1901–10', *International Journal of the History of Sport*, 19:1 (2002), 31–56.
30. Jennifer Hargreaves, 'Playing like Gentlemen Yet Behaving like Ladies: Contradictory Features of the Formative Years of Women's Sport', *British Journal of Sports History*, 2:1 (1985), 42.
31. For examples see Adburgham, *A* Punch *History of Manners and Modes*.
32. Good visual evidence of the increasing involvement of middle-class women in sporting activity between 1870 and 1900 can be found in the illustrations in magazines of the period such as the *Queen* and the *Graphic*.
33. Lowerson, *Sport and the English Middle Classes, 1870–1914*, p. 3.
34. *Punch* (27 Nov. 1875), 217.
35. For a short discussion of the depiction of flirting in *Punch* see Jihang Park, 'Sport, Dress Reform and the Emancipation of Women in Victorian England: A Reappraisal', *International Journal of the History of Sport*, 6:1 (1989), 17.
36. *Punch* (18 May 1872), 41.
37. In the 1870s the membership of the Wimbledon All-England Croquet Club was dominated by military gentlemen.
38. *Punch* (13 June 1868), 260.
39. Ibid. (28 June 1894), 39.
40. On the reproduction of such cartoons in the course of debates in New Zealand about the social transgressions of the 'New Woman' see Clare Simpson, 'Respectable Identities: New Zealand Nineteenth-Century "New Women" – on Bicycles', *International Journal of the History of Sport*, 18:1 (2001), 57.
41. *Punch* (25 June 1887), 306.
42. Ibid. (24 March 1894), 141.

43. Ibid. (6 Dec. 1899), 268.
44. See, for example, Mangan, *Athleticism in the Victorian and Edwardian Public School*.
45. *Punch* (6 Sept. 1873), 94.
46. See J.A. Mangan, 'Lamentable Barbarians and Pitiful Sheep: Rhetorics of Protest and Pleasure in Late Victorian Oxbridge', in T. Winnifrith and C. Barrett (eds), *Leisure in Art and Literature* (London: Macmillan Press, 1986); T.J. Chandler, 'Games at Oxbridge and the Public Schools, 1830–1880: The Diffusion of an Innovation', *International Journal of the History of Sport*, 8:2 (1991), 174.
47. *Punch* (15 June 1872).
48. See J.A. Mangan, 'Oars and the Man: Pleasure and Purpose in Victorian and Edwardian Cambridge', *British Journal of Sports History*, 1:3 (1984), 245–71.
49. *ASHH* is discussed in detail in Bailey, *Popular Culture and Performance*, Ch. 3.
50. *ASHH* (13 July 1895).
51. Ibid. (11 June 1885).
52. Ibid. (20 July 1895).
53. Ibid. (6 June 1885). See also Bailey, *Popular Culture and Performance*, p. 70.
54. *ASHH* (4 July 1885).
55. Ibid. (6 June 1885).
56. Ibid. (18 July and 8 Aug. 1885).
57. Ibid. (3 Oct. 1885).
58. Ibid. (9 March 1895).
59. Bailey, *Popular Culture and Performance*, pp. 151–74.
60. *ASHH* (27 April 1895).
61. Ibid. (8 June 1895).
62. See, for example, Gary Whannel, *Fields in Vision: Television Sport and Cultural Transformation* (London: Routledge, 1992).
63. This field is explored further in Mike Huggins, *Sport and the Victorians* (London: Hambledon Press, forthcoming).
64. Jeff Hill, 'Cocks, Cats, Caps and Cups: A Semiotic Approach to Sport and National Identity', *Culture, Sport, Society*, 2:2 (1999), 1–21.
65. See G. Armstrong and M. Young, 'Fanatical Football Chants: Creating and Controlling the Carnival', in G.P.T. Finn and R. Giulianotti (eds), *Football Culture: Local Contests, Global Visions* (London and Portland, OR: Frank Cass, 2000), pp. 173–211.
66. Bailey, *Popular Culture and Performance*, pp. 194–211, was among the first to explore this field.

Chapter 7

1. Gwyn Thomas, *Selected Short Stories* (Bridgend: Seren, 1992), p. 46.
2. Jack Jones, *Black Parade* (London: Faber and Faber, 1935), pp. 228–9.
3. As W.E. Gladstone is reported to have remarked in the House of Commons in 1891, 'The Nonconformists of Wales were the people of Wales': cited in K.O. Morgan, *Wales in British Politics, 1868–1922* (Cardiff: University of Wales Press, 1980), p. 92.
4. P. Morgan, 'From Long Knives to Blue Books', in R.R. Davies, R.A. Griffiths, I.G. Jones and K.O. Morgan (eds), *Welsh Society and Nationhood: Historical Essays Presented to Glanmor Williams* (Cardiff: University of Wales Press, 1984).
5. See, for instance, T. Phillips, *Wales: The Language, Social Condition, Moral Character, and Religious Opinions of the People* (London: J.W. Parker, 1849); H. Richard, *Letters on the Social and Political Condition of the Principality of Wales* (London: Jackson, Walford and Hodder, 1866).
6. Peter Bailey, '"Will the Real Bill Banks Stand Up?" Towards a Role Analysis of Mid-Victorian Working-Class Respectability', *Journal of Social History*, 12:3 (1979), 337–8; also in Peter Bailey, *Popular Culture and Performance in the Victorian City* (Cambridge: Cambridge University Press, 1998), Ch. 2.
7. Ibid.
8. J. Weeks, *Sex, Politics and Society: The Regulation of Sexuality since 1800* (Harlow: Longman, 1981), p. 88.
9. A recent example of a work that does pay due attention to the multiple nature of such contexts is

Mike Huggins, 'Second-Class Citizens? English Middle-Class Culture and Sport, 1850–1910: A Reconsideration', *International Journal of the History of Sport*, 17:1 (2000), 1–35, especially 25–8.

10. Russell Davies, *Secret Sins: Sex, Violence and Society in Carmarthenshire, 1870–1920* (Cardiff: University of Wales Press, 1996), p. 156. This book is by far the best account of 'the disreputable' in Victorian Wales.

11. G.A. Williams, *The Merthyr Rising* (London: Croom Helm, 1978), Ch. 1.

12. *Merthyr Telegraph* (23 Nov. 1861).

13. *Merthyr Express* (18 July 1896).

14. Ibid. (3 July 1880).

15. *Merthyr Telegraph* (31 Aug. 1861).

16. For more on poaching see D.J.V. Jones, 'The Poacher: A Study in Victorian Crime and Protest', *Historical Journal*, 22:4 (1977), 825–60.

17. *Cambrian News* (1881), cited in Davies, *Secret Sins*, p. 130. It should be noted that class was never a straightforward predictor of respectability. One poacher who recorded his adventures claimed that two members of his gang were magistrates: G.E. Jones, *Confessions of a Welsh Salmon Poacher* (Holborn, 1897), cited in Davies, *Secret Sins*, p. 131.

18. *Aberdare Times* (11 June 1881).

19. A. Hawkins, 'The Discovery of Rural England', in R. Colls and P. Dodd (eds), *Englishness, Politics and Culture, 1880–1920* (London: Croom Helm, 1986).

20. O.M. Edwards, *A Short History of Wales* (London: T. Fisher Unwin, 1906), p. 128. For a discussion of Edwards's thought see E. Sherrington, 'O.M. Edwards, Culture and the Industrial Classes', *Llafur*, 6:1 (1992), 28–41. See also P. Morgan, 'The *Gwerin* of Wales: Myth and Reality', in I. Hume and W.T.R. Pryce (eds), *The Welsh and their Country* (Llandysul: Gomer, 1986); C. Harvie, 'The Folk and the *Gwerin:* The Myth and Reality of Popular Culture in Nineteenth-Century Scotland and Wales', *Proceedings of the British Academy* 80 (1993), 19–48.

21. *Bye-Gones Relating to Wales and the Border Countries* (19 April 1899).

22. *Cnappan* could still be found in the market town of Narbeth in West Wales as late as 1881: *Red Dragon*, 6 (1884), p. 284. For more on the rowdy aspect of the game see *Bye-Gones Relating to Wales and the Border Countries* (2 March 1887), 263–4.

23. R. Suggett, 'Festivals and Social Structure in Early Modern Wales', *Past and Present*, 152 (1996), 88.

24. J. Howells, 'Glamorgan Revel' (1884), cited in Suggett, 'Festivals and Social Structure', 88.

25. 'J. H.', 'Reminiscences of Merthyr Tydfil', *Red Dragon*, 2 (1882), 338.

26. For a discussion of late-Victorian understandings of public drunkenness see Andy Croll, *Civilising the Urban: Popular Culture and Public Space, Merthyr 1870–1914* (Cardiff: University of Wales Press, 2000), Ch. 3.

27. The construction of golden ages by those horrified by the vices and crimes of their contemporaries has been a recurring feature of modern British history: see G. Pearson, *Hooligan: A History of Respectable Fears* (London: Macmillan, 1983).

28. For a discussion of this revolution in the realm of sport see Neil Tranter, *Sport, Economy and Society in Britain, 1750–1914* (Cambridge: Cambridge University Press, 1998), Ch. 3.

29. In 1895 the British Ladies Football Club played a match in Cardiff before a crowd of 3,000: B. Lile and D. Farmer, 'The Early Development of Association Football in South Wales, 1890–1906', *Transactions of the Cymmrodorion Society* (1984), 203.

30. S. Kern, *The Culture of Time and Space, 1880–1918* (London: Weidenfeld and Nicolson, 1983), p. 111.

31. For a wider view of the social panic created by cycling see Pearson, *Hooligan*, pp. 66–9. See also Clare Simpson, 'Respectable Identities: New Zealand Nineteenth-Century "New Women" – on Bicycles', *International Journal of the History of Sport*, 18:1 (2001), , 54–77.

32. *Merthyr Express* (10 July 1897).

33. Ibid. (29 May 1897).

34. Ibid. (21 May 1898).

35. For a history of pugilism see D. Brailsford, *Bareknuckles: A Social History of Prize Fighting* (Cambridge: Lutterworth Press, 1989).

36. J. Kneale, '"A Problem of Supervision": Moral Geographies of the Nineteenth-Century British Public House', *Journal of Historical Geography*, 25:3 (1999), 333–48.

37. *Merthyr Express* (28 Jan. 1893).

38. B. Glover, *The Prince of Ales: The History of Brewing in Wales* (Stroud: Alan Sutton, 1993), p. 50.

39. Andy Croll, 'Street Disorder, Surveillance and Shame: Regulating Behaviour in the Public Spaces of the Late Victorian British Town', *Social History*, 24:3 (1999), 260–1.
40. D.S. Kamper, 'Popular Sunday Newspapers, Class, and the Struggle for Respectability in Late Victorian Britain', in Martin Hewitt (ed.), *Leeds Centre Working Papers in Victorian Studies*, Vol. 4: *Unrespectable Recreations* (Leeds: Leeds Centre for Victorian Studies, 2001), pp. 81–94.
41. For histories of 'roughs' and their street culture see S. Humphries, *Hooligans or Rebels? An Oral History of Working-Class Childhood and Youth, 1889–1939* (Oxford: Blackwell, 1981) and A. Davies, *Leisure, Gender, and Poverty: Working-Class Culture in Salford and Manchester, 1900–1939* (Buckingham: Open University Press, 1992).
42. *Merthyr Express* (9 and 16 May 1903).
43. Davies, *Secret Sins*, pp. 156, 164.
44. *Merthyr Telegraph* (12 April 1856).
45. Ibid. (25 Aug. 1855).
46. E.F. Roberts, *A Visit to the Iron Works and Environs of Merthyr Tydfil in 1852* (London: William Edward Painter, 1853), p. 26.
47. Ibid., pp. 24, 41.
48. Ibid., p. 24.
49. Ibid., p. 42.
50. *Merthyr Telegraph* (22 Dec. 1855).
51. See Peter Bailey, *Leisure and Class in Victorian England: Rational Recreation and the Contest for Control, 1830–1885* (London: Routledge, 1978); R.W. Malcolmson, *Popular Recreations in English Society, 1700–1850* (Cambridge: Cambridge University Press, 1973).
52. *Merthyr Times* (10 Feb. 1893).
53. Russell Davies notes the tendency of people in packed courtrooms 'to find entertainment and comedy in the agony of others': *Secret Sins*, p. 167.
54. Alan Mayne, *The Imagined Slum: Newspaper Representation in Three Cities, 1870–1914* (Leicester: Leicester University Press, 1993), p. 150.
55. K. Strange, 'In Search of the Celestial Empire: Crime in Merthyr, 1830–1860', *Llafur*, 3:1 (1980), 44–86.
56. See, for example, the work of the 'social explorer' George R. Sims, who visited South Wales in 1907: *Western Mail* (27 and 28 June 1907). For another evocation of the slums of the South see *Western Mail* (8 and 10 Dec. 1898).
57. *Merthyr Telegraph* (1 Sept. 1866).
58. See, for example, *Merthyr Telegraph* (2 Feb. 1856); *Merthyr Express* (14 April 1894).
59. *Merthyr Express* (27 Sept. 1884).
60. Ibid. (4 Oct. 1884).
61. For more on the impact of the revival on popular leisure see Croll, *Civilising the Urban*, pp. 184–9.
62. J.V. Morgan, *The Welsh Religious Revival 1904–5: A Retrospect and Criticism* (London: Chapman and Hall, 1909), p. 161.
63. Ibid., pp. 141–5.
64. *Pontypridd Observer* (3 June 1905). The authors are grateful to Deborah James for this reference. For more on the gendered nature of late Victorian respectability see Deborah James, 'Virtue and Vice: Women, Respectability and Disorder in the South Wales Coalfield, 1870–1914', PhD thesis, University of Glamorgan, forthcoming.
65. See Caradoc Evans [pen-name of David Evans], *My People* (first published 1915; new edition, with introduction by J. Harris, Bridgend: Seren, 1987).
66. *Western Mail* (13 Nov. 1915), cited in J. Harris, 'Introduction: "The Banned, Burned Book of War"', in Evans, *My People*, p. 38. This paragraph relies heavily on Harris's introduction.
67. Harris, 'Introduction', pp. 41–2.

Chapter 8

1. U.A. Titley and A.R. McWhirter, *Centenary History of the Rugby Football Union* (London: RFU, 1970), p. 9. On the social context of the early development of rugby see Tony Collins, *Rugby's Great Split* (London and Portland, OR: Frank Cass, 1998); and Eric Dunning and Ken Sheard,

Barbarians, Gentlemen and Players (New York: New York University Press, 1979).

2. Richard Holt, *Sport and the British* (Oxford: Clarendon Press, 1989), pp. 98 and 174.
3. See Keith Sandiford, *Cricket and the Victorians* (Aldershot: Scolar Press, 1994); Wray Vamplew, *Pay Up and Play the Game* (Cambridge: Cambridge University Press, 1988); Derek Birley, *The Willow Wand* (London: Sportspages, 1989).
4. Letters of Arthur Shrewsbury to Alfred Shaw (14 March and 22 June 1888), in the Arthur Shrewsbury archive at Trent Bridge Cricket Ground, Nottingham; *Yorkshire Owl* (18 November 1895); *Yorkshireman* (2 May 1888).
5. *Yorkshire Post* (11 March, 4 Oct. and 13 Dec. 1893).
6. The key text is J.A. Mangan, *Athleticism in the Victorian and Edwardian Public School* (London and Portland, OR: Frank Cass, 2000).
7. Thomas Hughes, *Tom Brown's Schooldays* (first published 1857; Oxford: Oxford University Press [World's Classics edition], 1989), pp. 97–8.
8. Quoted in Jennifer Macrory, *Running with the Ball* (London: Collins Willow, 1991), p. 111.
9. For example, see the article by Arthur Pearson in *Rugby Football* (3 Nov. 1923).
10. *Yorkshire Evening Post* (12 Jan. and 9 Feb. 1901).
11. *Bell's Life* (2 and 9 Jan. 1859). For the minutes of the FA's early meetings see Macrory, *Running with the Ball*, pp. 170–80.
12. *Times* (23 Nov. 1870).
13. *Times* (30 Nov. 1870); see also letters in the *Times* (26 and 28 Nov. 1870). For a broader discussion of medical opposition to the various codes of football see Roberta J Park, '"Mended or Ended?": Football Injuries and the British and American Medical Press, 1870–1910', *International Journal of the History of Sport*, 18:2 (June 2001).
14. On the circumstances of the formation of the RFU and the text of its first rules see O.L. Owen, *The History of the Rugby Football Union* (London: Playfair, 1955), pp. 59–72.
15. *Yorkshire Evening Post* (1 and 8 Dec. 1900).
16. Ibid. (12 Jan. and 22 Feb. 1901).
17. *Yorkshireman* (7 Nov. 1885); Grundy quoted in John Lowerson, *Sport and the English Middle Classes* (Manchester: Manchester University Press, 1993), p. 84. On the Corinthians' 'robust' style of play see Tony Mason, *Association Football and English Society, 1863–1915* (Brighton: Harvester, 1981), pp. 207–09; and Derek Birley, *Land of Sport and Glory* (Manchester: Manchester University Press, 1995), p. 34.
18. *Yorkshire Evening Post* (15 Jan. 1900).
19. Ibid. (15 Dec. 1900, and 9 and 22 Feb. 1901).
20. Ibid. (27 Feb. 1904 and 21 March 1903); *Yorkshireman* (29 Sept. 1883).
21. *Yorkshire Post* (2 April 1886).
22. C. B. Fry, 'Some Famous Footballers', *Windsor Magazine* (Jan. 1899), 20.
23. Campbell quoted in Derek Birley, *Sport and the Making of Britain* (Manchester: Manchester University Press, 1993), p. 259; *Wakefield Express* (23 Nov. 1872); *Athletic News* (30 Nov. 1876).
24. *Clarion* (7 Oct. 1893).

Chapter 9

1. Richard Holt, *Sport and the British: A Modern History* (Oxford: Clarendon Press, 1989), p. 347.
2. See Colin Shields, *Runs Will Take Place Whatever the Weather – The Centenary History of the Scottish Cross Country Union* (Glasgow: SCCU, 1990) for a brief history of the early development of Scottish cross-country running.
3. Brian McAusland, *Clydesdale Harriers – A Centenary History 1885–1985* (Glasgow: published by the author, 1988), p. 5.
4. *Scottish Sport* (8 Oct. 1897).
5. See Hamish Telfer, 'Cross Country Running in Scotland: The Genesis and Context of Organised Club Running in the Late Nineteenth Century', unpublished paper presented at the second International ISHPES Seminar (Oslo/Lillehammer, 1994); Hamish Telfer, 'The Genesis of the Harrier Tradition in Scotland', unpublished paper presented at the tenth Commonwealth and International Scientific Congress (Victoria, 1994).
6. *Scottish Athletic Journal* (21 Sept. 1886), 17.

7. Information taken from members' yearbooks of Clydesdale Harriers and the West of Scotland Harriers.
8. *Scottish Sport* (27 Dec. 1895).
9. Ibid. (18 Oct. 1895), 17.
10. There were strong connections between venues associated with the military and harriers clubs in Dundee and Edinburgh, as well as in Glasgow. Public baths were used extensively, as were Masonic halls.
11. *Scottish Sport* (6 Jan. 1899).
12. Ibid. (7 Jan. 1890).
13. Ibid. (10 Feb. 1899), 6.
14. Ibid. (10 Sept. 1897).
15. Ibid. (24 Feb. 1899), 5.
16. Ibid. (26 Feb. 1897), 14.
17. The West of Scotland Harriers made Sir John Stirling Maxwell a patron of the club. He owned large estates on the south side of Glasgow, including what is now Pollock Estate, an area that was used by the West of Scotland Harriers for club runs.
18. *Scottish Sport* (4 Feb. 1898), 6.
19. See McAusland, *Clydesdale Harriers*.
20. Neil Wigglesworth, *The Evolution of English Sport* (London and Portland, OR: Frank Cass, 1996), pp. ??.
21. Charles C. Smith, *Historic South Edinburgh*, Vol. 2 (Skilton: Edinburgh, 1979), p. 202.
22. Neil Tranter, 'The Patronage of Organised Sport in Scotland', *Journal of Sport History* 16:3 (1989), 243.
23. *Scottish Sport* (31 Jan. 1890), 10.
24. Ibid. (15 Jan. 1897).
25. Ibid. (28 Jan. 1898).
26. *Scottish Athletic Journal* (23 Sept. 1886), 17.
27. McAusland, *Clydesdale Harriers*.
28. *Scottish Athletic Journal* (28 Sept. 1886), 14.
29. *Scottish Sport* (13 Oct. 1899).
30. Ibid. (5 Jan. 1897), 10.
31. Gerry P.T. Finn, 'Faith, Hope and Bigotry: Case Studies of Anti-Catholic Prejudice in Scottish Soccer and Society', in Grant Jarvie and Graham Walker (eds), *Scottish Sport in the Making of the Nation – Ninety-Minute Patriots?* (Leicester: Leicester University Press, 1994).
32. The temperance cause was further enhanced at this time by teams from temperance movements taking part in sport. Both football and cross-country running had clubs formed by total abstainers.
33. Finn, 'Faith, Hope and Bigotry'.
34. Bill Murray, *The Old Firm: Sectarianism, Sport and Society in Scotland* (Edinburgh: Donald, 2000), p. 88. For further examples of issues linked to Protestant popular culture see the excellent work of Graham Walker and Tom Gallagher (eds), *Sermons and Battle Hymns: Protestant Popular Culture in Modern Scotland* (Edinburgh: Edinburgh University Press, 1990).
35. *League Journal* (8 Jan. 1898), 25–26.
36. *Scottish Umpire* (4 Feb. 1889).
37. Hugh Keevins and Kevin McCarra, *100 Cups: The Story of the Scottish Cup* (Edinburgh: Mainstream Publishing, 1985), p. 42.
38. Wray Vamplew, *Pay Up and Play the Game: Professional Sport in Britain, 1875–1914* (Cambridge: Cambridge University Press, 1988).
39. *Scottish Sport* (5 Feb. 1897), 6.
40. See the short but illuminating article, 'Training for Distance Races', *Scottish Sport* (7 Feb. 1896), 13.
41. *Scottish Athletic Journal* (1 Feb. 1887), 13.
42. *Scottish Sport* (23 Dec. 1898), 6.
43. For a synthesis of the social and sporting achievements of the West of Scotland Harriers at this time see Hamish Telfer, 'Of Trails, Whips and Smokers – Gentlemen Harriers of the Late Nineteenth Century', *Proceedings of the 10th Commonwealth & International Scientific Congress* (Victoria, British Columbia: University of Victoria, 1994), pp. 93–95.

Epilogue

1. Geoffrey Best, *Mid-Victorian Britain, 1851–70* (London: Collins, 1979), p. 282.
2. See, for example, Mike J Huggins, 'More Sinful Pleasures: Leisure, Respectability and the Male Middle Classes in Victorian England', *Journal of Social History*, 33:3 (2000), 585–600.
3. Essays in the present collection illustrate this well, but much material remains to be explored that shows how a respectable public face could hide a less respectable private world. For example, the private diaries of Absolom Walkin, a self-made Manchester businessman, reveal a great deal about infidelities and excessive drinking among members of his family.
4. Patrick Joyce, 'Work', in F.M.L. Thompson (ed.), *The Cambridge Social History of Britain, 1750–1950*, Vol. 2, *People and their Environment* (Cambridge: Cambridge University Press, 1990), pp. 140–3.
5. David Cannadine, *The Rise and Fall of Class in Britain* (New York: Columbia University Press, 1999), p. 194.
6. Patrick Joyce, *Visions of the People: Industrial England and the Question of Class, 1848–1914* (Cambridge: Cambridge University Press, 1991).
7. See E.P. Thompson, *The Making of the English Working Class* (Harmondsworth: Penguin, and New York: Vintage, 1963).
8. Peter Bailey, 'The Politics and Poetics of Modern British Leisure', *Rethinking History*, 3:2 (1999), 159.
9. See Peter Bailey, *Popular Culture and Performance in the Victorian City* (Cambridge: Cambridge University Press, 1998).
10. For a discussion of this point see J.A. Mangan, 'Epilogue: Many Mansions and Many Architectural Styles', in J.A. Mangan and Fan Hong (eds), *Sport in Asian Society: Past and Present* (London and Portland, OR: Frank Cass, 2002).
11. Parliamentary Papers 1852 XVII, Report of the Select Committee on Wine Duties, qu. 3817.
12. Douglas A. Reid, 'Playing and Praying', in Martin Daunton (ed.), *Cambridge Urban History of Leisure*, Vol. 3 (Cambridge: Cambridge University Press, 2000), p. 782.
13. Bailey, 'Politics and Poetics', 134; see also Bailey, *Popular Culture and Performance*.
14. Peter Bailey, *Leisure and Class in Victorian England: Rational Recreation and the Contest for Control* (London: Routledge, 1978), pp. 102, 84.
15. See, for example, D. Kift, *The Victorian Music Hall: Culture, Class and Conflict* (Cambridge: Cambridge University Press, 1996), which explores the complex relationship between the Tory attitudes of owners and managers, and music hall's role as a foundation for a 'Labour' working-class identity.
16. See Patrick Joyce, *Work, Society and Politics: The Culture of the Factory in Later Victorian England* (Brighton: Harvester Press, 1980).
17. David Nash, *Secularism, Art and Freedom* (Leicester: Leicester University Press, 1992), pp. 97–9.
18. On Australia see K. Dunstan, *Wowsers* (Sydney: Angus and Robertson, 1968), pp. 206, 211.
19. See Kift, *The Victorian Music Hall*.
20. See Mike Huggins, *Flat Racing and British Society* (London and Portland, OR: Frank Cass, 2000).
21. See Lynda Nead, *Victorian Babylon: People, Streets and Images in Nineteenth-Century London* (New Haven, CT: Yale University Press, 2000).
22. Hugh Cunningham, 'Leisure and Culture', in F.M.L. Thompson (ed.), *The Cambridge Social History of Britain, 1750–1950*, Vol. 2, *People and their Environment* (Cambridge: Cambridge University Press, 1990), pp. 296–8.

Select bibliography

Prologue: All mere complexities

Mike Huggins and J.A. Mangan

Peter Bailey, *Leisure and Class in Victorian England: Rational Recreation and the Contest for Control, 1830–1885* (London, Routledge, 1978; 2nd ed., London: Methuen, 1987)

Richard Holt, *Sport and the British: A Modern History* (Oxford: Clarendon Press, 1989)

John Lowerson, *Sport and the English Middle Classes, 1870–1914* (Manchester: Manchester University Press, 1993)

Neil Wigglesworth, *The Evolution of British Sport* (London and Portland, OR: Frank Cass, 1996)

1 Bullies, beatings, battles and bruises: 'Great days and jolly days' at one mid-Victorian public school

J.A. Mangan

A.G. Bradley, A.C. Champneys and J.W. Baines, revised and continued by J.R. Taylor, H.C. Brentnall and G.C. Turner, *A History of Marlborough College* (London: John Murray, 1923)

Sir Lionel Earle, *Turn Over The Page* (London: Hutchinson, 1935)

Edward Lockwood, *The Early Days of Marlborough College* (London: Simpkin, Marshall, Hamilton, Kent, 1893)

J.A. Mangan, *Athleticism in the Victorian and Edwardian Public School* (London and Portland, OR: Frank Cass, 2000)

2 Bloods, blues and barbarians: some aspects of late Victorian Oxbridge

J.A. Mangan

Edward Paice, *Lost Line of Empire: The Life of 'Cape to Cairo' Grogan* (London: HarperCollins, 2001)

J.A. Mangan, 'Oars and the Man: Pleasure and Purpose in Victorian and Edwardian Cambridge', *History of Higher Education Annual*, Vol. 4, 1984

J.A. Mangan, *The Games Ethic and Imperialism: Aspects of the Diffusion of an Ideal* (London and Portland, OR: Frank Cass, 1998)

J.A. Mangan, *Athleticism in the Victorian and Edwardian Public School: The Emergence and Consolidation of a Victorian Ideology* (London and Portland, OR: Frank Cass, 2000)

3 Dandy rats at play: the Liverpudlian middle classes and horse-racing in the nineteenth century

John Pinfold

E. Bradyll, *The Lays of Cotton Broking* (Liverpool: Harris, 1865)

G.J. Milne, *Trade and Traders in Mid-Victorian Liverpool: Mercantile Business and the Making of a World Port* (Liverpool: Liverpool University Press, 2000)

B.G. Orchard, *Liverpool's Legion of Honour* (Birkenhead: the author, 1893)

H. Shimmin, *Liverpool Life, Second Series* (Liverpool: Egerton Smith, 1857)

P. Thompson, *On the Turf* (Bebington: Quarry Publications, 1991)

J.K. Walton and A. Wilcox, *Low Life and Moral Improvement in Mid-Victorian England: Liverpool Through the Journalism of Hugh Shimmin* (Leicester: Leicester University Press, 1991)

4 Popular Sunday newspapers, respectability and working-class culture in late Victorian Britain

David Scott Kamper

Thomas Catling, *My Life's Pilgrimage* (London: John Murray, 1911)

Brian Harrison, *Peaceable Kingdom* (Oxford: Clarendon Press, 1992)

Richard Holt, *Sport and the British: A Modern History* (Oxford: Clarendon Press, 1989)

Newsagent and Bookseller's Review (selected issues, 1889, 1893, 1894 and 1899)

Sell's Dictionary of the World's Press (1891, 1892, 1895 and 1900)

5 Disreputable adolescent reading: low-life, women-in-peril and school sport 'penny dreadfuls' from the 1860s to the 1890s

John Springhall

Patricia Anderson, *When Passion Reigned: Sex and the Victorians* (New York: Basic Books, 1995)

Peter Haining (ed.), *The Penny Dreadful, or Strange, Horrid and Sensational Tales* (London: Gollancz, 1975)

Jeffrey Richards (ed.), *Imperialism and Juvenile Literature* (Manchester: Manchester University Press, 1989)

Joanne Shattock and Michael Wolff (eds), *The Victorian Periodical Press: Samplings and Sounding*s (Leicester: Leicester University Press, 1982)

John Springhall, *Youth, Popular Culture and Moral Panics: Penny Gaffs to Gangsta-Rap, 1830–1996* (Basingstoke: Macmillan, 1998)

E.S. Turner, *Boys Will Be Boys: The Story of Sweeney Todd, Deadwood Dick, Sexton Blake, Billy Bunter, Dick Barton et al.* (London: Michael Joseph, 1948)

6 Cartoons and comic periodicals, 1841–1901: a satirical sociology of Victorian sporting life

Mike Huggins

Alison Adburgham, *A* Punch *History of Manners and Modes, 1841–1940* (London: Hutchinson, 1961)

Richard Altick, Punch: *The Lively Youth of a British Institution, 1841–1851* (Columbus, OH: Ohio State University Press, 1997)

Peter Bailey, *Popular Culture and Performance in the Victorian City* (Cambridge: Cambridge University Press, 1998)

Peter Burke, *Eyewitnessing: The Use of Images as Historical Evidence* (London: Reaktion Books, 2001)

John Lowerson, *Sport and the English Middle Classes, 1870–1914* (Manchester: Manchester University Press, 1993)

J.A. Mangan, *Athleticism in the Victorian and Edwardian Public School* (London and Portland, OR: Frank Cass, 2000)

7 A heart of darkness? Leisure, respectability and the aesthetics of vice in Victorian Wales

Andy Croll and Martin Johnes

Peter Bailey, *Leisure and Class in Victorian England: Rational Recreation and the Contest for Control, 1830–1885* (London: Routledge, 1978)

Andy Croll, *Civilising the Urban: Popular Culture and Public Space, Merthyr 1870–1914* (Cardiff: University of Wales Press, 2000)

Russell Davies, *Secret Sins: Sex, Violence and Society in Carmarthenshire, 1870–1920* (Cardiff: University of Wales Press, 1996)

Caradoc Evans [pen-name of David Evans], *My People* (first published 1915; new edition, with introduction by J. Harris, Bridgend: Seren, 1987)

D.S. Kamper, 'Popular Sunday Newspapers, Class, and the Struggle for Respectability in Late Victorian Britain', in Martin Hewitt (ed.), *Leeds Centre Working Papers in Victorian Studies*, Vol. 4: *Unrespectable Recreations* (Leeds: Leeds Centre for Victorian Studies, 2001)

Alan Mayne, *The Imagined Slum: Newspaper Representation in Three Cities, 1870–1914* (Leicester: Leicester University Press, 1993)

8 Violence, gamesmanship and the amateur ideal in Victorian middle-class rugby

Tony Collins

Derek Birley, *Sport and the Making of Britain* (Manchester: Manchester University Press, 1993)

Tony Collins, *Rugby's Great Split* (London and Portland, OR: Frank Cass, 1998)

Eric Dunning and Ken Sheard, *Barbarians, Gentlemen and Players* (New York: New York University Press, 1979)

Richard Holt, *Sport and the British: A Modern History* (Oxford: Clarendon Press, 1989)

J.A. Mangan, *Athleticism in the Victorian and Edwardian Public School* (London and Portland, OR: Frank Cass, 2000)

Jennifer Macrory, *Running with the Ball* (London: Collins Willow, 1991)

9 Ludism, laughter and liquor: homosocial behaviour in late-Victorian Scottish harriers clubs

Hamish Telfer

Gerry P.T. Finn, 'Faith, Hope and Bigotry: Case Studies of Anti-Catholic Prejudice in Scottish Soccer and Society', in Grant Jarvie and Graham Walker (eds), *Scottish Sport in the Making of the Nation – Ninety-Minute Patriots?* (Leicester: Leicester University Press, 1994)

Brian McAusland, *Clydesdale Harriers – A Centenary History 1885–1985* (Glasgow: published by the author, 1988)

Colin Shields, *Runs Will Take Place Whatever the Weather – The Centenary History of the Scottish Cross Country Union* (Glasgow: SCCU, 1990)

Hamish Telfer, 'Cross Country Running in Scotland: The Genesis and Context of Organised Club Running in the Late Nineteenth Century', unpublished paper presented at the second International ISHPES Seminar (Oslo/Lillehammer, 1994)

Hamish Telfer, 'The Genesis of the Harrier Tradition in Scotland', unpublished paper presented at the tenth Commonwealth and International Scientific Congress (Victoria, 1994)

Graham Walker and Tom Gallagher (eds), *Sermons and Battle Hymns: Protestant Popular Culture in Modern Scotland* (Edinburgh: Edinburgh University Press, 1990)

Epilogue: The dogs bark but the caravan moves on

Mike Huggins and J.A. Mangan

Peter Bailey, *Popular Culture and Performance in the Victorian City* (Cambridge: Cambridge University Press, 1998)

Patrick Joyce, *Visions of the People: Industrial England and the Question of Class, 1848–1914* (Cambridge: Cambridge University Press, 1991)

D. Kift, *The Victorian Music Hall: Culture, Class and Conflict* (Cambridge: Cambridge University Press, 1996)

Lynda Nead, *Victorian Babylon: People, Streets and Images in Nineteenth-Century London* (New Haven, CT: Yale University Press, 2000)

F.M.L. Thompson (ed.), *The Cambridge Social History of Britain, 1750–1950*, Vol. 2, *People and their Environment* (Cambridge: Cambridge University Press, 1990)

Index